Music Business Research

Series Editors

Music business research is a new multidisciplinary field that puts a number of different analytical approaches into mutual dialogue. It is located at the intersection of economic, artistic, musical, cultural, social, legal, and technological understandings of this cultural industry and it aims to generate a better understanding of the creation, distribution and consumption of music as a cultural good. As a field it is therefore characterised by methodological diversity and involves linking academic research with music business practices. The book series welcomes monographs and edited volumes that feature groundbreaking research into this dynamic and exciting field.

Brian Long

Democratising Orchestras

What Happens When Musicians Run the Show?

Springer

Brian Long
School of Culture and Communication
University of Melbourne
Melbourne, VIC, Australia

ISSN 2522-0829 ISSN 2522-0837 (electronic)
Music Business Research
ISBN 978-3-032-17398-0 ISBN 978-3-032-17399-7 (eBook)
https://doi.org/10.1007/978-3-032-17399-7

This Springer imprint is published by the registered company Springer Nature Switzerland AG
The registered company address is: Gewerbestrasse 11, 6330 Cham, Switzerland

This book is dedicated to my wife Eva and daughter Guinevere.

Attribution

Major sections of this book are based on my doctoral dissertation that I presented and defended on 27 October 2019 at the University of Melbourne, Australia. Reused with permission.

Competing Interests: My research was generously supported by an Australian Government Research Training Program Scholarship.

The author has no competing interests to declare that are relevant to the content of this manuscript.

Ethics Approval: The research for this book was approved by the University of Melbourne (approval number 14432150).

Informed consent to participate and publish was obtained from all individual research participants.

Acknowledgements

It is said that raising a child requires a village. Certainly, a small village helped bring this book to completion, and I am immensely grateful for all the help. Kate MacNeill was a fount of wisdom throughout the development of its early stages. Many others, in order of appearance, including Amanda Coles, Christiaan De Beukelaer and Guy Morrow, each brought their own invaluable contributions while also stoking the intellectual hearth at the centre of the village and ensuring the flames never dropped too far. My heartfelt thanks go to one and all.

The interviewees are at the heart of this research. Without them, I would have nothing to say. Their generous and enthusiastic support of the research gave it life. I am very grateful for their invaluable contributions. Dr Campbell Aitken provided invaluable editing services on an early version of the book.

Such a project would be impossible without a very supportive family, and none could be more wonderfully supportive and patient than my partner Eva and our daughter Guinevere. Their unquestioning and painstaking support provided an unshakeable foundation on which I was able to build.

We are democrats, not because the majority is always right,
but because democratic traditions are the least evil ones of which we know.
Karl Popper

Contents

List of Abbreviations

CEO	Chief executive officer
FBO	Freiburg Baroque Orchestra
LMF	Labour-managed firm
LSO	London Symphony Orchestra
OAE	Orchestra of the Age of Enlightenment
OCB	Organisational citizenship behaviour
PC	Producer cooperative
PGO	Player-governed orchestra
UK	United Kingdom
US	United States

Chapter 1
Introduction

1.1 Encountering a Manager and Violist in One

The seeds of this book were sown in 1991. I was a conducting student newly arrived in Vienna and keen to attend rehearsals of the Vienna Philharmonic. Walter Blovsky, the orchestra's general manager at the time, kindly approved and suggested I drop by his office to introduce myself beforehand. After a brief wait, I was surprised when he rushed in with a viola in hand. Here was a manager who divided his time between the viola section and the general manager's office. He had been elected manager by the orchestra's players.

This was new to me and my thoughts started racing. Was the success of this great orchestra somehow boosted by players influencing and voting on management and governance decisions? Were the players more engaged when they were akin to shareholders in their orchestra? Did better concerts result? What was life as an orchestra manager like when your position relied on electoral support among your playing colleagues? Did the famously complex interplay between conductor and orchestra change when the general manager was sitting in the orchestra and the players got a say in who conducted? What else might be different and even better in such a democratically organised orchestra? What happens when players run their orchestras? These and a lot of other questions flooded in. Many years passed before the investigations that produced this book. In the interim my conducting career went nowhere. Instead, I studied political science and started teaching arts management. But those questions from my brief Vienna encounter never let me go.

Orchestras meld organisational traits and work practices that strive for closely coordinated performance among a group of individuals. Traditional orchestras were built on strict control and top-down authority. They reflect ideas from the nineteenth century, when the modern orchestra emerged (Holoman, 2012). Management theorists, including Peter Drucker, nonetheless often portray orchestras and their decision-making as exemplars for modern management (Drucker, 1993; Khodyakov,

B. Long, *Democratising Orchestras*, Music Business Research,
https://doi.org/10.1007/978-3-032-17399-7_1

2007; Savage and Symonds 2018). Out of this understanding grew a small industry based on conductors training chief executive officers (CEOs) in leadership (Atik, 1994; Beau, 2014). My interest centres, though, on orchestras that make extensive use of democratic participation in governance and management decision-making so as to renegotiate the customary hierarchies of orchestras. More collaboration than charisma!

Today's orchestras face conflicting drivers, logics, and practices. For most, public funding remains essential (Flanagan, 2012). Generating the box-office income needed to balance budgets is hard when audiences are spoilt for choice in a crowded cultural and entertainment landscape (Newton, 2022). Many orchestral musicians report physical and psychological stress caused by performance pressure, precarious employment and economic insecurity, unhealthy working conditions, and unergonomic instruments (Bennett, 2008; Breda & Kulesa, 2012; Halleland et al., 2009; Sternbach, 1995; Voltmer et al., 2012). Orchestras need, then, responsive and agile systems for reaching management decisions.

Some professional orchestras and ensembles have closed or been merged. But others are being launched. Many of these are the creations of conductors trying to realise their musical ideas and professional goals. However, an important subgroup among today's new orchestras and ensembles embodies the dreams and entrepreneurship of musicians. Such player-governed orchestras (PGOs) stand on foundations of participatory, democratic decision-making, strong player engagement, and joint responsibility. They have instituted and refined models of governance and management that give musicians greater say over their professional destinies while building organisations with reputations for excellent music-making.

A duality is germane to orchestras. They must balance art and commerce. Orchestras embody, realise, and negotiate the logics of music performance while operating subject to labour law, the dynamics of various labour markets, to demands for compliant and effective governance structures and processes, and to the parameters of various markets (Newton, 2022). This book reflects this duality. To write it, I examined the principles, practices, and challenges of labour-management and governance in the context of orchestras so as to identify the ways in which participatory decision-making is sustained in PGOs and what we can learn from how they achieve it. Art, commerce, and democracy make for a heady mix.

Governance structures in orchestras cover a wide array of approaches, ranging from those that allow players little or no input into decision-making, to those for whom ultimate decision-making authority rests with the musicians. The latter group has a long tradition, dating back at least to the foundation of the Vienna Philharmonic in 1842 (Hellsberg, 1992). Some of the world's most prestigious orchestras—including the Berlin Philharmonic, the Vienna Philharmonic, and all of London's four independent symphony orchestras—are governed by their respective musicians using democratic processes (Galinsky & Lehman, 1995; Lehman, 2002). These orchestras were, however, established more than one hundred years ago and in very different cultural, economic, and political environments than those into which their contemporary counterparts are emerging. To establish an orchestra or ensemble now is a different proposition than it was for the founders of the orchestras of the late nineteenth and early twentieth centuries. This book focuses on the governance systems of orchestras and ensembles that were founded under today's conditions and that sought to adopt player-governance.

The first player-run orchestra was established in 1842 when members of the orchestra at the Vienna Court Opera mounted a series of matinee concerts to complement their work as pit musicians playing for the opera and ballet (Hellsberg, 1992). From the start, the musicians wanted to retain control of the new enterprise. Thus was the Vienna Philharmonic born, and today the essential features of that early initiative remain in place. Its musicians are still drawn from the orchestra of what is now the Vienna State Opera, and the orchestra's governance remains the responsibility of a democratically elected committee of players (Hellsberg, 1992).

The London Symphony Orchestra was likewise built on democratic foundations (McVeigh, 2013). It was launched in 1904 by a group of disgruntled musicians who broke away from an existing orchestra after a dispute with the conductor about employment rights (ibid). The Berlin Philharmonic similarly traces its roots back to an "act of rebellion" (Berlin Philharmonic, 2025) when in 1882 musicians refused *en masse* to sign contracts they had been offered by a conductor and promoter, instead establishing their own orchestra. Cooperative orchestras were quite common in early twentieth-century America (Mueller, 1951).

Despite the use of player-governance in these now well-established and high-profile orchestras, there is little systematically collated information on how the model works. Existing research focuses almost exclusively on long-established orchestras (Lehman, 2002; Maitlis, 1988, 1997). There is very little analysis of player-governance among recently established orchestras.[1] Yet these new orchestras are at the vanguard of repertoire renewal, audience development, and the enrichment of performance practices in the orchestral landscape. Not only that, the very nature of PGOs as recently established organisations means that it is possible to study first-hand the experience of player-led decision-making. This includes the challenges presented across the entire lifespan of the respective orchestras.

In this book, I analyse and map the establishment, development, and evolution of five PGOs and one contemporary music ensemble. This examination begins with a focus on the setup phase. I then consider the full operationalisation of orchestra governance through to the period of generational change, when the last founding member completes their handover to their successors, at which point additional governance sustainability challenges emerge. The challenge this book addresses concerns the conditions under which player-governance structures work in recently established orchestras. I seek to find out whether, and in which ways, these models, along with the orchestras and ensembles that use them, are sustainable. Clearly, an organisation that cannot be sustained beyond a few years is of little use. I hope that

[1] Orpheus is a notable exception. It was established in 1972 as the Orpheus Chamber Orchestra (Seifter & Economy, 2001) and has been the subject of extensive interest and various studies (Banai et al., 2000; Khodyakov, 2007; Lehman, 2002; Seifter & Economy, 2001; Vredenburgh & He, 2003).

in doing so the results are instructive and enlightening for musicians, managers, and students who want to see orchestras thrive.

1.2 Overview of the Book

The next chapter begins the book's central inquiry by considering possible alignments between labour-management theories and the basic features of orchestras as organisations. It opens by detailing orchestras' labour practices, authority structures, and commercial strategies. The discussion highlights the web of internal and external rationales and pressures that shape the modern orchestra. Musicians, conductors, and management staff bring their interests and priorities to bear, while cultural and artistic dynamics, market and funding imperatives, and legal frameworks comprise the most compelling external factors. Establishing how orchestras embody such an array of drivers sets up the study for the subsequent assessment of their suitability as sites of control by workers.

A consideration of labour-management's viability in the orchestral context follows. Different industries have distinct suitabilities as sites of labour control (Jensen, 2013; Jensen & Meckling, 1979). Labour-managed firms seem more likely to find a foothold in "certain industries, regions, and time periods" (Dow, 2003, p. 230). A central task of Chap. 2, then, is to discover areas of alignment between orchestras and the labour-management viability conditions proposed by Dow and other theorists. The final section highlights areas of overlap as well as aspects of orchestral operations that place them outside existing thinking of labour-management.

While Chap. 2 tests the basic theoretical suitability of orchestras as candidates for labour-management, Chap. 3 introduces the case study organisations that I look at and the people whom I spoke to in my quest to understand PGOs in practice. The chapter begins by staking out the boundaries of important terms such as "labour-managed firm", "cooperative", "partnership", and, most importantly, "player-governed orchestra".

Chapter 4 then foregrounds the role of setup decisions and initial operationalisation in the sustainability of player-governance. The breakdown of the chapter mirrors the bifurcated structure of typical orchestras. The operations of most orchestras have an artistic and cultural aspect next to a business management strand (Glynn, 2000). At the executive level, orchestras usually have an artistic/musical director and a chief executive or general manager (Glynn, 2000). The chapter's first section covers the place of artistic logics in the realisation of player-governance. In the second, the attention shifts to the part played by economic thinking, pressures, and dynamics. It focuses on how insecure work among orchestral musicians influences the founding of PGOs. The chapter's third theme concerns the enfranchisement ideas at the heart of player-governance, in particular the allocation of voting rights solely to musicians and the engagement of management staff as hired labour. Decisions made at the foundation stage set the parameters for player-governance and its sustainability, the primary aspects of later chapters.

Participatory decision-making takes the spotlight during Chap. 5. It identifies three elements that are germane to participation in the PGOs I studied: its facilitation, channelling, and harnessing. Other writers have shown that labour-managed firms (LMFs) are characterised by their workers' high levels of engagement, commitment, and sense of responsibility for their firms (de Jong & Van Witteloostuijn, 2004; Weber et al., 2009). My interviewees' statements reveal the essentially circular nature of participation. Player-governance creates opportunities for democratic decision-making, while the engagement and commitment that members experience in turn contribute to the sustainability of player-governance. The chapter's final section investigates such affective responses in PGOs. How these firms put democratic decision-making to work through the channelling of participation forms the core of the chapter.

Maintaining high levels of performance is a central component of any orchestra's operations and governance. Chapter 6 examines the ways in which PGOs optimise performance from three angles: performance monitoring, generational change, and recruitment. All three are essential in sustaining player-governance; labour-management's principles, practices, and challenges then influence all three of these activities. One of the critical questions for player-governance is whether it supports effective performance optimisation. I begin the chapter by considering performance monitoring, a crucial element in achieving and preserving artistic quality. It is also an area in which player-governance has a radical effect on traditional and hierarchical optimisation practices.

Similar impacts related to generational change also emerged during the writing of this book. Much research has documented the effects of musicians' age-related loss of performing proficiency (Gembris & Heye, 2014; Manturzewska, 1990), though a recent book by Brodsky (2025) questions this orthodoxy. In the PGOs I studied while writing this book, addressing such a complex problem in the context of mutual monitoring poses significant challenges, as became apparent during the interviews I did with musicians and managers. Recruitment represents the third strand in the study of performance optimisation in PGOs. Here too, the flat hierarchies and democratic decision-making of player-governance add complexity to the process. In Chap. 6 I observe how these PGOs balance the conflicting demands of performance monitoring, ensure that generational change is dealt with sensitively, and maintain recruitment processes that are efficient but thorough in establishing the suitability of members from multiple perspectives.

Chapter 7 reveals the essential features of the PGO as a type of LMF. The chapter's sections highlight the logics behind the creation of voting franchises and principles of membership in these PGOs, the operation of labour-management incentives and forms of utility, and the negotiation of authority and leadership in the player-governed context. By outlining how these firms deal with such critical aspects of governance, these three conceptual clusters constitute some of the book's most valuable contributions to ideas about labour-management in the creative industries.

Chapter 8 returns to the book's core investigation of how PGOs sustain their governance structures. The chapter begins by highlighting the risk of degeneration in labour-management. The greatest threat to the sustainability of player-governance results from a tendency toward hierarchy that is common in the performance structures and processes of orchestras. Dilution of musicians' control may also occur if departing members are replaced by recruits who are agnostic about player-governance.

The fundamental question of Chap. 8, and the book as a whole, is how, in light of such challenges, PGOs sustain their governance systems. The chapter argues that three elements support governance sustainability in the PGOs at the heart of this book. The ability of these firms to adapt the basic ideas and principles of control by labour to the practices of orchestral management is fundamental to sustaining player-governance. Flexibility and responsiveness are crucial strategies. Equally vital are the democratisation and collective identity-making that emerged from the interviews. The chapter's third section addresses the intra-organisational identities that players in PGOs give to their orchestras and ensembles. Engaging, committing, and sensing responsibility all presuppose the existence of organisational identities with which people can identify. Among PGOs, such constructs are, however, created in the context of collective decision-making. Player-governance presents challenges when developing organisational identities. The model's sustainability rests on the successful navigation of these complexities. The last part of Chap. 8 shows the links between governance sustainability and the management of musical quality in the PGOs studied.

The book makes a pioneering contribution to the understanding of labour-management in the not-for-profit creative and cultural industries, an under-researched field. By foregrounding the debate surrounding governance sustainability and the threat of degeneration in labour-management, the study highlights how PGOs adapt the ideas of control by musicians to the exigencies of orchestral management and the challenges that arise. Orchestras are complex enterprises that unite artistic goals with economic rationales. Adding labour-management to such a combination creates a set of fascinating and multifaceted firms. Studying these PGOs throws light on a little-understood segment of LMFs and on their potential.

References

Atik, Y. (1994). The conductor and the orchestra: Interactive aspects of the leadership process. *Leadership & Organization Development Journal, 15*(1), 22–28. https://doi.org/10.1108/01437739410050123

Banai, M., Nirenberg, J., & Menachem, M. (2000). Leadership in self-managing organizations: Orpheus and a date plantation. *Journal of Leadership & Organizational Studies, 7*(3), 3–17. https://doi.org/10.1177/107179190000700301

Beau, G. (2014). Beyond the leader-centric approach: Leadership phenomena and aesthetics in a conductorless orchestra. *Society and Business Review, 11*(1), 62–79. https://doi.org/10.1108/SBR-10-2015-0060

Bennett, D. (2008). *Understanding the classical music profession: The past, the present and strategies for the future*. Ashgate.

Berlin Philharmonic. (2025). *The beginning, an orchestra becomes independent*. Berliner Philharmoniker, Berlin, Germany. Accessed October 19, 2025. https://www.berliner-philharmoniker.de/en/about-us/orchestra/history/beginning/.

Breda, J., & Kulesa, P. (2012). In Institute, Symphony Orchestra (Ed.), *Stress and job satisfaction among symphony musicians*. Symphony Orchestra Institute.

Brodsky, W. (2025). *Seasoned musicians playing beyond the 5th decade: A case study on symphony orchestra lifestyle and ageing*. Oxford University Press. https://doi.org/10.1093/9780198956501.001.0001

de Jong, G., & Van Witteloostuijn, A. (2004). Successful corporate democracy: Sustainable cooperation of capital and labor in the Dutch Breman Group. *Academy of Management Executive, 18*(3), 54–66. https://doi.org/10.5465/ame.2004.14776169

Dow, G. (2003). *Governing the firm: Workers' control in theory and practice*. Cambridge University Press.

Drucker, P. (1993). Tomorrow's manager: More of an orchestra conductor than an administrator. *Success, 40*(8), 80.

Flanagan, R. (2012). *The perilous life of symphony orchestras: Artistic triumphs and economic challenges*. Yale University Press.

Galinsky, A. D., & Lehman, E. V. (1995). Emergence, divergence, convergence: Three models of symphony orchestras at the crossroads. *The European Journal of Cultural Policy, 2*(1), 117–139. https://doi.org/10.1080/10286639509358005

Gembris, H., & Heye, A. (2014). Growing older in a symphony orchestra: The development of the age-related self-concept and the self-estimated performance of professional musicians in a lifespan perspective. *Musicae Scientiae, 18*(4), 371–391. https://doi.org/10.1177/1029864914548912

Glynn, M. (2000). When cymbals become symbols: Conflict over organizational identity within a symphony orchestra. *Organization Science, 11*(3), 285–298. http://www.jstor.org/stable/2640262

Halleland, H., Harris, A., Sørnes, S., Murison, R., & Ursin, H. (2009). Subjective health complaints, stress, and coping in orchestra musicians. *Medical Problems of Performing Artists, 24*(2), 58–62. https://www.jstor.org/stable/48710793

Hellsberg, C. (1992). *Demokratie Der Könige: Die Geschichte Der Wiener Philharmoniker*. Schweizer Verlagshaus.

Holoman, D. K. (2012). *The orchestra: A very short introduction*. Oxford University Press.

Jensen, A. (2013). The labor managed firm? A theoretical model explaining emergence and behavior. Chapter 11. In D. Kruse (Ed.), *Sharing ownership, profits, and decision-making in the 21st century*. Emerald. https://doi.org/10.1108/S0885-3339(2013)0000014020

Jensen, M., & Meckling, W. (1979). Rights and production functions: An application to labor-managed firms and codetermination. *Journal of Business, 52*(4), 469–506. https://www.jstor.org/stable/2352442

Khodyakov, D. (2007). The complexity of trust-control relationships in creative organizations: Insights from a qualitative analysis of a Conductorless orchestra. *Social Forces, 86*(1), 1–22. https://www.jstor.org/stable/4495025

Lehman, E. V. (2002). Models of self-governance and workplace democracy: A comparison of select orchestras in Germany, the U.S. and U.K. (Doctoral dissertation) City University London, UK. http://openaccess.city.ac.uk/7618/.

Maitlis, S. (1988). Symphonic dances: A study of decision making in British symphony orchestras. Doctoral dissertation The University of Sheffield, UK. https://ethos.bl.uk/OrderDetails.do?uin=uk.bl.ethos.493277.

Maitlis, S. (1997). Decision making in British symphony orchestras: Formal structures, informal systems, and the role of players. *Harmony, 4*. http://www.polyphonic.org/wp-content/uploads/2012/02/Decision_British_Maitlis.pdf

Manturzewska, M. (1990). A biographical study of the life-span development of professional musicians. *Psychology of Music, 18*(2), 112–139. https://doi.org/10.1177/0305735690182002

McVeigh, S. (2013). The London symphony orchestra: The first decade revisited. *Journal of the Royal Musical Association, 138*(2), 313–376. https://doi.org/10.1080/02690403.2013.830476

Mueller, J. H. (1951). *The American symphony orchestra, a social history of musical taste*. Indiana University Press.

Newton, T. (2022). *Orchestra management handbook: Building relationships in turbulent times*. Oxford University Press. https://doi.org/10.1093/oso/9780197550670.001.0001

Savage, K., & Symonds, D. (2018). *Economies of collaboration in performance: More than the sum of the parts*. Palgrave MacMillan.

Seifter, H., & Economy, P. (2001). *Leadership ensemble, lessons in collaborative management from the world's only conductorless orchestra*. Times Books.

Sternbach, D. J. (1995). Musicians: A neglected working population in crisis. In S. L. Sauter & L. R. Murphy (Eds.), *Organizational risk factors for job stress*. American Psychological Association. https://psycnet.apa.org. https://doi.org/10.1037/10173-018

Voltmer, E., Zander, M., Fischer, J., Kudlieka, B. M., Richter, B., & Spahn, C. (2012). Physical and mental health of different types of orchestra musicians compared to other professions. *Medical Problems of Performing Artists, 27*(1), 9–14. https://pubmed.ncbi.nlm.nih.gov/22543317/

Vredenburgh, D., & He, I. Y. (2003). Leadership lessons from a conductorless orchestra. *Business Horizons, 46*(5), 19. https://doi.org/10.1016/S0007-6813(03)00067-3

Weber, W. G., Unterrainer, C., & Schmid, B. E. (2009). The influence of organizational democracy on employees' socio-moral climate and prosocial behavioral orientations. *Journal of Organizational Behavior, 30*(8), 1127–1149. https://doi.org/10.1002/job.615

Chapter 2
Orchestras and Democracy: The Theory

2.1 How Orchestras Are Organised

An orchestra embodies myriad competing interests, practices, and logics as it navigates complex and often competing external economic, political, and cultural forces (Newton, 2022). Introducing labour-management into such a multilayered and delicate constellation unavoidably and deeply changes operations. How well, then, do orchestras and player-governance align? Are orchestras viable as enterprises controlled by their workers, or does labour-management distort their finely balanced models? What are the challenges to sustaining labour-management in an orchestra? This chapter begins by highlighting relevant aspects of work in orchestras and surveying key ideas in labour-management. The main task here is to determine the basic viability of orchestras as sites of worker decision-making. Do features of orchestras and their working methods foster or hinder control by their players? What are the challenges facing workers who seek to sustain control of their orchestras? The chapter addresses such questions as a prelude to the consideration of player-governance in practice.

Orchestras and music-making have long served as examples of hierarchical organisation in tandem with charismatic and inspiring leadership (Young & Vaupel, 1981). On the subject of authority in a "combined organism", Karl Marx averred that "all combined labour on a large scale requires more or less, a directing authority" (2011, p. 363). The well-known thinker on management Peter Drucker found parallels between the work of conductors and corporate chief executives as well as between orchestras and other enterprises (1985, 1988, 1993). Some orchestra–conductor collaborations have turned such comparisons into management training and brought business leaders into rehearsals (Bathurst et al., 2007; Kammerhoff et al., 2019; Mintzberg, 1998). However, such thinking has also fed misunderstandings and spawned dubious metaphors about orchestras and the work of musicians (Hunt et al., 2004; Spitzer, 1996). Writers seeking such analogies often oversimplify or

B. Long, *Democratising Orchestras*, Music Business Research,
https://doi.org/10.1007/978-3-032-17399-7_2

romanticise orchestras (Hunt et al., 2004; Savage & Symonds, 2018). What are then the main features of work and control in orchestras?

2.1.1 Organisational Dualities

Every professional orchestra has its own mission, governance, processes, and operating environment. Nonetheless, such orchestras have much in common and an operating model with two halves is discernible: the musical and the managerial; art and commerce. Artistic operations such as the roles of conductors, programming formats, and even player seating arrangements were largely standardised by the early twentieth century and have changed little since (Holoman, 2012; Spitzer & Zaslaw, 2004). Conductors decide the most important interpretative questions (Khodyakov, 2007; Koivunen & Wennes, 2011; Krause, 2015; Lewis, 2012). Unified playing takes precedence. Musicians play the same score at the same time and in the same location. Few other activities call for such conformity and high levels of collaboration.

On the corporate and commercial side, greater variety characterises the management of orchestras. It is, nevertheless, possible to sketch a frequently observed model. Working behind the scenes of an orchestra has evolved in line with trends in the wider economy, law, and management (Newton, 2022; Salvaggio, 2024). Chief executive roles overlap with those in other industries, and supervisory boards are common (Cairnduff, 2026). Managing independent[1] orchestras calls for specialists from fields found in other sectors: marketing, human resources, financial management, sponsorship and partnerships, the law, and operations (Newton, 2022). Such workers can move into and out of the orchestra world more readily than players, who have very specific skills (Bennett, 2008). Behind-the-scenes workers share organisational goals with musicians, but their work routines differ as most are not generally tied to rehearsals and evening performances. Management teams operate differently from their playing colleagues.

Atop an orchestra's musical side stands an artistic/musical director or a chief conductor. Sustained success and even simple survival of an orchestra call for close cooperation between its CEO and artistic leader (Glynn, 2000, 2008). Chief executives oversee financial controlling, marketing, fundraising, the recruitment and supervision of management staff, stakeholder relations—including with sponsors, donors, and public funding bodies—and legal aspects of the firm. Musical directors oversee the recruitment and management of playing personnel as well as an orchestra's profile (Bibu et al., 2018). They also lead rehearsals and performances of their programmes and may be involved in the choice of guest conductors (ibid). Decision-making on the two sides often overlaps, and both depend on the other's successful

[1] Independent orchestras are those that are constituted as free-standing legal entities separate from organisations such as opera houses, theatres, or ballet companies.

functioning. Understanding the artistic–operational bifurcation helps us grasp the basic structures of orchestras and ensembles.

Orchestra management has evolved in line with broader economic trends. Marketing and brand-building are essential. Many orchestras have high levels of labour organising (Ayer, 2005; Flanagan, 2010; Williamson & Cloonan, 2016). Larger orchestras negotiate enterprise agreements, while industry-wide bargaining features in some jurisdictions (Broughton, 2001; Flanagan, 2010). Health and safety statutes demand responses, as do social security regulations and labour laws. Industry-specific software finds wide use. The chief executive's role may look like those of senior managers in other industries, but the economics of orchestras create special challenges and set atypical boundaries. Foremost among these challenges is the demand for players.

Management's control over the number of musicians in an orchestra's different instrumental groups varies between the strings and other sections. String-section complements are determined by conductors or performance directors in consultation with managers, but within tight limits set by industry standards and traditions. Most composers before the twentieth century did not stipulate the exact number of each string instrument required to play one of their works. In the case of the cello, for instance, composers typically wrote just a single musical line. Whether two, four, six, or eight celli were used, they mostly played the same notes and additional musicians only amplified and enriched the sound. The desirable number of string players has grown over the centuries as performance venues have become larger. Some variance between orchestras still occurs, even when playing the same work. String sections thus present some limited possibilities for conductors and executives to reduce expenditure without changing the repertoire.

The composer sets the number of woodwind or brass instrument players required to play an orchestral work, however. To all intents and purposes, management cannot change these requirements. The orchestral repertoire revolves around Ludwig van Beethoven's symphonies (Herman, 2023). They include separate parts for each instrument in the woodwind family, typically two flutes, two oboes, two clarinets, and two bassoons. Performing Beethoven's fifth symphony with, say, just one flautist is impossible without omitting some of the score; no professional orchestra would do that. Performing most Beethoven symphonies requires at least eight woodwind players. On the other hand, the tuba was invented after Beethoven's death in 1827, and performing his music never calls for a tuba player. Executives have practically no room to vary the woodwind, brass, and percussion personnel engaged for performances of a particular work.

The challenge of programming while providing the necessary player complement produces complex rosters in tenured orchestras. In freelance orchestras, "fixers" book different player cohorts between projects and in many cases from piece to piece in a single concert as an orchestra shrinks or grows to meet the demands of different works. Managers and artistic leaders in a freelance orchestra can reduce the number of players by, for instance, programming Mozart symphonies rather than those of Gustav Mahler. The latter require around double the players. But managers cannot program a Mahler symphony with only the number of players required for one by Mozart. The performing personnel required by an orchestra is dictated by musical factors rather than commercial thinking. Indeed, the number of players is largely outside the manager's control.

A direct relationship exists, of course, between the number of players needed to perform a chosen work and the resulting wage costs, though this relationship is different in tenured and freelance orchestras. But such a link does not exist between player numbers and ticket sales (Luksetich & Lange, 1995). For a freelance orchestra, musicians' fees for the approximately 85 players required to perform a Tchaikovsky symphony are more than double those required for one by Mozart (around 35 musicians). The larger orchestra is, though, unlikely to earn twice as much ticket revenue. Some works that need large numbers of musicians can generate high ticket sales, but music demanding many fewer players can do that too. Limited ticket price variation can apply but is unlikely to equate to the large orchestra's greater costs (Pompe et al., 2013). Managers thus have little influence over the relationship between wages and revenue. Putting on more players does not boost sales. Delicate balancing of labour and economic factors underlies a concert season, while repertoire must appeal to a range of potential listeners and maintain an orchestra's profile. All forms of orchestral governance face this challenge, but programming's centrality gives musicians a strong interest in it. Repertoire choice plays a critical role in an orchestra's success and sustainability (Herman, 2023).

2.1.2 Artistic Hierarchies and Performance Monitoring

Today's orchestral production model evolved during the mid-nineteenth century (Holoman, 2012; Spitzer & Zaslaw, 2004). Work practices in orchestras have changed little in the intervening two centuries, though entitlements have improved in tandem with the spread of modern welfare states in most rich-world economies. Artistic decision-making and routine onstage operating in orchestras occur with little input from managers, although programming and high-level planning involve more liaising. Conductors or lead instrumentalists decide practically all musical questions, sometimes with section leaders. Decision hierarchies are omnipresent, and most players have very little room for input. An ideal of musical unity plays a key role, as does controlling individuality. String players in particular must align their playing with their section colleagues, but all players must work toward a shared sound ideal. The work of most orchestral musicians remains rooted in hierarchies and the sublimating of individuality.

Reaching and maintaining high playing standards pose the greatest artistic challenge for any orchestra or ensemble pursuing long-term success. Concert audiences and listeners to orchestral recordings demand the highest possible performing and presentation standards (Roose, 2008). Orchestras compete for the best soloists and conductors as much as for residencies and bookings from major festivals, promoters, venues, and opera houses. Attracting and retaining sponsors, donors, and public funding depend on the quality of performances. Recruiting the best players is also a function of an orchestra's performance quality because musicians seek to play with the best orchestras and ensembles (Faulkner, 1973, 1974). Performance quality dictates an orchestra's artistic and economic success.

Playing in an orchestra involves great physical and psychological demands. It calls for excellent motor skills and cognition. Research among German musicians demonstrated that such attributes can start to diminish among players in their late forties or early fifties (Gembris & Heye, 2014). Manturzewska (1990) showed that Polish musicians displayed similar characteristics, and that their proficiency peaked between the ages of 25 and 45. Players may develop skills to at least partly offset age-related declines in proficiency (Brodsky, 2025), but sooner or later most struggle to consistently produce the required performance (Brandfonbrener, 2003; Gembris & Heye, 2014).

High performance, and its hierarchical monitoring, characterises orchestras. Music directors, conductors, and section leaders have the strongest voice. Other musicians have little say. This hierarchical performance monitoring aligns the artistic side of orchestras with practices in other industries. Musicians must ensure their playing aligns with unitary ideas on interpretation, sound, and performance practice (Dobson & Gaunt, 2013). Programming involves artistic leaders and managers, but most musicians interact little with managers during their routine work. Top-down decision-making and performance monitoring set the tone.

Orchestral musicians provide creative labour. The features and logics of their work discussed above shape the orchestral firms in which they work. In the next section, I explore earlier ideas on orchestral musicians as workers. How do the interests and priorities of musicians, as well as the challenges they face, influence the potential of orchestras as sites of labour-management or governance? Understanding and charting the characteristics of work in orchestras is a prerequisite for analysing player-governance.

2.2 Orchestral Work as Creative Labour

Over the last 65 years, extensive writing on creative labour, and specifically on musicians as workers, has emerged. Westby's, 1960 study of career mobility in orchestras contributed early insights. He noted how "the musician's professional identity, developed over long years of training, is constantly being buttressed and reinforced, holding to a minimum the possibilities of pursuit, or even consideration, of other possible ways of life" (Westby, 1960, p. 227). Arian, a musician in the Philadelphia Orchestra who later became a political scientist, foregrounded alienation[2] among orchestral musicians (1971, 1974). Writing of his former orchestra, he

[2] Arian borrows this term from the behavioural sciences and the writing of Erich Fromm, rather than from Marxist theories.

observed that players experienced alienation from management as well as from their own work (Arian, 1971).

Arian (1971) located the roots of player's alienation from their work in the "routinization of the traditional symphonic format ... which blocks the individual's needs for self-expression, recognition, and sustained interest in his [sic] work" (p. 74). An image of orchestral musicians as workers locked into alienating and routine careers began to emerge from these early studies. It became clear that in important ways, orchestral players do not provide the "*concrete and named* labour of the artist" (Ryan, 1991, p. 42 emphasis in the original). Rather than resisting "the abstractness and alienation that Marx attributes to pretty much all other work under capitalism" (Hesmondhalgh & Baker, 2011, p. 84), much orchestral work, Arian (1971) observed, produced in musicians "both an alienation from the work which they perform and an alienation from the management of the organization in which they perform it" (p. 74). Orchestral work thus represents a particularly complicated and conflicted form of creative labour.

Economic and managerial thinking grew in importance for cultural firms over the same period. Arian (1971) called attention to the spread of bureaucracy—the "process wherein organizational policies and procedures are rationalized and routinized to conform to economic necessity" (pp. 15–16). Bureaucratic thinking, he warned, meant that "economy and efficiency, the deadly enemies of unstructured charismatic leadership, become the ascendant values" (ibid.). Arian thus articulated one of the key tensions afflicting cultural industries firms and their workers: the friction between economic and creative–cultural logics. Later authors, including Ryan (1991), Hesmondhalgh and Baker (2011), and Banks (2010), have continued to investigate this basic characteristic of creative firms.

Faulkner (1973) expanded the early writing in this area with his research on players' attitudes in an orchestral sector he described as "one of the most complex, competitive, and stratified organizational sets in existence" (p. 336). Allmendinger and her colleagues (1996) studied "life and work" in 78 symphony orchestras in the United States, the United Kingdom, and pre-reunification Germany. Their findings included the insight that "orchestra players are ... fuelled by their own pride and professionalism" (Allmendinger et al., 1996, p. 201). Despite, or perhaps because of, this, their general job satisfaction ranked mid-field among thirteen groups of workers and the average rating of their satisfaction with professional growth opportunities sat at 4.9 on a seven-point scale (ibid.).

Concerns about the health and well-being effects of orchestral work have also generated extensive research (Ackermann et al., 2014; Gembris & Heye, 2018; Vastamäki et al., 2023; Abréu-Ramos & Micheo, 2007; Rotter et al., 2020). Piperek's 1981 study of "medical, psychological, sociological, and legal strain factors" in the Vienna Symphony Orchestra pioneered insights in this field and wide-ranging studies followed. Much of this research congealed around themes of mental health and stress (Herman & Clark, 2023; Halleland et al., 2009; Parasuraman & Purohit, 2000), injury (Rotter et al., 2020) and hearing loss (Behar et al., 2006; Walter, 2009).

Surveying these diverse studies highlights the following three elements of orchestral work that are particularly relevant to player-governance: security, affective resonances, and the economic–creative nexus.

2.2.1 *Security*

Widespread agreement exists that creative work is often precarious (Murray & Gollmitzer, 2012). Hesmondhalgh and Baker (2011), in their study of three cultural industries, found that insecurity is "arguably worse in the cultural industries than many other sectors, because of the uncertain and short-term nature of many cultural-industry job contracts, and the high level of subjective investment that many creative workers have in what they do" (p. 114). A lack of employment security characterises much creative work.

The insecurity observed in segments of the cultural industries also shapes the working conditions and experiences of orchestral players. The problem appears to be perennial. Writing as far back as 1960, Westby found that in the United States, "symphony musicians are an occupational group exhibiting considerable anxiety over their jobs on a number of dimensions, most prominently performance and security" (p. 223). Orchestral musicians experience security and its absence through multiple prisms (Long, 2015). Williamson and Cloonan (2016) found that in 2013 just over half of the orchestral players who were also members of the Musicians Union in the United Kingdom worked as freelancers. This situation is likely to have been exacerbated by the Covid-19 pandemic (Nørholm Lundin, 2023). However, such findings risk oversimplifying secure and precarious work (Hesmondhalgh & Baker, 2011). No matter what their contractual status is, injuries, as noted above, and early age-related declines in playing proficiency threaten the work of players. There is little current research on organisational responses to such threats in the orchestral context. In a report sponsored by the Musicians Union, Oakland (2014) interviewed orchestral musicians in the United Kingdom and concluded that there appeared to be "little meaningful dialogue between management and players as to how individuals could approach retirement with dignity and self-esteem" (p. 38). Job security remains a pervasive concern for many orchestral musicians.

2.2.2 *Affective Resonances*

An array of concepts shares a focus on psychological or affective responses to the core activity or organisational and industrial parameters of creative labour. These ideas include identification, absorption, job satisfaction, commitment, engagement, ownership, and self-realisation. Hesmondhalgh and Baker (2011) observed how creative workers might enjoy "states of pleasurable absorption in their work that are the opposite of the alienated clock-watching many of us dread in labour" (p. 132).

Self-realisation often goes hand in hand with such ideas of absorption or engagement. For Hesmondhalgh and Baker, self-realisation:

> involves a sustained sense of good work, so that work may contribute to a sense that a person might have — and other people might also share — that they are developing, flourishing, achieving excellence in forms of work activity that are valuable. (2011, p. 140)

Surveying earlier writing reveals a multifaceted picture of how orchestral musicians develop affective states such as absorption, job satisfaction, self-realisation, and identification. Breda and Kulesa (2012) surveyed 698 players in the United States. They established that "younger musicians are more stressed, less satisfied, and more critical of their orchestras and their profession than older musicians" (ibid., p. 24). National differences also play a role. Allmendinger, Hackman, and Lehman surveyed musicians in the United Kingdom, the United States, and the former West and East Germany (1996). They charted different attitudes between players in these countries in a range of satisfaction factors, including general satisfaction, as well as satisfaction with job security, pay, and management (Allmendinger et al., 1996). Mogelof and Rohrer (2005) looked for connections between satisfaction and differing levels of resourcing and established that "employment in a prestigious, resource-rich organization actually lowers … chances of deriving certain kinds of satisfaction" (p. 107). Johansson and Theorell (2003) produced similar results. Charting affective responses to the work of orchestral musicians is complicated by the sheer range of terms and concepts used (often with insufficient delineation or definitional precision) and by the diverging research findings.

Two research projects provided pertinent results (Wood, 2010; Young, 2017). Both researchers studied how job satisfaction among orchestral players correlates with taking on non-performing roles. Wood (2010) investigated the interplay of three factors and musicians' job satisfaction: conductor leadership style, employment status, and organisational participation. His work showed that musicians who "participated in the organization beyond the role of performance reported higher satisfaction ratings in 6 … of the 9 facets" (ibid., p. 164) of job satisfaction. Young (2017) also found that "musicians who hold unpaid non-performance roles report significantly higher job and role satisfaction levels than those musicians who do not have non-performance roles" (p. 69), though she also acknowledged that demonstrating causality required further research (ibid.).

Hesmondhalgh and Baker and others have observed how creative workers identify with their jobs (2011; Reid et al., 2016). The relationship between organisational identity and workers' satisfaction was emphasised by Watts (2010), who argued that job satisfaction in cultural organisations "can be improved by strengthening the level of identification between the employee and the organization" (p. 201). Orchestral musicians' identifying with their organisations as well as with their work is a core theme in the remaining chapters of this book.

2.2.3 *The Economic–Creative Nexus*

Portraying musicians as workers calls to mind debates about how economics and artistry interact in the cultural industries (Hesmondhalgh & Baker, 2011; Ryan, 1991). Some researchers foreground the economics of players' work (Case, 2013; Cloonan, 2014; Frith, 2017; Silva, 2017), but the "contradictions of the art-capital relation" (Ryan, 1991, p. 33) can never be entirely occluded. Ryan's Marxist approach teases out the contradictions by mapping the specifics of artistic labour. In particular, its irreducibility to "abstract value" (ibid. p. 44) means that "artistic workers … cannot be made to appear in the labour process as generalised, undifferentiated artists" (ibid.). In other words, musicians are not easily substitutable for each other. The reality of orchestral work observed by writers such as Arian (1971, 1974), and discussed above, suggests, however, that alienation is a common problem of artistic labour in orchestras. Musicians' work is characterised by its hybridity (2008; 2000) both between the routine, alienating work of Arian's "traditional symphonic format" (1971, p. 74) and players' desire for artistic control, and between the poles of the economic–creative nexus.

Navigating the confluence of economics and creativity while directing artistic workers requires an approach that Hesmondhalgh and Baker characterise as "unlike the top-down, inflexible supervision found in many industries" (2011, p. 84). However, most orchestras use vertical management structures and musicians routinely chafe at the authority exercised by conductors. Parasuraman and Purohit (2000) found that "disagreements with the conductor" and musicians' "perception that playing in the orchestra undermines their artistic integrity" (p. 78) "exacerbate(d) distress, boredom stress, and job dissatisfaction" (ibid. p. 80). Allmendinger et al. (1996) found that "symphony players … are not well satisfied with their managements" and "players in US Major orchestras score lower on this measure than do those in regional orchestras" (p. 203). Subsequently, Breda and Kulesa's (2012) research showed that orchestral musicians have a "general negative view of management, a mistrust of management, and the perception that management is more concerned with budgets than musical performance" (p. 12). Labour-managed orchestras bring alternative perspectives to the economic–creative nexus by giving control to workers, and this is a central focus of the interviews for this book.

Orchestral players thus constitute a heterogeneous group of workers. This section highlighted three sets of characteristics. It began by showing how musicians deal with myriad job security concerns that go beyond contracting and any division between tenured and freelance work. Musicians also experience a wide range of psychological states and affective resonances relating to their work and orchestras. Many of these—such as identification and absorption—are positive, but alienation and dissatisfaction are also common. When players form ensembles, balancing economic and artistic priorities is the third feature that frames player-governance.

2.2.4 Asset Ownership

Most orchestral musicians own their instruments, although orchestras often own or hire percussion gear. Orchestras are thus relieved of providing productive assets, even if some pay musicians modest instrument allowances. As a result, setting up an orchestra does not call for the large capital needed to, for example, open a factory. Players' owning assets means that orchestras' funding mostly covers operating rather than capital costs.[3] In terms used by Mirabel, the "sunk cost of physical capital and of human capital" (2024, p. 1) in an orchestra is borne almost entirely by the musicians. This form of asset ownership has other implications for orchestras and their workers. It eases freelancing because musicians own their tools of trade and can use them where and when they like. Furthermore, responsibility for maintaining an orchestra's assets is shifted from the company and onto its musicians. Orchestras do not generally finance their productive assets in the way that manufacturing companies own the machines and premises that their workers use, or most transport firms finance the vehicles their workers drive.

Nevertheless, other assets, including rights in recordings and brands, are valuable to orchestras. Attending a ticketed orchestral concert involves a discretionary and premium purchase for which buyers have high expectations. Brand recognition and loyalty characterise the market for concert tickets and recordings (Tong, 2016), but for musicians other than soloists, building and benefitting from a brand is only possible in an ensemble or orchestra. Players benefit from the repeat sales and regular income enjoyed by orchestras with strong brands. Although orchestras generally do not provide musicians with the productive assets (instruments) they use to work, they do offer chances to share the economic benefits of brands.

The friction in the economic–creative nexus can manifest itself in the work and life of individual musician decision-makers. Player-governance puts musicians at the centre of their firms' decision-making. It also brings the logics, priorities, and challenges of creative work into the heart of the organisations that players create and control. In the next two sections, I turn to the literature on labour-managed firms (LMFs) and assess whether orchestras—complete with their musicians—are viable sites of labour-management.

2.3 Conditions Supporting Labour-Management

This section outlines the foundational theories underlying the following empirical chapters and analysis. Dow's (2003) list of "conditions that have been said to favour LMF viability" (p. 256) provides the primary theory. The aim at this stage is not to determine the sustainability of labour-management in orchestras; that follows in the

[3] Player payments make up around 49 percent of costs for a typical US symphony orchestra (Flanagan, 2012).

later empirical chapters. Instead, in this section I assess whether, using the theories of Dow (2001, 2003, 2018) and Jensen and Meckling (1979), labour-managed orchestras are likely to emerge. I also consider the threat of degeneration in labour-management. The section highlights the challenges involved in implementing labour-management in orchestras.

Labour-managed firms come in various shapes and sizes. In 2023, Spain's Mondragon Cooperative Group had 92 cooperatives operating across more than 150 countries and more than 70,000 employees (Mondragon, 2024). The group spans banking, manufacturing, retail, and higher education. The John Lewis Partnership, one of Britain's largest retailers, posted sales of £12.8 billion in 2024 and had over 70,000 partners (John Lewis Partnership, 2025). Partnerships are common in the legal, accounting, medical, and consulting sectors (Leblebici & Sherer, 2015). At the other end of the spectrum sit countless two-person partnerships. Faced with such diversity, it is futile to search for a single model of LMFs beyond basic definitions. Nonetheless, conditions that appear to support the setting up and sustained success of LMFs can be observed and described. Dow (2001) called them "conditions under which LMFs may be expected to perform well in competition with capitalist firms" (p. 214). This section outlines these factors.

Many contributors observe greater labour-management viability and sustainability in some sectors than others. Dow (2003) found that LMFs tend to occur in the "professional services (law, accounting), craft manufacturing ... low-skill service tasks... and construction" sectors (p. 10). Jensen and Meckling (1979) also noted that partnerships were the dominant organisational form among professional services firms (see also Harlacher & Reihlen, 2014). For Alchian and Demsetz (1972), "team production in artistic or professional intellectual skills will more likely be by partnerships than other types of team production" (p. 790). Different types of enterprise interact with control by workers in distinct ways.

Pinning down conditions that facilitate or hinder labour-management across all firms is the first step toward describing the specific circumstances and practices that may or may not support labour-management in orchestras. Two key texts are germane to this investigation. Jensen and Meckling (1979) "criticize the claim that labor-managed systems are efficient" (p. 476) but go on to observe that

> the professional partnership form of labor-managed firms is more likely to dominate other organizational forms when:

1. The capital/labor ratio is small,
2. The ration of labor value added to all nonlabor costs is high
3. There are economies of scale to team production,
4. External monitoring costs are high and/or the monitoring of the productivity of team members is more cheaply performed internally,
5. The size of the team is small,

6. The returns to the human capital of the individual team members are farther from perfectly positively correlated,[4] and
7. The agency costs associated with the capitalization of future labor income are high.[5] (Ibid. p. 503)

The second key contribution comes from Dow (2003). He created a list that expands on Jensen and Meckling and encompasses wider industry conditions in which LMFs operate. Dow's list includes 18 characteristics that are conducive to labour-management:

1. Production technology and the market environment are common knowledge.
2. Production depends strongly on teamwork and information sharing.
3. Production does not require an extensive division of labor.
4. Production places workers in close geographic proximity.
5. Mutual monitoring is cheap and accurate compared with monitoring by supervisors.
6. Non-human assets are easily maintained and not highly vulnerable to abuse.
7. Non-human assets are not highly specialised.
8. High rates of investment in shared non-human assets are not required.
9. Minimum efficient scale is small, and the cost penalty for operating below minimum efficient scale is minor.
10. Workers have substantial wealth compared with the per capita financing needs of their firms, or external financing is readily available.
11. Workers are not strongly risk-averse, either because of their personal preferences or the availability of personal wealth that can be diversified through financial markets.
12. The industry is characterized by relatively stable import and output prices.
13. Rigidity in the face of short-run cost or demand shocks is not strongly penalized.
14. Workers prefer job security even at the expense of fluctuations in income or hours.
15. Egalitarian treatment of members does not conflict strongly with a need for internal incentives, or a need to recruit members on outside markets at unequal wages.

[4] In such cases, it is difficult to clearly isolate individual contributions to a team's output. This then means that fair and transparent reward and remuneration structures are equally difficult to implement. Orchestras provide a good example. The abilities of players naturally vary, particularly between experienced musicians and newcomers (though young players may have greater dexterity, stamina, and technical proficiency than their more experienced and older colleagues). But the collective, team-focused nature of orchestral music-making means that the "returns to human capital" (Jensen & Meckling, 1979, p. 503) of individual musicians cannot be isolated and cannot be correlated with reward structures. However, principal or solo players are an exception.

[5] One of the basic theoretical "asymmetries" (Dow, 2018) between capital-managed and labour-managed firms is their differing treatments of financial capital and labour. Capital suppliers can readily sell their entitlements to future returns on their investment. Labour suppliers cannot sell the future returns on their labour because doing so would result in a form of indentured labour. Such contracts are now generally illegal in Western countries (Dow, 2003).

16. Workers are relatively homogenous with respect to age, sex, and ethnic, cultural, or religious background.
17. Adverse-selection problems are minor because worker skills and the quality of non-human physical assets are easily ascertained in advance.
18. Exogenous worker turnover is infrequent. (Ibid. p. 256)

Because Dow's list expands upon the factors identified by Jensen and Meckling, I rely on it in the following analysis in which I identify five clusters of factors: (a) work practices, (b) assets and financing, (c) industrial and cultural factors, (d) organisational factors, and (e) markets. This grouping structures the following discussion.

2.3.1 Work Practices

Four of Dow's viability conditions relate to work practices. He argues that LMFs are more viable when teamwork plays a key role in production, the division of labour is minimal, "production places workers in close geographic proximity" (Dow, 2003, p. 256) and "mutual monitoring is cheap and accurate compared with monitoring by supervisors" (ibid.). Dow (2003) finds that labour control is viable when production "does not require an extensive division of labor" (p. 256). How extensive then is the division of labour in orchestras? The answer is not straightforward. The work of players and operations staff is clearly divided, though such separation is complicated when musicians take on operational roles such as executive positions.

Task specialisation features in the work of musicians. Each player is a highly trained expert and seldom plays more than one type of instrument. Some players double on instruments from the same family (oboists may play cor anglais and percussionists play a range of percussion instruments), but specialising is common within an orchestra's woodwind and brass groups. Every horn, trumpet, or trombone player requires special skills. The principal or solo player of each wind or brass instrument performs solos demanding skills rarely called for among their colleagues. String players are different. A player in the first violins might work alongside as many as 15 colleagues all playing the same part; together, they strive for unity. For string instrumentalists, conforming replaces specialising. Division of labour occurs among woodwind and brass musicians but much less among the strings.

Despite these divergent experiences of specialising, many aspects of musicians' work bring regimentation and counteract any division of labour. Players work in close physical proximity. Most start and stop at the same time, though some are only required if the score calls for their instrument. Their playing is uniformly directed by common control structures. They have a shared goal: realising one musical score. The team-focused nature of orchestral music-making counteracts demands for specialising. In some respects, the division of labour among musicians is low and suggests that orchestras may suit labour control along the lines listed by Dow in his writing on LMFs more broadly (2003).

Much has been made of orchestras as teams (Scholz & Schmitt, 2008; Vredenburgh & He, 2003). Players' work depends on and aligns closely with that of colleagues. More experienced or proficient players cannot, of course, work with greater efficiency and finish early, though mistakes can waste time. Musicians are expected to master their parts before a project begins. Rehearsals serve as information exchanges (Parton, 2014). Conductors and players share ideas on tempos, balancing, articulating, and phrasing notes and the coordinating of individual parts with others (Koivunen & Wennes, 2011). Dow (2003) argued that workers' "close geographic proximity" (p. 256) or production's dependence on "teamwork and information sharing" (ibid.) both facilitate labour-management. In these respects, work practices in orchestras make them viable sites of labour control.

The lists of LMF viability conditions created by Dow (2003) and Jensen and Meckling (1979) highlight the capacity for successful mutual monitoring. A firm's success depends on optimising production. Monitoring plays a key role in this optimisation. Labour-management has an advantage when workers monitor each other, and the result is cheaper or more accurate than using monitors from outside a team (Dow, 2003). Monitoring raises three essential questions: *What* gets monitored? *How* is it monitored? And, *who* monitors it? Monitoring in LMFs concentrates on the *who*. Workers monitoring each other's productivity typifies LMFs, but capital-controlled or externally governed firms rarely apply it (Hansmann, 1996). Most writing in the field characterises LMFs' ability to successfully implement mutual monitoring as a strength (Ben-Ner, 1988; Bowles & Gintis, 1990, 1993, 1996; Jensen, 2000; McCain, 2007). However, questions remain about the viability of peer-to-peer monitoring in orchestras and ensembles.

Some types of work are harder to monitor than others. In these cases, reciprocal monitoring may achieve greater efficiency than hierarchical types. Creative and knowledge-intensive labour can present challenges for external monitors and may benefit from peer-to-peer monitoring. The "ambiguities of the results produced" (Alvesson, 2004, p. 64) characterise sectors such as the performing arts, law, accounting, and consulting. These ambiguities suggest that lawyers are best placed to evaluate and monitor the work of other lawyers, accountants can best monitor the work of their peers, and musicians may be able to successfully evaluate the work of other players. Peer monitoring can bring benefits if workers have information or perspectives that are unavailable to monitors from outside a work group and if it is suited to the type of activity being monitored.

Worker-to-worker monitoring may falter, however, if incentives to undertake it are weak, especially when it creates burdens for workers. To be viable, such monitoring in LMFs must balance the responsibilities it imposes on workers with benefits to them and their firms. In much thinking on LMFs, financial returns to members represent the primary benefits. Jensen and Meckling (1979) made such a connection in noting how "profit sharing will … tend to be more efficient when the team members themselves have a comparative advantage over an outsider in monitoring the behavior of other team members" (p. 502). In not-for-profits such as orchestras, surpluses cannot be shared and other incentives become necessary if mutual monitoring is to be sustained. Here, the query concerns whether incentives other than profit-sharing suffice to make such monitoring viable in the face of any resistance from workers who take on the burdens it imposes.

2.3.2 Assets and Financing

Establishing a firm requires financial and human capital, productive assets, or intellectual property. Some firms and sectors are more capital-intensive than others. An indicator of a firm's capital requirements is provided by comparing them to ongoing labour costs. High capital-to-labour ratios inhibit labour-management if workers cannot raise the funds needed and banks or other financiers refuse to lend to workers or to their LMFs (Dow, 2003; Jossa & Cuomo, 1997). Dow (2003) proposed that LMF viability is favoured when firms do not require "high rates of investment" (p. 256), when assets are "easily maintained" (ibid.), "not highly specialised" (ibid.), and when workers have "substantial wealth compared with the per capita financing needs of their firms" (ibid.). To what extent do these conditions show up in orchestras?

As noted earlier, most musicians own their instruments, though some orchestras purchase unusual ones. Instruments are very specialised, but orchestras do not need to pay for their primary productive assets.[6] Asset financing in orchestras thus aligns with Dow's (2003) theorising that the absence of demands for "high rates of investment in shared non-human assets" (p. 256) favours labour-management. Jensen and Meckling (1979) also argued that firms with low capital–labour ratios are more likely to succeed as LMFs. Owning their tools of trade incentivises players to maintain and protect them from abuse. Labour-management theories maintain that such incentives bolster the viability of musicians controlling an orchestra. The asset and financing models found in orchestras appear to make them viable as candidates for control by workers. Problems nonetheless arise when trying to establish whether workers in orchestras have "substantial wealth compared with the per capita financing needs of their firms" (Dow, 2003, p. 256). As just outlined, the capital and asset-funding requirements of orchestras are low; however, the personal wealth of orchestral musicians has not been reliably mapped. What can be said is that when orchestral musicians own expensive tools of the trade—their instruments—at least these assets can count as wealth in a comparison with the financing needs of their firms.

[6] The small instrument allowances some orchestras pay to players are operating costs rather than capital expenditure.

2.3.3 Industrial and Cultural Factors

Dow's (2003) LMF viability conditions include workers' preferencing job security without being "strongly risk-averse" (p. 256) when it comes to personal wealth. His list also identified the "egalitarian treatment of members" and the "relatively homogenous" cultural, ethnic, religious, age, and sex backgrounds of members (Dow, 2003, p. 256).[7] Dow (2003) argued that control by labour is supported when "workers are not strongly risk-averse, either because of their personal preferences or the availability of personal wealth that can be diversified through financial markets" (p. 256) and when "workers prefer job security even at the expense of fluctuations in income or hours" (ibid.). All enterprises involve risk. The important question in the context of labour-management is who takes the risk: capital providers or labour providers? In capital-controlled firms, capital owners assume most risk and receive rewards in the form of financial returns. Labour-management transfers uncertainty to workers, either because they provide the firm's capital or the firm hires such capital and workers risk losing collateral used to secure the loaned capital (Jossa & Cuomo, 1997). For labour, the rewards may be financial, but workers may also opt to "take out their income from the enterprise not in the form of monetary or other physical returns but rather in the form of intangibles" (Vanek, 1970, p. 12). Greater job security can be such an intangible benefit.

Labour-management firm members face the dilemmas of incentives and risk, the financial stability of their organisations and horizon problems[8] (Ellerman, 1986). (These concerns were an element of my empirical research and are covered in the analytical chapters of this book.) Remuneration and reward policies attempt to balance these factors and are key elements in the viability of labour-management in orchestras. Finding a sustainable equilibrium is especially challenging in a labour-managed context, in part because of the diversity of risk appetites and portfolios among decision-making members (Dow, 2001). New members with long careers ahead of them, for example, may have greater openness to risk-taking than those who expect to retire in the near term (Jensen & Meckling, 1979).

Insecure work manifests itself very differently among orchestral musicians. As Cloonan (2014) observed, orchestras represent "one of the few places to guarantee permanent contracts for musicians" (p. 19). Nonetheless, many players of orchestral instruments work without the security offered by large, publicly funded orchestras,[9] either because they are yet to secure a contract with such an employer or because

[7] For further research into the interaction between diversity and cooperation, see Huberman and Glance's work on diversity and collective action in civil society contexts (1993, 1998).

[8] A horizon problem arises when decision-makers prefer increased near-term benefits at the cost of long-term payoffs. This might, for example, occur if workers choose an immediate increase in wages over investment in assets that promise future returns (1993, 1998, Dow, 2003).

[9] Terminology plays a role in these discussions. Secure work is the norm if the term "orchestral musician" is taken to mean only those employed by large, tenured orchestras. When the term includes all musicians who play orchestral instruments, it encompasses early-career players seeking a secure orchestral position as well as those who work as freelancers.

they work in sectors in which tenure is rare. Such sectors include historically informed performance, contemporary music ensembles, and chamber orchestras, all of which feature in my research cohort. The orchestras and ensemble studied for this book only offer freelance contracts, and the focus thus falls on the freelance segment of the orchestral sector.

The precarious working lives of many freelance orchestral musicians often mirror uncertainties created by programming. Even when an orchestra or ensemble performs regularly, there may be no need for a specific musician if the scheduled works do not call for their instrument. Large, publicly funded orchestras offer year-long contracts that smooth the peaks and troughs of scheduling, while providing musicians with regular salaries. Freelance orchestras like those featured in this research do not, however, provide similar security. Jensen and Meckling suggested that such variability and insecurity may foster labour-management. They found that in circumstances in which a disproportionately large fraction of an individual's wealth is represented by his human capital and when the cash flows on that human capital are highly uncertain from period to period we also expect to see profit-sharing partnerships arise. (Jensen & Meckling, 1979, p. 502)

Such circumstances apply in the professional lives of many musicians in the orchestras studied. The freelance nature of their work, coupled with the variability of demand for players, can mean individuals may not be engaged for weeks at a time. The desire to reduce workers' cash-flow variability and bolster job security may incentivise musicians to control their firms, even if full employment security is only partly achievable. As Dow (2018) noted, "LMFs may attract a subset of workers whose preferences for job security is unusually strong" (p. 113). Workers' attitudes to security and risk are central to theories on labour-management. They also play a key role in the empirical chapters of this book. Important overlaps exist between labour-management theory and the experience of orchestra workers. The security and risk-focused conditions for LMF viability listed by Dow and Jensen and Meckling suggest orchestras may, in these respects, be viable as LMFs.

2.3.4 Organisational Factors

The last group of LMF viability conditions consists of organisational factors. These include the ability to successfully function at a small "minimum efficient scale" (Dow, 2003, p. 256), infrequent "exogenous worker turnover" (ibid.), and the ease with which "worker skills and the quality of non-human physical assets" can be "ascertained in advance" (ibid.), thus minimising adverse selection. All firms have an interest in establishing the skills of potential workers before they engage them. In LMFs, doing so has added weight because new members share control. As Dow (2003) wrote, "in their roles as decision-makers, residual claimants, and asset owners, LMF insiders take a keen interest in the characteristics of any new member" (p. 159). Poor recruiting can be costly for firms. But choosing new hires presents challenges, particularly when an information asymmetry exists between a firm and a potential employee or LMF member. Orchestras' discovering players' proficiency in advance is, however, boosted by a well-developed system of auditioning and extended probations. By vetting an applicant's credentials as a member as well as a player, recruiting plays a key role in the governance of labour-managed orchestras.

Chamber orchestras and ensembles can operate at a small "minimum efficient scale" (Dow, 2003, p. 256), if the repertoire is selected appropriately. For example, with 16 players, Ensemble Musikfabrik has the smallest membership of the firms in my study. The average number of members in the research cohort is 34. All the firms studied engage supernumerary players as required by repertoire-driven changes in demand for musicians. PGOs outside the research group, including the London Symphony Orchestra or the Berlin Philharmonic, regularly have between seventy and ninety musicians on stage.

Worker turnover can be a problem for LMFs if it creates horizon problems. Such problems arise if, for example, a soon-to-depart member prefers short-term returns over long-term investing in the firm. However, horizon problems can be limited if turnover among workers is low (Dow, 2003). Low worker turnover helps LMFs make long-term commitments that contribute to governance and organisational sustainability. What, then, does the literature say about turnover among orchestral musicians? Allmendinger et al. (1996) found that "relative to other professions, there is not much career mobility for symphony orchestra musicians" (p. 204) and that "retirement is far and away the most common reason for departure among major orchestra players" (p. 206). The highly specialised skills of musicians, coupled with the high rates of precarious work in the sector, also keep down job turnover among orchestral musicians (Flanagan, 2012), though many players undertake regular freelance session playing or teaching with other employers (Cottrell, 2004). That orchestras enjoy low worker turnover suggests further alignment with Dow's list of viability conditions. By minimising the risk of horizon problems, low turnover among musicians may also contribute to the viability of labour-managed orchestras.

2.3.5 Markets

The remaining three of Dow's viability conditions describe markets for a firm's products or services as well as LMF responses to changes in those marketplaces. He observed that worker control is viable when firms can absorb "short run cost or demand shocks" (Dow, 2003, p. 256); when an industry enjoys "relatively stable" prices and when "production technology and the market environment are common knowledge" (ibid.). All of these conditions apply in orchestras, if to varying degrees. Demand for performances, tours, or projects varies considerably and can be difficult to predict (Pompe et al., 2013). The result can be "short run cost or demand shocks" (Dow, 2003, p. 256) when individual projects require large resources or involve repertoire outside the mainstream that achieves lower-than-expected revenue. Nonetheless, non-performance revenues such as sponsorships, as well as public and philanthropic funding,[10] can allow orchestras to absorb short-term losses and even deficits from whole seasons (Flanagan, 2012; Salvaggio, 2024).

Orchestras do not seek competitive advantage through their production technology—there is very little variation in how concerts are prepared and presented. Instead, they usually seek to differentiate themselves through marketing and to a lesser extent through pricing (Courty & Pagliero, 2014; Seaman, 2006). The essential non-human elements of an orchestra's production system—the instruments and playing techniques—are common knowledge and were more or less standardised by the early twentieth century. In recent years, leading orchestras have begun video-streaming their concerts as well as experimenting with other enhancements to the audience experience (Janer et al., 2016; Prockup et al., 2013). Limited technology-based competition may emerge between well-resourced orchestras if more sophisticated websites, software, or other technologies confer advantages over their rivals. However, selling tickets to live events remains an orchestra's core business. Here, the "production technology" (Dow, 2003, p. 256) remains widely adopted and common knowledge. Similarly, the core market environment for orchestral performances is public knowledge. Any observer can easily estimate the number of tickets sold for a particular performance. In terms of market dynamics, orchestras' operating models thus align with the relevant conditions of labour-management viability proposed by Dow. Critical features of their markets make orchestras viable as sites of labour governance.

2.4 The Degeneration Threat

Important writers on labour-management also consider the potential for degeneration in LMFs. Michels (2000 (1915)) observed a degenerative tendency in democratic political systems and labelled it an "iron law of oligarchy" (pp. 224–35). Pencavel (2013) noted how "the belief that worker co-ops lose their distinctive participatory and democratic character over time and either close or convert to conventional capitalist firms is widely held" (online article, no page). Cornforth (1995) observed that "historically there has been a good deal of pessimism about the possibility of sustaining genuinely democratic forms of organization" (p. 487). Such loss is often tied to a drift away from high-participation decision-making toward control by a small subset of workers. Stryjan (1989) isolated two degenerative "processes":

> … the one, a gradual restriction and, eventually, elimination of all steering inputs, save for loyalty; a restriction commonly legitimated by reasons of expedience; and the other, a

[10] Public funding varies greatly between orchestras. The Mahler Chamber Orchestra, for example, received practically no "substantial and long-term public funding" (Mahler Chamber Orchestra, 2018) during the first 20 years of its operation. The London Mozart Players adopted player-governance in 2014 when all of its public funding and that of its major sponsor were cut entirely (Hewett, 2014).

> successive deterioration in the quality of membership, through selective exit of involved members. (p. 87)

Jossa (2017) also warned that "the most proactive members of a cooperative and those interested in rapid and efficient decision-making may be tempted to gain full control of the firm by ousting the other members one by one" (p. 185). For many researchers in the field, degeneration threatens governance sustainability in LMFs.

The threat of degeneration in labour-management is, nonetheless, debated. Dow (2018) takes issue with the idea that a transition from labour-management to capital-management is degenerative. The lack of agreement among theorists on suitable measures to address threats to democratic decision-making hampers any axiological evaluation of transitions from democratic to oligarchic governance in orchestras as much as in the economy as a whole. What this research seeks to understand is how PGOs, as a type of LMF, resist the threat of degeneration and sustain control by workers. I consider specific aspects of the degeneration threat and responses to them throughout the book.

2.5 Orchestras and Labour-Management

This chapter provided unique perspectives into the possibilities and perils of labour-management in orchestras. Establishing whether orchestras make viable candidates for labour-management lies at the heart of this opening investigation. It combined and contrasted the theories on labour-management and the conditions found in these firms. The following questions guided the chapter: What does the theoretical work say about the potential of labour-managed orchestras as they begin operating? Do orchestras' practices, structures, and markets facilitate or hinder workers' potential to control such firms?

The study highlighted five features of orchestras with parallels in LMF theory: (1) work practices, including the division of labour and teamwork; (2) assets and financing; (3) industrial and cultural factors; (4) organisational factors; and (5) markets. The orchestral operating model, with its work practices, entrepreneurial dynamics, incentives, hierarchies, and boundaries, makes these firms viable sites for control by workers, though questions remain. The mixed messages emerging from the current chapter's study of orchestras as sites of labour-management need further scrutiny.

Viability does not guarantee longevity. The long-term viability of labour governance in orchestras—its sustainability—still requires investigation. Additional rationales and drivers may undermine labour governance in orchestras as these firms evolve and develop. The following research into the sustainability of labour-management in orchestras congeals around three broad themes: realising and operationalising labour-management in orchestras, facilitating and channelling participation, and optimising performance. Within these zones of interest, critical questions emerge concerning the importance of players exercising artistic control, boosting job security as a critical form of utility for workers, and creating sustainable governance structures. Bolstering workers' participation in decision-making by renegotiating hierarchies at the same time as navigating affective responses such as commitment, engagement, and identification form further focal points. The challenges of optimising performance in a labour-governed context (in particular, mutual monitoring) are also central to the insights that emerge from the empirical study presented in the remaining sections.

The focus now shifts from the theoretical analysis of the current chapter to the empirical and qualitative research I undertook in seeking to establish what underpins and supports the sustainability of worker governance in the orchestras and ensemble I studied. Labour-management theory necessarily blends out the work of individuals. The remaining chapters, on the other hand, prioritise the insights and perspectives of workers—in this case, orchestral players and management staff. Their thinking tends to get lost in theoretical studies, but studying workers' ideas about job security, work practices, monitoring, teamwork, and other features of work in orchestras enriches the understanding of labour control in practice. The attitudes, experiences, and ideas that orchestral workers voiced about their work and firms take centre stage in the remainder of the book.

References

Abréu-Ramos, A., & Micheo, W. (2007). Lifetime prevalence of upper-body musculoskeletal problems in a professional-level symphony orchestra: Age, gender, and instrument-specific results. *Medical Problems of Performing Artists, 22*(3), 97–104. https://doi.org/10.21091/mppa.2007.3022

Ackermann, B. J., Kenny, D. T., O'Brien, I., & Driscoll, T. (2014). Sound practice—improving occupational health and safety for professional orchestral musicians in Australia. *Frontiers in Psychology, 5*, 1–11. https://doi.org/10.3389/fpsyg.2014.00973

Alchian, A. A., & Demsetz, H. (1972). Production, information costs, and economic organization. *The American Economic Review, 62*(5), 777–795. https://www.jstor.org/stable/1815199

Allmendinger, J., Hackman, J. R., & Lehman, E. V. (1996). Life and work in symphony orchestras. *The Musical Quarterly, 80*(2), 194–219. https://doi.org/10.2307/742362

Alvesson, M. (2004). *Knowledge work and knowledge-intensive firms*. Oxford University Press.

Arian, E. (1971). *Bach, Beethoven, and bureaucracy: The Case of the Philadelphia Orchestra*. University of Alabama.

Arian, E. (1974). Some problems of collective bargaining in symphony orchestras. *Labor Law Journal, 25*(11), 666–672.

Ayer, J. (2005). *More than meets the ear: How symphony musicians made labor history*. Syren Book Company.

Banks, M. (2010). Autonomy guaranteed? Cultural work and the 'Art-Commerce Relation. *Journal for Cultural Research, 14*(3), 251–269. https://doi.org/10.1080/14797581003791487

Bathurst, R., Williams, L., & Rodda, A. (2007). Letting go of the reins: Paradoxes and puzzles in leading an artistic enterprise. *International Journal of Arts Management, 9*(2), 29–38. https://www.jstor.org/stable/41798995

Behar, A., Wong, W., & Kunov, H. (2006). Risk of hearing loss in orchestra musicians: Review of the literature. *Medical Problems of Performing Artists, 21*(4), 164–168. https://doi.org/10.21091/mppa.2006.4035

Ben-Ner, A. (1988). The life cycle of worker-owned firms in market economies. *Journal of Economic Behavior & Organization, 10*(3), 287–313. https://doi.org/10.1016/0167-2681(88)90052-2
Bennett, D. (2008). *Understanding the classical music profession: The past, the present and strategies for the future*. Ashgate.
Bibu, N., Brancu, L., & Teohari, G. A. (2018). Managing a symphony orchestra in times of change: Behind the curtains. *Procedia – Social and Behavioral Sciences, 238*, 507–516. https://doi.org/10.1016/j.sbspro.2018.04.030
Bowles, S., & Gintis, H. (1993). A political and economic case for the democratic enterprise. *Economics and Philosophy, 9*(1), 75–100. https://doi.org/10.1017/S0266267100005125
Brandfonbrener, A. (2003). From the editor: Old musicians never die: Issues of aging in orchestral musicians. *Medical Problems of Performing Artists, 18*(4), 135–136. https://doi.org/10.21091/mppa.2003.4023
Breda, J., & Kulesa, P. (2012). *Stress and job satisfaction among symphony musicians*. Symphony Orchestra Institute.
Brodsky, W. (2025). *Seasoned musicians playing beyond the 5th decade: A Case study on symphony orchestra lifestyle and ageing*. Oxford University Press. https://doi.org/10.1093/9780198956501.001.0001
Broughton, A. (2001). Collective bargaining in the arts and culture sector: An examination of symphony orchestras in Germany and the UK. *European Journal of Industrial Relations, 7*(3), 327–345. https://doi.org/10.1177/095968010173006
Cairnduff, S. (2026). *Harmonising cultural leadership in professional orchestras*. Taylor and Francis.
Case, K. (2013). The commoditization of symphony orchestra musicians. *The Horn Call: Journal of the International Horn Society, 43*(3), 71–72. https://journals.lib.unb.ca/index.php/MC/article/view/22354
Cloonan, M. (2014). Musicians as workers: Putting the UK Musicians' Union into context. *MUSICultures, 41*(1), 10–29. https://journals.lib.unb.ca/index.php/MC/article/view/22354
Cornforth, C. (1995). Patterns of cooperative management: Beyond the degeneration thesis. *Economic and Industrial Democracy, 16*(4), 487–523. https://doi.org/10.1177/0143831X95164002
Cottrell, S. (2004). *Professional music-making in London: Ethnography and experience*. Ashgate.
Courty, P., & Pagliero, M. (2014). The pricing of art and the art of pricing: Pricing styles in the concert industry." Chapter 13. In V. A. Ginsburgh & D. Throsby (Eds.), *Handbook of the economics of art and culture*. Elsevier. https://doi.org/10.1016/B978-0-444-53776-8.00013-1
Dobson, M. C., & Gaunt, H. F. (2013). Musical and social communication in expert orchestral performance. *Psychology of Music*, 1–19. https://doi.org/10.1177/0305735613491998
Dow, G. (2001). Allocating control over firms: Stock markets versus membership markets. *Review of Industrial Organization, 1*(2), 201–218. https://www.jstor.org/stable/41798995
Dow, G. (2003). *Governing the firm: Workers' control in theory and practice*. Cambridge University Press.
Dow, G. (2018). *The labor-managed firm: Theoretical foundations*. Cambridge University Press.
Drucker, P. (1985). Playing in the information-based 'orchestra'. *The Wall Street Journal Western Edition*, 4 June.
Drucker, P. (1988). The coming of the new organization. *Harvard Business Review, 66*(1), 45–53.
Drucker, P. (1993). Tomorrow's manager: More of an orchestra conductor than an administrator. Success.
Ellerman, D. P. (1986). Horizon problems and property rights in labor-managed firms. *Journal of Comparative Economics, 10*(1), 62–78. https://doi.org/10.1016/0147-5967(86)90119-8
Faulkner, R. (1973). Career concerns and mobility motivations of orchestra musicians. *The Sociological Quarterly, 14*(3), 334–349. https://doi.org/10.2307/4105682
Faulkner, R. (1974). Coming of age in organizations: A comparative study of career contingencies and adult socialization. *Work and Occupations, 1*(2), 131–173. https://doi.org/10.1177/073088847400100201

Flanagan, R. (2010). Symphony musicians and symphony orchestras. Chapter 8. In C. Brown, B. J. Eichengreen, & M. Reich (Eds.), *Labor in the era of globalization*. Cambridge University Press.

Flanagan, R. (2012). *The perilous life of symphony orchestras: Artistic triumphs and economic challenges*. Yale University Press.

Frith, S. (2017). Are workers musicians? *Popular Music, 36*(1), 111–115. https://doi.org/10.1017/S0261143016000714

Gembris, H., Heye., A., & Seifert, A. (2018). Health problems of orchestral musicians from a life-span perspective: Results of a large-scale study. *Music and Science, 1*, 1–20. https://doi.org/10.1177/2059204317739801

Gembris, H., & Heye, A. (2014). Growing older in a symphony orchestra: The development of the age-related self-concept and the self-estimated performance of professional musicians in a lifespan perspective. *Musicae Scientiae, 18*(4), 371–391. https://doi.org/10.1177/1029864914548912

Glynn, M. (2000). When cymbals become symbols: Conflict over organizational identity within a symphony orchestra. *Organization Science, 11*(3), 285–298. http://www.jstor.org/stable/2640262

Glynn, M. (2008). Maestro or manager? Examining the role of the music director in a symphony orchestra. In J. Lampel, J. Shamsie, & T. Lant (Eds.), *The business of culture: Strategic perspectives on entertainment and media*. Taylor & Francis.

Halleland, H., Harris, A., Sørnes, S., Murison, R., & Ursin, H. (2009). Subjective health complaints, stress, and coping in orchestra musicians. *Medical Problems of Performing Artists, 24*(2), 58–62. https://www.jstor.org/stable/48710793

Hansmann, H. (1996). *The ownership of enterprise*. The Belknap Press of Harvard University Press.

Harlacher, D., & Reihlen, M. (2014). Governance of professional service firms: A configurational approach. *Business Research, 7*(1), 125–160. https://doi.org/10.1007/s40685-014-0006-8

Herman, A. (2023). *Orchestra management: Models and repertoires for the symphony orchestra*. Routledge.

Herman, R., & Clark, T. (2023). It's not a virus! reconceptualizing and de-pathologizing music performance anxiety. *Frontiers in Psychology, 14*. https://doi.org/10.3389/fpsyg.2023.1194873

Hesmondhalgh, D., & Baker, S. (2011). *Creative labour: Media work in three cultural industries*. Routledge. https://doi.org/10.4324/9780203855881

Hewett, I. (2014). *London Mozart Players: The Ultimate Comeback Kids*. The Telegraph, 28 May, Accessed 19 October 2025. https://www.telegraph.co.uk/culture/music/classicalmusic/10858384/London-Mozart-Players-the-ultimate-comeback-kids.html

Holoman, D. K. (2012). *The orchestra: A very short introduction*. Oxford University Press.

Huberman, B. A., & Glance, N. (1993). Diversity and collective action. In H. Haken & A. Mikhailov (Eds.), *Interdisciplinary approaches to nonlinear complex systems*. Springer. https://doi.org/10.1007/978-3-642-51030-4_5

Huberman, B. A., & Glance, N. S. (1998). Beliefs and cooperation. In P. A. Danielson (Ed.), *Modeling rationality, morality, and evolution*. Oxford University Press.

Hunt, J., Stelluto, G., & Hooijberg, R. (2004). Toward new-wave organization creativity: Beyond romance and analogy in the relationship between orchestra-conductor leadership and musician creativity. *Leadership Quarterly, 15*(1), 145–162. https://doi.org/10.1016/j.leaqua.2003.12.009

Janer, J., Gomez, E., Martorell, A., Miron, M., & de Wit, B.. (2016). "Immersive Orchestras: Audio Processing for Orchestral Music Vr Content," paper presented at 2016 8th International Conference on Games and Virtual Worlds for Serious Applications (VS-GAMES), 7–9 Sept. 2016.

Jensen, M. (2000). *A theory of the firm, governance, residual claims, and organizational forms*. Harvard University Press.

Jensen, M., & Meckling, W. (1979). Rights and production functions: An application to labor-managed firms and codetermination. *Journal of Business, 52*(4), 469–506. https://www.jstor.org/stable/2352442

Johansson, Y. L., & Theorell, T. (2003). Satisfaction with work task quality correlates with employee health. *Medical Problems of Performing Artists, 18*(4), 141–149. https://www.jstor.org/stable/48710968

John Lewis Partnership. (2025). *Annual report and accounts 2025*. John Lewis Partnership. https://www.johnlewispartnership.co.uk/content/dam/cws/pdfs/Juniper/ARA2025/JLP-plc-ARA-2024-25.pdf.

Jossa, B. (2017). *Labour managed firms and post-capitalism*. Routledge. https://doi.org/10.4324/9781315299518

Jossa, B., & Cuomo, G. (1997). *The economic theory of socialism and the labour-managed firm: Markets, socialism, and labour management*. Edward Elgar.

Kammerhoff, J., Lauenstein, O., & Schütz, A. (2019). Leading toward harmony—different types of conflict mediate how followers' perceptions of transformational leadership are related to job satisfaction and performance. *European Management Journal, 37*(2), 210–221. https://doi.org/10.1016/j.emj.2018.06.003

Khodyakov, D. (2007). The complexity of trust-control relationships in creative organizations: Insights from a qualitative analysis of a conductorless orchestra. *Social Forces, 86*(1), 1–22. https://www.jstor.org/stable/4495025

Koivunen, N., & Wennes, G. (2011). Show us the sound! Aesthetic leadership of symphony orchestra conductors. *Leadership, 7*(1), 51–71. https://doi.org/10.1177/1742715010386865

Krause, D. (2015). Four types of leadership and orchestra quality. *Nonprofit Management and Leadership, 25*(4), 431. https://doi.org/10.1002/nml.21132

Leblebici, H., & Sherer, P. D. (2015). Governance in professional service firms, from structural and cultural to legal normative views. In L. Empson, D. Muzio, & J. Broschak (Eds.), *The Oxford handbook of professional service firms*. Oxford University Press.

Lewis, L. (2012). The incomplete conductor: Theorizing the conductor's role in orchestral interpretation in the light of shared leadership practices. (Doctoral dissertation) Royal Holloway, University of London, UK. https://pure.royalholloway.ac.uk/portal/files/11821983/2012lewislaphd.pdf.

Long, B. (2015). Forms of precarity and the orchestral musician. *The Asia Pacific Journal of Arts and Cultural Management, 12*(1), 3–13. http://apjacm.arts.unimelb.edu.au/article/view/207/0

Luksetich, W., & Lange, M. (1995). A simultaneous model of nonprofit symphony orchestra behavior. *Journal of Cultural Economics, 19*(1), 49–68. http://www.jstor.org/stable/41810532

Mahler Chamber Orchestra. (2018). 5 Questions for Michael Hoffmann-Becking. Accessed October 18, 2025. https://mahlerchamber.com/news/5-questions-for-michael-hoffmann-becking.

Manturzewska, M. (1990). A biographical study of the life-span development of professional musicians. *Psychology of Music, 18*(2), 112–139. https://doi.org/10.1177/0305735690182002

Marx, K. (2011). *Capital, volume I: A critique of political economy*. Translated by Moore, Samuel, and Edward Aveling. Dover.

McCain, R. (2007). Cooperation and effort, reciprocity and mutual supervision in worker cooperatives. In S. Novkovic & V. Sena (Eds.), *Cooperative firms in global markets: Incidence, viability and economic performance*. Emerald. https://doi.org/10.1016/S0885-3339(06)10007-1

Michels, R. 2000 (1915). *Political parties: A sociological study of the oligarchical tendencies of modern democracy*. Translated by Paul, Eden, & Cedar Paul. Batoche Books.

Mintzberg, H. (1998). Covert leadership: Notes on managing professionals. *Harvard Business Review, 97*(6), 140–147. https://hbr.org/1998/11/covert-leadership-notes-on-managing-professionals

Mirabel, T. (2024). Do sunk costs nip worker-owned firms in the bud? *Economic and Industrial Democracy*. https://doi.org/10.1177/0143831X241284832

Mogelof, J. P., & Rohrer, L. H. (2005). Rewards and sacrifices in elite and non-elite organizations: Participation in valued activities and job satisfaction in two symphony orchestras. *International Journal of Manpower, 26*(1), 93–109. https://doi.org/10.1108/01437720510587307

Mondragon. (2024). *Humanity at work, annual report*. Mondragon Corporation. https://www.mondragon-corporation.com/people/site/assets/files/103207/annual-report-2023.pdf

Murray, C., & Gollmitzer, M. (2012). Escaping the precarity trap: A call for creative labour policy. *International Journal of Cultural Policy, 18*(4), 419–438. https://doi.org/10.1080/10286632.2011.591490

Newton, T. (2022). *Orchestra management handbook: Building relationships in turbulent times*. Oxford University Press. https://doi.org/10.1093/oso/9780197550670.001.0001

Nørholm Lundin, A. (2023). "Where is your fixed point?" dealing with ambiguous freelance musician careers. *Cultural Trends, 32*(3), 231–246. https://doi.org/10.1080/09548963.2022.2075715

Oakland, J. (2014). *Ageing and retirement: Towards and understanding of the experiences of symphony musicians as they approach retirement.* https://doi.org/10.13140/RG.2.1.1385.8408

Parasuraman, S., & Purohit, Y. S. (2000). Distress and boredom among orchestra musicians: The two faces of stress. *Journal of Occupational Health Psychology, 5*(1), 74–83.

Parton, K. (2014). Epistemic stance in orchestral interaction. *Social Semiotics, 24*(4), 402–419. https://doi.org/10.1080/10350330.2014.929389

Pencavel, J. (2013). The economics of worker cooperatives. In *Elgar research reviews in economics*. Edward Elgar. https://doi.org/10.4337/9781784710545

Pompe, J., Tamburri, L., & Munn, J. (2013). Symphony concert demand: Does programming matter? *Journal of Arts Management, Law & Society, 43*(4), 215–228. https://doi.org/10.1080/10632921.2013.818085

Prockup, M., Grunberg, D., Hrybyk, A., & Kim, Y. E. (2013). Orchestral performance companion: Using real-time audio to score alignment. *IEEE Multimedia, 20*(2), 52–60. https://doi.org/10.1109/MMUL.2013.26

Reid, A., Petocz, P., & Bennett, D. (2016). Is creative work sustainable? Understanding identity, motivation, and worth. *Australian Journal of Career Development, 25*(1), 33–41. https://doi.org/10.1177/1038416216637089

Roose, H. (2008). Many-voiced or unisono? An inquiry into motives for attendance and aesthetic dispositions of the audience attending classical concerts. *Acta Sociologica, 51*(3), 237–253. http://www.jstor.org/stable/20460057

Rotter, G., Noeres, K., Fernholz, I., Willich, S. N., Schmidt, A., & Berghoefer, A. (2020). Musculoskeletal disorders and complaints in professional musicians: A systematic review of prevalence, risk factors, and clinical treatment effects. *International Archives of Occupational and Environmental Health, 93*(2), 149–187. https://doi.org/10.1007/s00420-019-01467-8

Ryan, Bill. (1991). *Making capital from culture: The corporate form of cultural production.* De Gruyter.

Salvaggio, S. A. (2024). *Orchestra management in practice*. Routledge. https://doi.org/10.4324/9781032629636

Savage, K., & Symonds, D. (2018). *Economies of collaboration in performance: More than the sum of the parts*. Palgrave MacMillan.

Scholz, C., & Schmitt, A. (2008). Orchester Als Hochleistungsteams?. Chapter 18. In P. Pawlowsky & P. Mistele (Eds.), *Hochleistungsmanagement*. Gabler. https://doi.org/10.1007/978-3-8349-9878-1_18

Seaman, B. (2006). Empirical studies of demand for the performing arts. Chapter 14. In V. A. Ginsburg & D. Throsby (Eds.), *Handbook of the economics of art and culture*. Elsevier. https://doi.org/10.1016/S1574-0676(06)01014-3

Silva, M. D. (2017). Are musicians "Ordinary Workers"? Labor organization and the question of "Artistic Value" in the first years of the Portuguese musicians' class association: 1909–1913. *Popular Music & Society, 40*(5), 518–538. https://doi.org/10.1080/03007766.2017.1348671

Spitzer, J. (1996). Metaphors of the orchestra—the orchestra as a metaphor. *The Musical Quarterly, 80*(2), 234–264. http://www.jstor.org/stable/742364

Spitzer, J., & Zaslaw, N. (2004). *The birth of the orchestra: History of an institution (1650–1815)*. Oxford University Press.

Stryjan, Y. (1989). *Impossible organizations: Self-management and organizational reproduction*. Greenwood Press.

Tong, E. (2016). Passion, identity, and the model of goal-directed behaviour in a classical music context. (Doctoral dissertation) RMIT, Australia. https://researchbank.rmit.edu.au/view/rmit:161659

Vanek, J. (1970). *The general theory of labor-managed market economies*. Cornell University Press.

Vastamäki, M., Heliövaara, M., Vastamäki, H., & Ristolainen, L. (2023). Orchestra musicians' work environment and health versus general workforce. *Journal of Occupational & Environmental Medicine, 65*(4), 344–348. https://doi.org/10.1097/JOM.0000000000002763

Vredenburgh, D., & He, I. Y. (2003). Leadership lessons from a conductorless orchestra. *Business Horizons, 46*(5), 19. https://doi.org/10.1016/S0007-6813(03)00067-3

Walter, J. S. (2009). Sound exposure levels experienced by university wind band members. *Medical Problems of Performing Artists, 24*(2), 63–70. https://www.proquest.com/scholarly-journals/sound-exposure-levels-experienced-university-wind/docview/196339352/se-2

Watts, S. (2010). Identification and the cultural organization: How the concept of identification can impact the constituencies who work within cultural organizations. *Journal of Arts Management, Law & Society, 40*(3), 200–216. https://doi.org/10.1080/10632921.2010.506173

Westby, D. L. (1960). The career experience of the symphony musician. *Social Forces, 38*(3), 223–230. https://www.jstor.org/stable/2574085

Williamson, J., & Cloonan, M. (2016). *Players' work time: A history of the British Musicians' Union, 1893–2013*. Manchester University Press.

Wood, R. (2010). Correlation of conductor leadership style, musician employment status, organizational participation to orchestra musician job satisfaction. (Doctoral dissertation) University of Phoenix. https://www.proquest.com/dissertationstheses/correlation-conductor-leadership-style-musician/docview/911029205/se-2

Young, A. (2017). Job satisfaction of orchestral musicians: The effects of non-performance organizational roles. (Doctoral dissertation) University of Miami. https://scholarlyrepository.miami.edu/oa_dissertations/1825.

Young, D., & Vaupel, J. W. (1981). Organization and orchestra: Lessons from the pit. *Journal of Policy Analysis & Management, 1*(2), 264–267.

Chapter 3
What Is a Player-Governed Orchestra? The Case Studies

3.1 Themes and Definitions

3.1.1 Governance, Management, Orchestras

It is first important to clarify the concepts of "governance" and "management". These terms are routinely used to refer to different loci of decision-making within firms and organisations. Perhaps the most widely accepted understanding of the two terms comes from principal–agent theories.

Principals are defined here as people who are typically the owners of firms or the bearers of legally constituted authority in cases of not-for-profit companies or public bodies, and who are the ultimate controllers of these entities but who also engage agents or managers to implement their decisions (L'Huillier, 2014). In this understanding, governance refers to the decision-making of principals that sets an organisation's strategy, while management involves decision-making concerning how to realise the strategic objectives set at the governance stage. The sustainability of a particular system of control is at the heart of my interest in labour-management in orchestras. Most of my analysis concerns what Dow (2003) called "ultimate" control (p. 5), and, in keeping with agency theory, I use the term "governance" to refer to such high-level decision-making.

The players in my research cohort mostly make governance-level decisions, that is, they are principals in the principal–agent scheme who leave the realisation of their decisions to agents in the form of management staff. It was against this background that I chose to describe the structure I consider in this research as a player-governed orchestra rather than player-managed orchestra. Similarly, I avoid the terms "self-managed orchestra" and "self-governed orchestra" because the word "self" is too vague and these terms do not sufficiently differentiate between board members who are recruited from outside the organisation and musicians who are also governance officers. My study thus focuses on the sustainability of

B. Long, *Democratising Orchestras*, Music Business Research,
https://doi.org/10.1007/978-3-032-17399-7_3

organisational structures in which ultimate control—labelled "governance"—is exercised by musician members of orchestras and ensembles. Musicians serve on boards and board committees that make governance decisions, while leaving the implementation of decisions to managers.

I should also comment briefly on the use of the term "orchestra" to refer to both orchestras and ensembles. Though the terms "orchestra" and "ensemble" are often used interchangeably, differences exist. The differences between orchestras and ensembles concern musical instrumentation and are not relevant to organisation theory. The rewards and challenges of player-governance I found manifested in the orchestras and ensemble I studied are sufficiently uniform to make the adoption of a single collective term reasonable. I thus refer to them as player-governed orchestras. This term refers to both orchestras and ensembles that use player-governance.

3.1.2 LMFs, Partnerships, Coops

I will now consider three specific types of governance, namely LMFs, partnerships, and cooperatives, all of which share a commitment to participatory and democratic governance but that also diverge from one another in a number of ways.

The framework for my study of player-governance comes from work on LMFs. Analysing governance sustainability in PGOs, in turn, contributes to the understanding of labour-management more widely. However, the LMF is only one form of democratic and participatory organisation, and PGOs have elements in common with other types, particularly professional partnerships and cooperatives. PGOs do not neatly align with any one type; instead, they borrow elements from all three. In this subsection, I briefly define LMFs, professional partnerships, and cooperatives before highlighting some of their key commonalities and differences. I also highlight the elements that PGOs borrow from them.

Dow (2018b) defined a firm as "an organized set of individual agents who participate in a common production process and sell the resulting outputs on a market" (p. 3). LMFs are a subset of all firms, one in which "ultimate control is held by labor suppliers" (Dow, 2018b, p. 4). Stryjan (1989) took a similar approach when he defined the "self-managed enterprise" as "any enterprise that is managed democratically by its workers by virtue/right of their labour" (p. 3). A different understanding focuses on ownership rather than the supply of labour. Ben-Ner (1988), for example, defined a "worker-owned firm" as "an organization in which the ultimate right to decision-making rests principally with workers" and in which this right is a "reflection of workers' individual or collective ownership of a dominant share of the firm's equity" (p. 288). The essential feature of an LMF is, then, the legitimation of control, decision-making and democratic management by workers based on their providing labour or their ownership of the firm.

Professional partnerships are a type of organisation that is recognised in many jurisdictions. They frequently appear in professional services such as accounting, legal advising, management consulting, architecture, and medicine. Jensen and

Meckling (1979) as well as Dow (2003) view professional partnerships as a type of LMF. For Levin and Tadelis (2005), "the defining feature of a partnership" is the "redistribution of profits among the partners" (p. 131). An important point of commonality between PGOs and professional partnerships is their extensive use of non-member hired labour (Greenwood et al., 1990), a feature that the theoretical literature on labour-management regards as a threat to the sustainability of the governance model (Dow, 2018b). Using hired labour ignores one of the key principles of cooperative organisation but is also a common practice—if to a lesser extent—among PGOs. Levin and Tadelis (2005) identified other features of professional partnerships. Those shared by PGOs include that "they are not capital intensive" (ibid., p. 159) and, in some cases, the "unlimited liability of the partners"[1] (ibid., p. 162). PGOs thus also have some characteristics of professional partnerships.

The idea of the cooperative has a longer pedigree than the LMF and benefits from more institutional infrastructure, including legal definitions in many jurisdictions. The International Co-operative Alliance (2015) developed a widely adopted terminology that defines a cooperative as an "autonomous association of persons united voluntarily to meet their common economic, social and cultural needs and aspirations through a jointly owned and democratically-controlled enterprise" (no page).

Professional partnerships, cooperatives, and LMFs have features and characteristic practices that go beyond these definitions. Table 3.1 presents the characteristics that are most relevant for my study. It also includes a fourth column that shows how PGOs combine elements of the three organisational types. Some features (rows in the table) deserve particular mention. The use of hired labour is especially important. The use of non-member hired labour in LMFs and cooperatives is widely regarded as a potential source of degeneration in their organisational models and is discouraged by theorists (Dow, 2018a). It is, however, extensively used in professional partnerships and is typical of PGOs, which usually recruit management staff as hired labour as well as supernumerary players for specific projects. Profit distribution is also an important point of difference. Allowing workers to share in profits is a central rationale for labour-management (Kruse, 2013) but PGOs are usually constituted as not-for-profits because this is a condition of eligibility for public and philanthropic funding. This means that, even when a PGO produces a financial surplus, paying bonuses or dividends to members is not an option and is therefore not a motivation for the introduction or continued use of player-governance. A key part of my study sought to establish whether other factors sustain player-governance in the absence of the profit-sharing motivation that is so important to other LMFs.

[1] The FBO and the Mahler Chamber Orchestra both use the legal form of a *Gesellschaft bürgerlichen Rechts*, the German equivalent of a professional partnership.

Table 3.1 Summary comparison of organisational characteristics observed in LMFs, professional partnerships, cooperatives, and PGOs

	LMFs	Prof. partnerships	Coops	PGOs
Labour membership	Yes	Yes	Yes	Yes
Consumer membership	No	No	Yes	No
Democratic and participatory decision-making by members	Yes	Yes	Yes	Yes
Hired labour is:	Discouraged	Widely used	Discouraged	Widely used
Are profits distributed?	Yes	Yes	Generally not	No
Is non-member investment possible?	Yes (This may be unusual but is not theoretically excluded. See Dow (2018b) (pp. 248–66))	Generally not	No	No
Are entitlements to profit-sharing tradeable to other members?	Yes	Yes	No	Not applicable
Is there limited liability for members?	Yes	Not in all cases	Yes	Not in all cases

3.1.3 Degeneration

Various dangers threaten the sustainability of labour-management, and in the case of this book, the governance systems player-governed orchestras (PGOs) use. Arguably the most pressing is that a subset of members gradually takes control. They could do so by ensuring that new workers are engaged as hired labour with no voting rights or other membership entitlements, rather than as members who participate in decision-making. Taken to its end point, this practice could lead to the transformation of what started as a labour-managed firm (LMF) into one that is controlled by an individual, or into "a form of dictatorship run in the interests of a single dominant constituency" (Dow, 2003, p. 278). At the latest then, such a firm ceases to be labour-managed in any meaningful sense. Such a development might be accepted as being the result simply of rational decision-making and evidence of a tendency towards hierarchical bureaucracy of the type that Max Weber (1947) observed.[2] In my research, I do not attempt to establish whether player-governance is "better" than other forms of organisation and control. Labour-management has strengths, benefits, and pay-offs in the orchestras studied, leading members to consider it

[2] See Rothschild and Whitt (1986) for a comprehensive treatment of the tension between Weber's analysis and "organisational democracy and participation" (p. 19).

worth sustaining once it has been adopted. Avoiding and countering the risk of degeneration in the commitment to player-governance is an essential element in sustaining such a model, and the book approaches the questions that arise from several different angles.

The oldest of the five orchestras and one ensemble that I studied—the Orchestra of the Age of Enlightenment—turned 40 in 2026. The others have also sustained their governance structure for between 11 and 36 years.[3] At first glance, and using a simple measure such as years of operation using a specified model, player-governance in orchestras and ensembles thus seems sustainable and resilient against the threat of degeneration. However, the reasons why this is so are less immediately apparent.

Orchestras and ensembles are a special type of firm. They embody complex and interactional sets of economic, social, organisational, and cultural logics that do not perfectly match any other type of organisation. Some of the factors that enable labour-managed orchestras to sustain their governance structures are *sui generis*. Nonetheless, many more do resonate with other labour-controlled firms and suggest that researching how PGOs sustain player-governance is a valuable undertaking that will enrich understanding of LMFs. The core investigation at the heart of this book thus asks how do player-governed orchestras sustain their governance structures?

3.1.4 Members, Workers, Freelancers

Researchers in the field of labour-management use the term "member" (and sometimes "partner") to refer to workers who have voting rights in their firms, as distinct from workers who are not enfranchised. Collectively, the latter group is usually referred to as hired labour. I, too, use the term "member" exclusively to mean a worker with voting rights. Colloquially, a "member of an orchestra" is simply a musician who plays with it. In this book, the phrase refers to a musician who has the right to vote and stand for election to a governance role. All the organisations studied engage additional musicians as hired labour. I refer to such players as "supernumeraries". PGOs also engage management and administrative staff as hired labour. Those engaged in the activity of PGOs can thus be allocated to one of three groups:

1. Members: musicians with voting rights.
2. Supernumeraries: musicians with no voting rights.
3. Management and Administrative Staff: Workers with No Voting Rights[4]

The following question also emerged: What is the best terminology for the actors at the centre of this study, the people who founded and ran/run the orchestras and

[3] A list of major PGOs is provided in Appendix A.

[4] I explore the logics behind the existence of these three groups in the PGOs studied, and in particular the fact that management and administrative staff are not engaged as members, in Sect. 4.4.

ensemble I researched? My focus was exclusively on people who are remunerated for performing music or management tasks. By virtue of this remuneration, they are routinely referred to as "professionals". This term is often used by working musicians and by researchers who study them. However, the economics literature and specifically literature dealing with labour-management uses the generic term "worker" to label a person who is remunerated for their activity within an organisation. In an economic sense, professional musicians are indeed workers (Williamson & Cloonan, 2016). This term can, however, be unhelpfully reductive, though professional musicians certainly see themselves as undertaking work (Coulson, 2012). Moreover, in most contexts, orchestral musicians do not easily identify with the term "worker" (Cloonan, 2014; Silva, 2017), and a choice to label them as such would reflect the preferences of writers and researchers.

To prefer the label "worker" when referring to professional musicians in PGOs would then not only run the risk of adopting a term that hews more closely to the thinking of researchers at the cost of perspectives held by interviewees and other sector actors. It would also elide the hybrid nature of membership in a PGO. The book spans the intellectual worlds of professional music performance, economics, organisation theory, and organisational psychology. It also ranges across the terminologies of these various fields. In the process, the different terms I use may jar. This friction is in a sense welcome, as it reflects the complexities of the field of research, and the multiple identities and roles that PGO members assume.

The people at the centre of this research have multiple roles. They are musicians who in one moment may be absorbed in the activity of playing music with other people. Shortly after they might be called on to make commercial decisions about their firm. Some have governance roles that call on them to lead discussions that can involve conflicting interests. In such moments they share many of the rewards and challenges of people in other LMFs, and they might more meaningfully be labelled "workers". The desire to understand this duality, the ability of the interviewees to navigate multiple professional roles and identities, underlies the research underlying this book. I embrace this multiplicity because doing so mirrors that found in the fields I researched. It also reflects the complex self-conceptualisations that many professional musicians balance and maintain as they work (Bennett, 2008; Cottrell, 2004). I reserve the term "worker" for the discussion of people in generic contexts and will use the terms "musician" and "player" to refer to performers in the PGOs I discuss. I will now outline the rationale for selecting the PGOs in the research cohort.

The five orchestras and one ensemble in my study only offer their musicians freelance contracts, even to those who are members. The concept of freelancing therefore looms large in this research, and I discuss it further in Sect. 4.2. However, both the interviewees and much of the relevant writing use the term "freelance" without defining it. The use of other, related terms such as "casual", "self-employed", "atypical" and "precarious" work further clouds discussion of contracting among orchestral musicians. Dividing lines between different classifications are also blurred. As an example, take a musician who holds a tenured position with an orchestra (Org. A) that provides social security cover, annual and sickness leave, but who also undertakes short-term engagements with other musical employers (Org.

B), and is paid on a fee-for-service or freelance basis with no additional entitlements. In a study of Org. B, this player could be regarded as a freelance player. From the perspective of Org. A, the same musician would be regarded as securely employed. It can be difficult to determine whether such players should be considered freelance, self-employed, or even precariously employed, because some of their income is unpredictable and comes without the entitlements associated with secure employment. Now consider other musicians who have tenured positions with full entitlements but only on a part-time basis equivalent to 1 day per week. The rest of their work is on a fee-for-service basis with no additional entitlements. This work accounts for over 70 percent of their income. These players could reasonably be considered as freelance or securely employed, yet their position is quite different from that of the first case (Lewchuk et al., 2013, 2014).

I do not offer my own definition of the term "freelance"; others, such as Lewchuk et al. (2013), have done so. Though it was used widely by the musicians I interviewed, my discussions with them did not focus on their understanding of it. It would be misleading for me to impose a single definition across this wide range of usages. It will suffice to note that none of my player interviewees has a guaranteed number of hours per year with their respective PGOs, all are remunerated on a fee-for-service basis calculated using the number of rehearsals or performances completed, and all have more than one source of income.

3.2 Who Is This Book About?

3.2.1 Choosing the PGOs

A survey of the literature on player-governed orchestras suggested that focusing on a segment of the larger PGO cohort[5] would help close a gap in the research that exists concerning more recently established PGOs. Large, long-established symphony orchestras such as the London Symphony Orchestra (LSO) and the Berlin Philharmonic were the most common targets of investigation. They both featured in Lehman's PhD research (2002), which is the only substantial academic work specifically on PGOs that predates my study. The Berlin Philharmonic's election of its chief conductor has drawn extensive commentary and has been the subject of a documentary film (Iturriagagotia & Smaczny, 2002), while the LSO has been the subject of a monograph (Mulder, 2015).

The Orpheus Chamber Orchestra, an approximately 26-member orchestra established in New York in 1972, was also one of Lehman's case studies and has been the subject of other research (Banai et al., 2000; Wood, 2010), as well as a book co-authored by one of its former executive directors (Seifter & Economy, 2001). Similarly, the managing director of the Deutsche Kammerphilharmonie Bremen—a

[5] See Appendix A for a list.

PGO established in 1980 and with around 40 members currently—co-authored a book about the orchestra's operating model and portrayed it as a high-performance team built on player-governance (Scholz & Schmitt, 2011). There has been, however, very little research on player-governance among the crop of more recently established orchestras[6] that appear in Appendix A, and none examining PGOs as a type of LMF or the sustainability challenges that are central to the theoretical writing on labour-management. Initial evaluation of the literature on PGOs thus suggested that this was an area deserving of attention.

Theoretical sampling was an additional approach that guided my selection of PGOs for study from among the larger population. The goal here was to select a research cohort that was as homogeneous as possible and adhered to governance sustainability factors. Studying a PGO that has existed for more than a century next to one that has 20 years of experience with player-governance risked creating a very heterogeneous cohort that would be more appropriate to answering a different research question. Similarly, treating PGOs with 80 or more members as meaningfully equivalent to those with 20 or 30 would risk creating a widely divergent and internally incoherent research cohort.

With a research gap in mind, and theoretical sampling as a guiding principle, I first set out to broadly align my work with the literature on LMFs. Initially, I wanted to ensure that the PGOs I studied really were ongoing concerns that replicated sufficient features of LMFs so as to be able to contribute to this field. I decided that, to qualify as such, orchestras and ensembles had to

1. Be professional
2. Operate continuously
3. Perform frequently and regularly
4. Be legally constituted as a distinct entity independent of any other institution.

I have included more details on these criteria in Table 3.2.

Table 3.2 Detailed description of initial cohort selection features

Selection feature	Detailed description
Professional	Remunerates musicians by contractually agreed amounts equivalent to at least 75 per cent of the rate recommended by the relevant industrial organisation representing musicians
Continuous organisational operation	Engages at least one management staff member for a minimum of 11 months each year
Regular performances	Publicly performs at least 25 times per year and at least once in each quarter of the year
Independent existence	Exists as an independently registered legal entity

[6] Juno-Delgado, McCulloch, and Sinapi (2015) considered the Orchestra of the Age of Enlightenment among a cohort of performing arts cooperatives.

Youth, training, and community orchestras were thus excluded because their missions, cost structures, market dynamics, funding mechanisms, and personnel policies differ from those of professional orchestras. Professional orchestras that only come together for, say, a music festival or to record a film soundtrack were also disregarded because they do not face the governance challenges of ongoing operation. Finally, I excluded orchestras that are constituted as departments of larger organisations and do not have their own independent governance structures. Typically, these are so-called "pit orchestras" that play as part of operas or ballets and exist as parts of larger performing-arts organisations. They include orchestras that are incorporated into public broadcasters. These parameters allowed me to isolate an initial research sample.

Next, I further distilled the sample by looking at how I might reduce the role of factors such as membership size and years of experience with player-governance. With an average of 34 members, my cohort is closer to the size of start-up companies in other sectors of the arts, as well as in the wider economy, than are the player-governed symphony orchestras studied by other researchers (e.g. Lehman, 2002). On average, the members of my cohort had 19 years of experience with player-governance. This also made their experience more relevant and interesting for other potential PGO or LMF founders. Such a period is long enough for trends, themes, and features to emerge, yet not so long that the knowledge of the governance development phase is buried in archival materials from times when the cultural, economic, and political framework was very different from that of today. The availability of interviewees who were able to speak about the establishment phase of player-governance, and how decisions made at that stage shaped governance sustainability, supported the idea of focusing on PGOs with relatively little experience of player-governance. The PGOs I studied thus brought new perspectives to the sustainability of labour governance and management more broadly, as well as to the sustainability of player-governance in orchestras.

My research cohort also constituted a subset of the broader LMF sector. Orchestras depend on high levels of human capital. The experience of the PGOs I studied has relevance to LMFs that are similarly dependent on attracting, retaining, managing, and supporting highly talented and creative workers (see Chap. 6). They are also all not-for-profit operations, as is typical of the publicly funded orchestral sector. This sets them apart from most LMFs, but demonstrates that labour governance and management can be sustainable and successful in the absence of profit-sharing as a core logic. Instead, other economic drivers—such as the desire to reduce the exposure to precarious work commonly found among orchestral musicians—substitute for profit-sharing in the operation of PGOs (see Chap. 4). The research cohort is then a specific type of LMF, one that has to date been subject to little, if any, study, but that, in its atypical combination of logics, rationales and priorities, contributes to our understanding of labour-management more broadly.

PGOs rely on their player members to undertake governance tasks on committees, boards, and working groups that are above and beyond their work as musicians. However, the number of governance roles is rarely proportional to the total membership. Large and small organisations can usually be governed by a similar number of officers. The Berlin Philharmonic, for example, is a PGO with around 128 members and a primary governance body of five players. The Mahler Chamber Orchestra—one of the PGOs featured in this book—has 45 members and the same number of player members on its governance team. Thus, PGOs with large memberships are better able to spread the governance workload. This may give larger PGOs operational and sustainability advantages simply because of their large memberships.

The memberships of the PGOs studied varied between 16 and 49; at the time of my research the average was 34. My focus was thus on PGOs that share similar operational and sustainability challenges related to their modest membership size, while I excluded PGOs that might have a sustainability advantage simply because of their large memberships.

Low-incumbency and small-membership professional PGOs operate in the United States[7] and European countries. However, I restricted my focus to German and London-based orchestras and ensembles because they exist in the orchestral music sectors with which I am most familiar.

I describe the participating PGOs in the next section, but a final point should be made about them. As small firms established in the contemporary market, political and funding context, their experiences approximate those of other types of companies looking for sustainable governance structures, either for new enterprises or for new governance structures in existing firms. This gives my research greater relevance for the broader LMF sector. With a research cohort established, I now turn to the approach I took when researching for this book.

3.2.2 Meet the PGOs

The PGOs in the research cohort have, as of 2025, used player-governance for an average of 28 years. In 2025, the average number of enfranchised player members[8] was 37. Table 3.3 presents basic information on these organisations.

Each of the organisations I studied adopted player-governance under different circumstances. In a subsequent chapter, I analyse the establishment rationales that emerged from the interviews I did with members and managers. At this point, I provide only a brief description of how each came to be player-governed, to highlight the diversity of approaches.

The Orchestra of the Age of Enlightenment (OAE) was founded by musicians who broke away from an existing orchestra. An early mission statement showed the breadth of objectives formulated by members as they established an orchestra that they controlled (Wallace, 2006). The themes that emerge from the statement

[7] Examples include Orpheus, The Knights, A Far Cry, and the East Coast Chamber Orchestra.

[8] The term "member" refers to enfranchised musicians or partners.

Table 3.3 Basic information on the organisations studied

Name	Year of formal establishment	Number of members (in 2025)	Operational base	Repertoire focus
Ensemble Musikfabrik	1990 (player-governed since 1995)	15	Cologne, Germany	Contemporary
Freiburg Baroque Orchestra	1990	22	Freiburg, Germany	Baroque and Classical
Kammerakademie Potsdam	2001	34	Potsdam, Germany	Comprehensive
London Mozart Players	1949 (player-governed since 2014)	48	London	Comprehensive
Mahler Chamber Orchestra	1997	47	Berlin	Comprehensive
Orchestra of the age of Enlightenment	1986	54	London	Baroque and Classical

resonate with those of the interviews I undertook and were shared by players from other orchestras. In particular, OAE set out to achieve artistic goals by addressing the "dangers implicit in playing as a matter of routine, pursuing exclusively commercial creative options, and under-rehearsal" (quoted in Wallace, 2006, p. 13). The roles of conductors and music directors were also prominent in this early mission statement. It cautioned against the "undue emphasis" that many musicians feel music directors impose (quoted in Wallace, 2006, p. 13). OAE is a resident orchestra of London's Southbank centre and regularly plays at the Glyndebourne Opera Festival. With more than 50 recordings, it has pioneered adventurous programming that ventures further into late nineteenth- and early twentieth-century music than do most of its peers.

The Freiburg Baroque Orchestra (FBO) first performed in 1987 and was formally established in 1990. Like OAE, it has been player-governed since its foundation. FBO won sections of the prestigious Gramophone Classical Music Awards in 1996, 2005, 2011, and 2012. The Mahler Chamber Orchestra (MCO) began in 1997 when former members of the Gustav Mahler Youth Orchestra decided to set up a professional orchestra. It, too, was player-governed from day 1. It won a Gramophone award in 2003 and the prize for Recording of the Year in the concerto category of the BBC Music Magazine Awards in 2015. The Ensemble Musikfabrik is a contemporary music ensemble that was established in 1990, but only adopted player-governance after its founders left in 1995. It has worked with many of today's leading composers.

The Kammerakademie Potsdam was established in 2001, when two ensembles merged. One of these consisted of former musicians of the Brandenburg Philharmonie Potsdam, a 67-member orchestra that was dissolved in 2000 after its public funding was withdrawn (Kaempf & Höbel, 1999). In 2022, the Kammerakademie was recognised as Orchestra of the Year as part of the Opusklassik awards. The London

Mozart Players was established by the conductor Harry Blech in 1949. In 2014, the orchestra came close to being wound up after its major sponsor withdrew and two sources of public funding were terminated (Hewett, 2014). However, its musicians were not prepared to accept its demise and they took control of its management and governance. In 2024, the orchestra celebrated its 75th year.

Each of the orchestras and ensembles has its own brand, repertoire strengths, and profile. Three of the PGOs studied have a comprehensive repertoire focus. They perform music from the last three centuries, stretching from the earliest music for the modern orchestra through to music by twenty-first-century composers. Two of the orchestras in my study specialise in music of the Baroque and Classical periods (approximately 1600–1820) and use historically informed practice. Ensemble Musikfabrik is a contemporary music ensemble that only plays works from the twentieth and twenty-first centuries. These varying foci present different concerns for governance and operation. However, a focus on the challenges that relate specifically to player-governance enables a coherent study of these PGOs as LMFs.

3.2.3 *Meet the People*

I conducted 18 semi-structured interviews with 20 musicians and management staff of six PGOs, and an additional interview with the managing director of a national association of orchestras. Also, 7 interviewees were female and 14 were male. The breakdown of their professional roles is shown in Table 3.4.

To protect the identities of the interviewees as far as possible, I use pseudonyms throughout the book when quoting statements made by them. Table 3.5 lists these pseudonyms.

Table 3.4 The professional roles of interviewees

Description	No. of interviewees	Additional information
Players with current governance roles	9	Includes one chief executive
Players with former governance roles	3	
Players who have never held a governance role with their respective organisations	2	
Chief executives (non-players)	3	Not enfranchised (These interviewees do not have voting rights under the rules of their respective firms)
Other management staff	3	Not enfranchised
Other professionals in the sector	1	Not employed by a PGO

Table 3.5 Interviewee pseudonyms and professional roles of interviewees quoted

Pseudonym	Role
Alvis	Player member
Angela	Player member
Daniel	Player member
Maria	Player member
Patrick	Player member
Richard	Player member
Robert	Player member
Sebastian	Player member
Simon	Player member
Sophie	Player member
Stephan	Player member
Susanna	Player member
Walter	Player member
Alex	Chief executive
Herbert	Chief executive
Mario	Chief executive
Martin	Chief executive
Claudia	Management staff
Kirsten	Management staff
Leo	Management staff

3.2.4 Limitations of the Interviewee Cohort

The biggest challenge to recruiting participants for the research was the freelance nature of the PGOs studied. This meant that players might go weeks without working for the PGO concerned, and thus be in other cities or countries and unavailable for interview. Hence, most interviewees were players or staff who were available during my visit. Such people were most likely to be senior players and those with governance or management roles, whose high levels of engagement in governance meant they were regularly in the office. The ratio of interviewees without governance roles to those with them does not match the ratio in the PGOs studied. The chief executives endeavoured to help me to speak to a wide cross-section of players, but it is unavoidable in social science research that sample cohorts reflect the availability and willingness of participants. That said, the interviewees who participated had many years of intimate knowledge of governance in PGOs, and this was the primary focus of my research.

Other Data In addition to undertaking interviews, I consulted the websites and marketing materials of the PGOs studied. The governance model used by an orchestra or ensemble is of little interest to most concertgoers and plays a minor role in publicity materials. In 2006, OAE published a history that provided a useful overview of the orchestra's early development (Wallace, 2006). I was also able to read its *Maintaining Standards Procedure and Handbook*. The websites and publications of the other PGOs also provided general background to their operations and corporate identities. Some of the interviewees thought that the benefits of player-governance manifested themselves in performances. However, I decided against conducting observational research in rehearsals or concerts. I wanted to put the interests, motivations, and perceptions of the interviewees at the heart of my study. Auxiliary observational research would have created what was in effect a second, parallel project that would have overcomplicated the project and occluded its findings.

The questions I posed in the interviews responded to my reading, and this was reflected in the nodes, categories, and themes that emerged from the investigation. However, some themes first became apparent during the analysis. The challenges of optimising performance in a PGO (Chap. 6) was the most prominent theme to emerge during the interviews and the subsequent analytical work. It was also one that was not suggested by my study of the literature. Indeed, as discussed in Chap. 6, the literature indicates that mutual monitoring should be a strength of LMFs (Ben-Ner, 1988; Dow, 2003, Hansmann, 1990, 1996). It was perhaps natural that the interviewees spoke often and at length about the themes that are summarised in the title of Chap. 4—realising and operationalising player-governance. But the extent and import of discussion about building engagement, commitment, and responsibility (Chap. 5) only became clear as my study of the discourse gathered steam. My approach to data analysis was characterised by a blend of "pre-understanding" (Hinton, quoted in Birks & Mills, 2015, p. 92) and reflective adaptation.

Analytical tightening of the research, by its nature, involves moving some themes and ideas to peripheral positions. Discussion of finances, for example, was less prominent in the transcripts than I anticipated before starting the interviews. This may reflect the reality that factors such as cost disease,[9] revenue generation, and fundraising concern all orchestras and ensembles and are not peculiar to PGOs (Herman, 2022; Flanagan, 2012). It also highlights an important feature of PGOs as a type of LMF: the fact that they operate on a not-for-profit basis. This means that profit-sharing, in the form of dividend payments, does not exist for the members of PGOs. As my analysis matured, a group of dominant themes emerged, while others took on subsidiary roles. These themes are described and discussed in detail in Chaps. 4–7. The next chapter opens the empirical study by looking at the decisions made at the setup stage.

[9] Baumol and Bowen (1966) theorised that performing arts companies were afflicted by cost disease when they were unable to increase revenue so as to cover rises in payments made to performers.

References

Banai, M., Nirenberg, J., & Menachem, M. (2000). Leadership in self-managing organizations: Orpheus and a date plantation. *Journal of Leadership & Organizational Studies, 7*(3), 3–17. https://doi.org/10.1177/107179190000700301

Baumol, W. J., & Bowen W. G. (1966). *Performing arts, the economic dilemma; a study of problems common to theater, opera, music, and dance*. Twentieth Century Fund.

Ben-Ner, A. (1988). The life cycle of worker-owned firms in market economies. *Journal of Economic Behavior & Organization, 10*(3), 287–313. https://doi.org/10.1016/0167-2681(88)90052-2

Bennett, D. (2008). *Understanding the classical music profession: The past, the present and strategies for the future*. Ashgate.

Birks, M., & Mills, J. (2015). *Grounded theory: A practical guide*. Sage.

Cloonan, M. (2014). Musicians as workers: Putting the UK Musicians' Union into context. *MUSICultures, 41*(1), 10–29. https://journals.lib.unb.ca/index.php/MC/article/view/22354

Cottrell, S. (2004). *Professional music-making in London: Ethnography and experience*. Ashgate.

Coulson, S. (2012). Collaborating in a competitive world: Musicians' working lives and understandings of entrepreneurship. *Work, Employment & Society, 26*(2), 246–261. https://doi.org/10.1177/0950017011432919

Dow, G. (2003). *Governing the firm: Workers' control in theory and practice*. Cambridge University Press.

Dow, G. (2018a). The theory of the labour-managed firm: Past, present, and future. *Annals of Public and Cooperative Economics, 89*(1), 65–86. https://doi.org/10.1111/apce.12194

Dow, G. (2018b). *The labor-managed firm: Theoretical foundations*. Cambridge University Press.

Flanagan, R. (2012). *The perilous life of symphony orchestras: Artistic triumphs and economic challenges*. Yale University Press.

Greenwood, R., Hinings, C. R., & Brown, J. (1990). "P2-Form" strategic management: Corporate practices in professional partnerships. *The Academy of Management Journal, 23*(4), 725–755. https://www.jstor.org/stable/256288

Hansmann, H. (1990). When does worker ownership work? ESOPs, law firms, codetermination, and economic democracy. *Yale Law Journal, 99*(8), 1749–1816. https://doi.org/10.2307/796676

Hansmann, H. (1996). *The ownership of enterprise*. The Belknap Press of Harvard University Press.

Herman, A. (2022). *Orchestra management: Models and repertoires for the symphony orchestra* (1st ed.). Routledge.

Hewett, I. (2014). London Mozart players: The ultimate comeback kids. *The Telegraph*, May 28, Accessed October 19, 2025. https://www.telegraph.co.uk/culture/music/classicalmusic/10858384/London-Mozart-Players-the-ultimate-comeback-kids.html.

International Cooperative Alliance. (2015). *Cooperative identity, values & principles*. International Cooperative Alliance. Accessed October 19, 2025. https://www.ica.coop/en/whats-co-op/co-operative-identity-values-principles.

Iturriagagotia, I., & Smaczny, P. (2002). *Maestros in democracy: Members of the Berlin philharmonic elect their conductor*. EuroArts Music

Jensen, M., & Meckling, W. (1979). Rights and production functions: An application to labor-managed firms and codetermination. *Journal of Business, 52*(4), 469–506. https://www.jstor.org/stable/2352442

Kaempf, S., & Höbel, W. (1999). "Versteppt Der Osten?" *Der Spiegel*, 7 June. http://www.spiegel.de/spiegel/print/d-13672937.html.

Kruse, D. (Ed.). (2013). *Sharing ownership, profits, and decision-making in the 21st century*. Emerald.

L'Huillier, B. M. (2014). What does "Corporate Governance" actually mean? *Corporate Governance: The International Journal of Effective Board Performance, 14*(3), 300–319. https://doi.org/10.1108/CG-10-2012-007

Lehman, E. V. (2002). Models of self-governance and workplace democracy: A comparison of select orchestras in Germany, the U.S. and U.K. (Doctoral dissertation) City University London, UK. http://openaccess.city.ac.uk/7618/.

Levin, J., & Tadelis, S. (2005). Profit sharing and the role of professional partnerships. *Quarterly Journal of Economics, 120*(1), 131–171.

Lewchuk, W., Lafleche, M., Dyson, D., Goldring, L., & Meisner, A. (Eds.). (2013). *It's more than poverty. Employment precarity and household wellbeing*. United Way.

Lewchuk, W., Procyk, S., Laflèche, M., et al. (2014). Is precarious employment low income employment? Changing labour market in southern Ontario. *Just Labour: A Candian Journal of Work and Society, 22*(Autumn), 52–73. http://www.justlabour.yorku.ca/volume22/pdfs/05_lewchuk_et_al_press.pdf

Mulder, C. (2015). The London Symphony Orchestra: Still afloat. In *Transcending capitalism through cooperative practices*. Palgrave Macmillan.

Rothschild, J., & Whitt, J. A. (1986). *The cooperative workplace: Potentials and dilemmas of organisational democracy and participation*. Cambridge University Press.

Scholz, C., & Schmitt, A. (2011). *Hochleistung Braucht Dissonanz: Was Teams Vom 5-Sekunden-Modell Der Deutschen Kammerphilharmonie Bremen Lernen Können*. Wiley-VCH.

Seifter, H., & Economy, P. (2001). *Leadership ensemble, lessons in collaborative management from the world's only conductorless orchestra*. Times Books.

Silva, M. D. (2017). Are musicians "Ordinary Workers"? Labor organization and the question of "Artistic Value" in the first years of the Portuguese musicians' class association: 1909–1913. *Popular Music & Society, 40*(5), 518–538. https://doi.org/10.1080/03007766.2017.1348671

Sinapi, C., & Juno-Delgado, E. (2015). Motivations for establishing cooperative companies in the performing arts: A European perspective. Chapter 3. In A. Kauhanen (Ed.), *Advances in the economic analysis of participatory & labor-managed firms*. Emerald. https://doi.org/10.1108/S0885-333920150000016017

Stryjan, Y. (1989). *Impossible organizations: Self-management and organizational reproduction*. Greenwood Press.

Wallace, H. R. (2006). *Spirit of the orchestra*. Orchestra of the Age of Enlightenment.

Weber, M. (1947). *The theory of social and economic organization*. Translated by Henderson, A, and Talcott Parsons. The Free Press.

Williamson, J., & Cloonan, M. (2016). *Players' work time: A history of the British Musicians' Union, 1893–2013*. Manchester University Press.

Wood, R. (2010). Correlation of conductor leadership style, musician employment status, organizational participation to orchestra musician job satisfaction. (Doctoral dissertation) University of Phoenix. https://pqdtopen.proquest.com/doc/911029205.html?FMT=ABS.

Chapter 4
Going for Democracy: Setup Decisions

4.1 Why Start a Player-Governed Orchestra?

Company founders must establish the most effective and efficient governance structures for their enterprise. Similar organisations may serve as models. However, risks abound for anyone introducing a borrowed control system that may not accommodate a firm's strengths and weaknesses, its operating context, or its stakeholders' interests. In labour-managed firms (LMFs), the range of interest groups and positions involved in participatory and democratic decision-making magnifies the challenges of honing a governance system (Cornforth, 2004).

This book's exploration of how player-governed orchestras (PGOs) optimise and sustain their governance structures moves now to the empirical study of their initial realisation. Moving from theoretical models about LMFs to the practices of operational PGOs entails observing the basic decisions that implement and institutionalise the interests, ideas, expectations, and ambitions that musicians bring to the setting up of a PGO. What dynamics and ideas shape governance in PGOs? To what extent have the PGOs that I studied managed to amalgamate the needs and interests of their members? My aim in this chapter is to answer such questions.

The desire of musicians to take artistic control and improve their job security were the most important of the logics that emerged from speaking with founding members. This chapter shows how the realisation and operationalisation of the PGOs in the book's research transforms the motivations and thinking of their founders—who are almost exclusively musicians—into functional governance structures and practices. The interests, aspirations, and thinking of founding members are a rich source of intellectual and social capital for starting PGOs, while the economic and practice-based parameters of the orchestral sector set boundaries for player-governance.

The PGOs featured in this book were either established by their musicians or players took over existing firms. Setting up an orchestra or taking control of one is

B. Long, *Democratising Orchestras*, Music Business Research,
https://doi.org/10.1007/978-3-032-17399-7_4

complex. It asks founders to commit resources with little certainty about future returns and benefits. Establishing a system of governance in which the workers have control is a greater challenge because the number of decision-makers, and with it the heterogeneity among them, is greater than in the case of a sole entrepreneur, such as a conductor, establishing an orchestra.

Cooperating with a group of like-minded and appropriately skilled co-founders can, nonetheless, help individuals realise plans and ambitions that would otherwise go untried. Alternatively, the readiness of workers to take control of a firm that is in serious difficulties might be driven by the immediate risk of its dissolution and job losses (Olsen, 2013). The labour markets in which PGOs operate also create parameters that shape the setting up of such orchestras. The interviews I undertook with PGO musicians provided insights that corroborate published thinking on LMFs, while others diverge from such theories. This chapter provides new and complementary perspectives into the setup phase of PGOs.

4.1.1 "Flexible, Open, and Self-Critical"

The evolution and life cycles of LMFs have attracted the attention of several writers. Theorists in the field highlight the risks of understanding the LMF as a static black box (Batstone, 1983; Ben-Ner, 1988; Lichtenstein, 1986). Instead, their writing explores LMFs' dynamic, evolutionary, and responsive nature. Batstone (1983) described the first phase of an LMF's life cycle as a "primitive democracy" rooted in the "communal effort of a few" who are "highly committed to the enterprise and its success" (p. 150). Lichtenstein (1986) observed an "unusually high degree of uncertainty" (p. 63) during an LMF's startup phase. Moreover, as in any enterprise, "the physical and financial resources available depend on the circumstances under which the … organization was established" (Lichtenstein, 1986, p. 62). Lichtenstein concluded that the primary attribute an LMF required to survive the establishment phase was "its ability to be flexible, open and self-critical" (1986, p. 63). The current chapter reveals how the musicians in the case study PGOs attempted to balance labour conditions in the orchestral sector, while working within the parameters of labour-management and instituting sustainable governance structures.

This chapter is divided into three sections. In the first two, I map the rationales, interests, and factors at play in the PGOs' establishment histories. The role of factors specific to professional music performance, along with the dynamics of a sector in which freelance work is common, is a central focus. In the first section, I observe that while players' exercising artistic control over their PGOs is one of their essential features, it is also bounded by the dynamics of programming and artistic planning that operate irrelevant of whether musicians or a music director–chief executive dyad make the decisions. The musicians I interviewed made clear that while players' taking control over an area of governance and management as important as artistic planning was central to the operation and sustainability of PGOs, it was not a panacea for the economic and musical challenges inherent in programming and long-term artistic planning.

Section 4.4 charts the thinking involved when PGOs create governance structures and decide whether all their employees should be enfranchised as members—as many LMF models suggest—or various groups of employees should be treated differently. The section also responds to questions surrounding membership size. Orchestras make regular use of supernumerary musicians. Decisions about optimal membership numbers, the relationship between PGOs and their supernumerary musicians, and the various types of involvement within an organisation create a complex interplay of theoretical, democratic, music-specific, and economic factors that are also relevant to the sustainability of player-governance. The interviewees emphasised their firms' approaches to defining membership as well as multiple rationales behind the determination of membership numbers. As the chapter unfolds, a picture of organisations characterised by flexibility, responsiveness, and a pioneering spirit emerges.

4.2 Taking Artistic Control

Governance sustainability in orchestras is a function of work practices, cultures, and structures. The operations of these orchestras create incentives for the implementation of labour-management, while also setting boundaries and parameters for its realisation. In this section, I show that while members taking artistic control is an essential part of establishing and running a PGO, governance sustainability also calls for a balancing of other factors. Taking control does not free members from balancing the economic and artistic considerations in a project or season. To remain sustainable, player-governance must align the desire of members to control decisions with the challenges of artistic planning and programming. The discussion also highlights the role of existing PGOs as models during a new PGO's setup phase. This interest stems from Dow's (2003) observation that "once it becomes known that an LMF has been successful in some industry, others are more inclined to replicate this organisational form" (p. 232). Comments made by the interviewees indicated that the experiences of others on the same path can indeed help PGOs navigate the challenges of player-governance. Nonetheless, a variety of unique circumstances confront each PGO, and they call for specific responses. Models in the form of other PGOs were of modest benefit.

4.2.1 Why Taking Artistic Control Is Critical

Player control of artistic planning and programming is a critical motivation for establishing a PGO. Martin (a general manager) felt that

> One of the really crucial elements of self-governance for the orchestra is not so much discipline and political procedure, grievance processes and maintaining standards, though all of these things are part of the orchestra and they are important and you can't avoid them. The really significant, defining element of self-governance is actually artistic.

For Martin, central to taking artistic control was the renegotiation of the leader dynamics of the traditional orchestra or "playing without a conductor, working with a conductor at its own discretion, not having an autocratic artistic director but actually taking artistic matters into their own purview and consideration". The resulting PGO embodied an important shift because "effectively, the player membership is the music director. They are the artistic director".

In most of the PGOs I studied, artistic decisions such as programming, the planning of seasons, and the selection of conductors and guest soloists are delegated to a committee or to the board. In some cases, the programming or curating of individual projects or concerts is entrusted to individual players. Such committees consist of members who are elected, usually for fixed terms of 2 or 3 years. Management staff advise such committees on financing and marketing questions that may arise from artistic decisions, but final decisions are the responsibility of the relevant committee.

Taking artistic control has far-reaching impacts. Leo described how it boosted motivation among musicians while he also made connections to the labour economics of PGOs: "If you decide your own programs, you have to be sure about the quality and that it will be great for the audience, because the players are their own employers in the end." The result for him was that the "motivation to have good programs and to perform them brilliantly is much higher than in an orchestra where you have to be there and someone else takes care of the program and the dramaturgy". Richard's description of a recent planning retreat gives an indication of the breadth and centrality of the artistic planning undertaken by players in his orchestra:

> Last time we talked more about programming, future scoping for the orchestra, focal points for coming years, things like where we are going, what can we do, what did we overlook in the past, what are the most pressing things that need to be dealt with. Such things are discussed intensively.

Handing control over artistic planning to players does not, however, shield it from economic and artistic forces. Successful programming and artistic planning harness many perspectives. The expertise of non-member management staff is central, even when the ultimate decisions are made by committees or boards consisting of or dominated by player members. This was clear when Susanna described meetings of her orchestra's artistic committee: "we do usually have someone from development and someone from marketing join us. Then you do get that: 'we're saying this piece, but you're saying box-office death, why is that? Why can't we program this piece?'" She described the outcome, noting how "it's not just players being idealistic and saying we're going to play this piece, why hasn't anybody come?"

Alvis concurred as he described the situation in his orchestra. He acknowledged that "to be honest, as lovely as it would be to do English Victorian music, there is probably a limited number of people who might be interested in that". In his PGO too, the artistic interests of player members are tempered by commercial realities and "it's not just a bunch of musicians being all artistic and saying we want to do this. Fundraising will also get involved in that". In some of the PGOs, this need to reconcile artistic planning with financial exigencies is cemented into the governance structure through the creation of an overlap between the membership of the artistic committee and the board. Robert noted how the perils of separate board and artistic planning shaped the governance of his PGO when he recalled that "it was realised from the start, that if you separated the governance from the artistic decisions completely, you might just have two groups of people arguing constantly over how to finance over-ambitious projects". In response to this risk, his PGO pursued "an idea … that by keeping an overlap between the membership and the governance of the board you would keep a certain amount of check and balance between the two". Behind this thinking lay the hope that

> The board would be able to understand the artistic planning much better because there are players on the board, and the players would understand the difficulties that their artistic decisions were having in terms of raising funding for some of the rather unusual and extraordinary projects.

Another of the PGOs takes these ideas a step further and gives responsibility for artistic planning to its board, which is elected from among the players. Reflecting on the use of an artistic planning committee, Sophie explained that

> We tried that in the past and it was too difficult to implement because a lot of the artistic planning/programming is tied to logistics questions, to finances, to everything, basically. It's the core activity, the core of everything, so we can't really manage well if it's separate. We have always kept it within the board.

The locating of artistic planning authority and its relationship to other decisions varies between these PGOs. These are fundamental elements that require careful alignment of artistic and commercial logics within governance.

4.2.2 How Musical Motivations Drive and Sustain Player-Governance

Players' desire to work regularly with specific colleagues was another key motivation for them to establish an orchestra that they control. My interviewees emphasised the team-focused collegiality and bonding that players bring to their PGOs as an important element in their success. They highlighted working with esteemed colleagues as a motivation for establishing an orchestra or converting an existing orchestra into a PGO. Alex acknowledged that "it's not the most obvious thing for the players to take over an orchestra. But we wanted to play as an orchestra. … we had a need to play together as an orchestra". Central to this ambition were the artistic bonds and affinity between the players. Alex felt that "our orchestra is made up of a really diverse group of people and they are some of the best players around". This realisation provided her with a strong interest in co-establishing her PGO: "we have the very best people there and we really enjoy making music together. … This is what it is all about." For her the result was a powerful motivation, which came across strongly when she said: "I'm in this job because I want to perform with *this* orchestra. … That is my starting point. That is the reason why I am doing it." Collegiality and connection to specific peers are strong motivations for musicians to control their orchestras.

As Walter spoke about setting up his orchestra, he recalled how the experience of performing together in a youth orchestra laid the foundations for a professional, player-governed chamber orchestra:

> It was a good experience that we enjoyed. We had been playing together for four years and there was a stable core that was unusual in a youth orchestra … we did not want to stop and … we thought it was a good idea to carry on as a chamber orchestra separate from the youth orchestra.

Another of the PGOs emerged from a group of music students and graduates who met and played together in private, with few thoughts of establishing a professional orchestra. One of its members, Maria, highlighted the interactions between economic, artistic and social factors. She first described how members initially "just kept investing, money and time and energy, everything" though "at first we earned nothing, we just kept putting more in". Asked what drove this she replied, "Because it was fun. We were friends and wanted to try it. Others play in quartets because they enjoy it, and similarly we messed around with the old instruments and tried to see what works." Walter likewise emphasised the primacy of shared music-making in his PGO when he said that "the key to success, the core idea, the most important thing, is the artistic motivation. Nothing else can keep an orchestra like this together, I think". Other factors were less important for him:

> It's not financial success. It's not wanting to play a certain number of concerts, fame or anything like that. The key element of such an adventure is definitely the artistic motivation. If that's not there, it's going to be flawed from the beginning.

He also emphasised the resilience that players can draw from making music together and how it can help overcome challenges behind the scenes:

> Even in moments of difficulty, whenever they occur, the joy of playing together on stage is the most important. That keeps everything rolling. At the moment you are on stage to play a concert, everyone understands what it's all about. You're reminded once again that everything else you do is for that moment and that is the most important. The rest, we just have to find ways and make it come together.

Programming and artistic planning are complex, multifaceted, and largely unpredictable elements of orchestral management (Bathurst et al., 2007). In an externally governed orchestra, the decisions involved are typically the prerogative of the artistic director/chief conductor, senior management staff, guest conductors, and soloists, with minimal, if any, input from players. PGOs, on the other hand, allocate responsibility for artistic planning and programming to an artistic committee or board consisting of player members. The result is that "effectively the player membership is the music director" (Martin). The interviews showed that players' exercising control over artistic decision-making is, in Sophie's words, "the core of everything".

Project and programme planning, the selection and appointment of music directors, guest conductors, or performance directors determine an orchestra's ability to generate revenue through the sales of tickets and recordings. Programming and repertoire decisions also have immediate impacts on the demand for players and on wage costs. Long-term artistic planning also has other outcomes, such as establishing a profile and brand for an orchestra (Bathurst et al., 2007; Luksetich & Lange, 1995). In the next section, consideration shifts to the interest of musicians to improve their job security through the creation of a PGO and the realisation and operationalisation of player-governance.

4.3 Improving Job Security

Settings made during a firm's establishment period can influence and determine the sustainability of its governance model. To assess the sustainability of player-governance, it was essential to chart the logics, interests, and experiences of founding members as they began PGOs or instituted such a model in an existing orchestra or ensemble. The setup histories outlined in Sect. 3.2.2 display considerable diversity, but speaking to the interviewees who took part in this research revealed a range of shared economic motivations and rationales.

Workers' desire to share in profits generally undergirds labour-management (Bonin & Putterman, 1987; Bowles & Gintis, 1993; Dow, 2018; Pencavel, 2013; Vanek, 1970). However, profit-sharing does not provide such incentives in PGOs, which operate as not-for-profits. Instead, the interviewees revealed how reducing the insecurity of their employment takes priority. They also showed that reducing players' exposure to precarious work is neither straightforward nor fully realised in the PGOs studied. Balancing musicians' interest in job security and firms' need for commercial success is not obviated by giving players control. In all orchestras, the necessary negotiations take place within the limits of programming and shifting demand for musicians' labour. Offering musicians secure contracts depends on an orchestra's securing sufficient funding from sources such as public bodies, philanthropists, or sponsors, not on the governance model it uses.

The desire for job security must be balanced against a PGO's need to manage the constantly changing demand for the work of individual musicians. Robert described the trade-offs involved when he said that establishing a PGO attempted "to mitigate the disadvantages of the freelance world". He acknowledged that from an individual perspective the "advantage of the freelance world and the self-governing world is the independence, the ability to move fast, the ability to respond to a changing environment and the flexibility". Yet he also highlighted the trade-offs involved when he said that the "disadvantage is the lack of security, employment security". Against this background, he thought that "the self-governing orchestra tries, in a way, to provide a little bit more sense of security for the musicians that they can't just be thrown out at the whim of a conductor". Caution was nonetheless required because "the reality is that we are all freelancers and the legal position is that we do not have any job security". For Robert, his PGO was ultimately an attempt to "create an environment in which there is a sense of semi-permanence" though he "wouldn't put it any stronger than that". In the end he noted that "as a player, there is no guarantee that you will be used on every project. So, in some years you may be very busy, and in other years not". PGOs only go some of the way to addressing the desires of members for greater job security.

This thinking highlights the importance for players of trying to increase their employment security, even if only incrementally. The connection between the realities of playing in a freelance orchestra and the realisation of a "sense of semi-permanence" lies in orchestral musicians' drive to address the endemic insecurity of work that many experience and take responsibility for and control of their professional security. Maria highlighted the especially high rate of freelancing in subsectors of the orchestral labour market. She began by saying that

> There are, of course, no fixed positions in the early music scene. That means what we offer is the best thing that can happen to a player. Everything else means being freelance and totally dependent on being engaged by people.

The advantages of membership to Maria were a combination of modest employment security and various artistic rewards:

> At least we know that we can reckon with a certain number of days per year when we are booked to play, that we get to play with a good group, to play interesting concerts, nice programs and to get paid as well. That is very attractive.

The connection between employment security and artistic motivations was prominent in the earlier discussion of artistic control. For Maria, avoiding a dependence on "being engaged by people" overlaps and interacts with intrinsic factors such as musical fulfilment and professional development.

Susanna noted the role of industry standards in shaping attitudes to insecure work and attempts to deal with it:

> Part of it, of course, is being freelance. That also makes it so hard because you feel that your work is precarious anyway. If you are working for something like the Royal Opera House or the BBC, which have got strategies that you have in any business, then you know that certain things have to happen before you can be dismissed or ordered to prove yourself. In a way, I think that is what we are trying to model here. We are not "employed" in that business sense, but we can look at businesses and think, "OK, so that's why they do this, what can we take from how that works?" … In other orchestras for which I work, that is not appropriate, because if the director doesn't like you, they just won't book you.

Here too is an awareness of a freelance player's vulnerability and the power of directors (often conductors) who "just won't book you" if they are not satisfied with your work. Maria spoke of wanting to reduce the risk of total dependence "on being engaged by people", and Robert desired some protection against being "thrown out at the whim of a conductor". These three musicians are clearly quite conscious of the perils associated with freelance work, and their negative sentiments provide strong motivations and psychological drivers for the establishment of a PGO, even if such an organisation can only provide "a sense of semi-permanence". In important ways, founding a PGO is a response to the impact of precarious work. It is, however, only a partial response because the constantly variable nature of labour demand in orchestras means that full employment security with regular and fixed remuneration is difficult to sustain in the absence of substantial and continuing public or philanthropic funding or sponsorship.

The interview statements focus on the structural, organisational, and industry-level features of insecure work and PGOs' attempts to ameliorate its impact on their members. Player members spoke about additional effects of freelancing on individuals, their professional identities, and psychology. Walter was conscious of the limited security provided by his PGO: "One of the things we said right at the beginning was that in our minds we are permanently on trial. Being a member is not a guarantee of anything." Patrick thought that working with a freelance orchestra fostered specific psychological traits: "You are more self-centred as a freelance musician, bordering on narcissistic. That also means that you are also conscious of the fragility, but also the different possibilities that are open."

Herbert emphasised the responsibility felt by freelance players and how it was manifested within a PGO:

> The musicians who come to us are also freelance players who already bear considerable responsibility for their lives and those of their families, and so on. When they come to us they join a group of musicians that shares the risk.

In a similar vein, Walter stressed the resilience required of freelance players, the performance pressure under which they work, and the upshot that working in a freelance PGO creates demands that function like a filter on potential members:

> Any soloist, conductor or singer who has a career knows that. They can only count on themselves, that's all. If their standard drops, if they behave badly, eventually their career will suffer. It's the mentality of the musicians who join [our orchestra]. Those that stay agree with that, can cope with that, are strong enough in their minds and in their playing. … I think it is not for everyone. Some people can't cope with it and won't give their best under these conditions.

Hesmondhalgh and Baker (2011) showed how discussions of the dichotomy between freelance and secure employment in the cultural and creative industries are often overly simplistic. Walter's comments illustrated this. He observed that "nowadays, there is no such thing as security, even in big institutions. It's a bit of an illusion". In the face of such widespread insecurity, he felt that "it is an illusion to think you are protected and you are safe". Instead, membership of his PGO meant that

> We are just closer to the front row, or in the driving seat for some of us, and we know how quickly it happens. There is no such thing as security and I believe it is much better to know that right from the start. You know the truth; you know the risks.

The prevalence of freelance work among orchestral musicians is a key driver in the setting up of PGOs because doing that offers at least some control over players' work opportunities. The interviewees had a wide range of perspectives on the nature of freelancing and the ways in which it shapes their PGOs. Negative images of being dependent on work offers from capricious sources or being "thrown out at the whim of a conductor" are powerful drivers for players to seek greater control over their terms of employment by establishing a PGO. The interviewees were, nonetheless, also conscious of the freedoms and flexibility that they felt freelancing offered. For the sustainability of player-governance, perhaps the most interesting idea was that membership in a freelance PGO was "not for everyone" and might therefore function like a filter that goes some way to aligning the "mentality of the musicians who join" (Walter).

The focus of the next section is the regulation of essential governance elements in the PGOs researched, in particular, deciding who gets to vote, how decision-making functions in practice, and how the processes involved in such governance are optimised. The role of other PGOs as models is also briefly considered at the end of the section.

4.4 Creating Strong Governance

4.4.1 Avoiding Democratic Dilution

One of the greatest threats to the sustainability of labour-management arises from the creation of two groups of workers if members engage additional workers as hired labour without membership or voting rights. The use of such unenfranchised workers in an LMF threatens its democratic and participatory foundations as labour-management is diluted by a drop in the share of workers who are enfranchised (Dow, 2003). What might be thought of as the density of labour-management varies depending on the share of the total workforce that is enfranchised. At one end of such a density spectrum sit LMFs in which members provide all labour. Enfranchisement is 100 per cent of the workforce. Every worker can vote and be elected to governance roles. At the other end, the share of non-member workers is so high, and the firm is controlled by such a proportionally small group of workers, that the firm can no longer be meaningfully described as labour-managed (Batstone, 1983; Ben-Ner, 1988; Dow, 2003; Jensen, 2013).

Rothschild and Whitt (1986) warned of the risk that, "in search of growth, members are seduced into abandoning their principles. Internal democracy gives way to rule by a small group of elite members who are able, through the control of information and patronage, to make themselves indispensable" (p. 23). The opportunity to boost economic returns per member by reducing the number of members, to restrict decision-making to existing members as a firm expands by taking on new workers, or to limit the franchise to a group among a firm's workers are three of the prime motivations that can tempt members to restrict a firm's franchise and its number of members.

The parameters facing firms that experience fluctuating or seasonal demand for labour or whose work practices are characterised by a clear division of labour are, however, yet more complex. In practice, defining and maintaining a membership franchise with high levels of participation while allowing the hiring of non-member labour in clearly delineated and specific contexts is a key element of operationalising and sustaining labour-management. The demand for musicians' labour in PGOs is such a case because it results from a complex web of factors, some of which are economic, others artistic. The division of labour between musicians and management staff also raises challenges for the theoretical ideal of 100 per cent enfranchisement.

This section outlines the ways in which PGOs balance the competing demands of democracy, decision-making efficiency, and artistic control. The key query is whether a governance structure that enfranchises one group of workers (musicians) but not another (management staff) is more sustainable than one that enfranchises workers irrelevant of the type of work they perform. A further question also arises about the degree of enfranchisement among musicians and whether a governance system that offers membership to some musicians, while engaging others as supernumeraries, is more or less sustainable than one that offers—or even requires—membership for all players.

I argue that despite concerns that the employment of hired labour leads to the degeneration of labour-management, in the PGOs studied, the different labour market dynamics among management staff and musicians mean that such organisations are more efficient and sustainable when they engage management staff as hired labour. Doing so creates greater homogeneity of interests within the membership and avoids the risk of having two voting blocks that reflect the bifurcation of economic and artistic priorities between players and management staff.

The section begins by explaining how the interviewees and their respective organisations have sought to create a balanced and sustainable franchise that reflects the different types and level of engagement among PGO players and management staff and realises the desire to foster and sustain a democratic and participatory governance model.

Patrick summarised the challenge of establishing a franchise and balancing the interests of various groups:

> There are different [stakeholders[1]] and we have to then decide who we want our [stakeholders] to be. Do we want it to be just the members? Do we want it to be the office, maybe? Do we want it to be the people on the board of our foundation, because that might encourage them to take on more of a role? On the other hand, sometimes you see foundation boards become too powerful and then they start wanting to call the artistic shots. Do we also include our non-members who play with us a lot? They are also important to us, and so that they have some sense of having a stake?

Susanna described the challenges her orchestra confronted in defining full, enfranchised membership and the adjustments it made, including creating another category called "ordinary member" for those musicians who would only be hired on a project basis and would not be enfranchised:

---

[1] Patrick used the term "shareholder", but later in the interview, he said that the term he had wanted to use here was "stakeholder".

> When we changed [the governance] we knew that there would be some players who'd been playing quite a while with the orchestra who would not fall into the category of player member, because of where they are on the fixing lists.[2] They might well still come and play for the orchestra, but when you try to make a demarcation, the area around the line gets terribly messy. "Ordinary member" was a way of leaving it open for people who were not player members but who still wanted to have a connection with the orchestra and wanted to have a membership.

Claudia also described the need to optimise the various elements in a PGO's governance structure and ensure that enfranchisement of some, while others remain unenfranchised, did not create counterproductive gaps:

> What we've now come to [realise], is that you need much closer correlation (if that is the right word) with your board, your player representatives, your marketing, your development, your finances. They had to be brought closer together, and your development, of course. That is to do with the financial climate, the changes in industry and that sort of money not being around. It just meant we had to be a bit more clever and really work a bit more closely together, as to how we were going to manage that.

The experiences of these PGOs throw light on the divergent treatment of enfranchisement among players and between players and management. In most cases, the founding members or the people who drove the introduction of player-governance into an existing organisation were musicians. Administrative and management tasks were initially undertaken by musicians, and it was not until the initial setup was complete that they first considered creating specialist roles for management positions. Angela's recollections of the beginnings of her orchestra are typical: "It was run from a kitchen table. The early meetings felt like we were underground, having meetings around a table at various locations discussing whether we could create something like this, where we took charge of our musical destiny."

The proportion of musicians who are enfranchised as members in the PGOs studied, and therefore the proportion of those who are engaged as supernumeraries, reflects the interplay of artistic, business, and policy decisions. The challenge involved in establishing the ideal proportion of members has two sides. One concerns the absolute number of members. The other relates to the ratio between enfranchised and unenfranchised musicians. The number of musicians on stage for any performance is primarily a function of the demands made by individual musical works. Expanding beyond around 130 players makes neither musical nor economic sense for any orchestra because few musical works call for such numbers. In PGOs, these limitations and logics interact with the efficiency dynamics of democratic governance.

[2] Fixing lists record the order in which musicians are offered work in freelance orchestras.

4.4.2 Can There Be Too Many Members?

The theoretical writing on LMFs argues that their efficiency of decision-making suffers as the number of members grows. Too many enfranchised members may impede effective decision-making, and too few diminishes player-governance. As Stryjan (1989) observed, a "belief that size is detrimental to democracy, participation, and immediate personal relations between members is commonly shared by practitioners and students of self-management" (p. 138). In this section, I argue that to sustain player-governance, the PGOs must achieve a balance between the number of enfranchised and unenfranchised musicians which ensures that democratic decision-making remains viable and efficient.

Speaking of her chamber orchestra, Maria highlighted the dilemmas facing orchestras and ensembles trying to get the balance right between the numbers of enfranchised members (whom she refers to as "partners") and supernumeraries who would like to become members:

> At the moment we have, for example, eleven partner violinists. That is absolutely enough. There are certainly another five violins who would immediately become partners, where we know that they would like to become partners. But we don't have enough work. If they became partners, we would have to discuss who would be allowed to play for every project. We don't want that, rather, those who are members should, in principle, have the possibility of playing every project, and can decide for themselves what they don't want to play.

In the situation Maria described, members are keen to ensure that their income is not weakened by granting membership to supernumeraries. It is clear from Maria's comments how repertoire and programming decisions dictate that, for her PGO, 11 violinists are "absolutely enough" for the music they usually play. That number is dictated by artistic and financial considerations. A decision to play the same repertoire with the 11 violinist members and the 5 would-be member violinists that she mentioned would run up against artistic hurdles.

Herbert made it clear that taking on new members also represented a commitment by the orchestra to providing a minimum amount of work. Such a commitment requires careful planning and often reflects long-term repertoire plans. As Herbert noted:

> … when we consider taking on particular instruments in the partnership, then we also commit ourselves to offer these musicians work. Thus, we cannot have two horns and then say we are only playing string music for the next two years.

Describing the process through which his orchestra decided to expand what was originally a string orchestra into one including wind instruments, Herbert said that this was the result of a decision through which "we committed ourselves to taking a different approach to the repertoire". He added that

> The number of musicians is a function of our development. We started with thirteen: twelve strings and a harpsichordist. That was exactly the number required to play concerti grossi.[3]

[3] A concerto grosso is a musical form that was popular in the Baroque period.

> Later we started to play more music from the classical period as well as Baroque music with winds, and so we first added four winds, a flute, an oboe, a bassoon and a horn. In the next step we took on another four winds, the same instruments. That practically gave us the classical complement and we could play small Mozart, Haydn symphonies etc. with those forces. That put as at eight plus thirteen, makes twenty-one, and from there we added a few extra violins, another cello, a viola.

Like Maria's comments above, this quote shows the centrality of musical considerations such as programming and repertoire choice in deciding the numbers of player members in the PGOs studied. Expanding the repertoire led to an expansion of the membership. At the same time, Herbert, like Maria, highlighted economic considerations as he described how taking on previously supernumerary musicians as members entailed "commit[ing] ourselves to offer these musicians work". There is a direct connection between demand for players and the ability of a PGO to increase its membership.

These statements reveal artistic, financial, and efficiency factors involved in determining the optimal number of members in a PGO. Restricting the number of enfranchised members in an LMF may make governance processes more efficient (Dow, 2003). The situation observed in the music performance sector throws a different light on these debates. Factors other than the maximisation of profit and the distribution of residual earnings are decisive in determining the number of enfranchised members in a PGO. In this section, I argue that despite the risks that the employment of hired labour leads to degeneration of the self-governing ideal, the different labour market dynamics among management staff and musicians mean that PGOs are more efficient and sustainable if they engage management staff as hired labour.

As Maria and Herbert observed, the demand for musicians' labour in an orchestra or ensemble is primarily a function of its repertoire, individual programmes and projects. This situation poses a dilemma for PGOs, in particular those, such as the Freiburg Baroque Orchestra, that are constituted as partnerships without the protections of a limited liability firm. In such cases, members are individually liable for any financial losses incurred by the firm and there is an incentive to increase the number of members because doing so reduces the financial liability of existing members. Yet, even in such cases, the number of members is limited by other factors, as the interviews revealed. These PGO-specific factors contrast in several respects with the theoretical literature and reveal the complexity of operationalising the principles of labour-management in the context of orchestras.

4.4.3 "Perverse" Incentives

Some economists argue that LMFs have a "perverse" (Murat, 1987, p. 1619) incentive to reduce the number of members because doing so boosts the financial returns per member, an objective they argue is central to the formation of LMFs (Dow, 2003; Jensen, 2000; Meade, 1972). Members who are eligible to receive a share of residual income should, accordingly, resist an expansion of the membership so as to protect their financial interests. They should, then, cover any additional need for labour by hiring supernumerary workers at market wage rates and without granting them membership or a share of profits (Bonin et al., 1993; Dow, 2003; Jensen, 2000). However, in not-for-profit orchestras, members suffer no loss of profit-share when new members are admitted, though, as discussed below, their ability to influence other decisions, including those around artistic control and programming, may be watered down.

Similarly, the incentive to create additional capital for the firm or partnership through the expansion of the franchise to new capital-contributing members does not exist in PGOs. The future distribution of residual surpluses is precluded in not-for-profit companies such as almost all orchestras. In the absence of the potential for future financial returns, new members in PGOs have little incentive to contribute anything more than a token amount. Most musicians do, however, contribute capital to their orchestras by financing the instruments they own and bring to work. This is, though, true of all orchestras, irrelevant of governance type. Expanding the membership of a PGO does not increase capital or reimburse departing members for their putative share of retained surpluses. The incentive of boosting organisational capital by taking on new members is, then, neutralised in PGOs.

Other factors play a role in determining the optimum ratio of member to supernumerary musicians in a PGO. As the statements above highlight, taking on new members—as distinct from engaging additional players as supernumeraries—represents a commitment by the existing membership to satisfy reasonable expectations of work among new members. The PGOs I investigated for this book all operate on a freelance basis. This has important ramifications. One of the primary economic motivations for establishing a PGO is to reduce the exposure of musicians to insecure work (see Sect. 4.3). Yet increasing the number of members in a PGO does not normally lead to greater production or organisational earning capacity. Increasing the membership by, say, 25 percent does not automatically mean an equivalent rise in performances is possible or that ticket prices can be raised. So, extra members have to be allocated work from the existing quota of hours available. As Maria and Herbert both noted, this causes a reduction of hours for existing members, unless the total number of hours increases.

Existing PGO members do thus have an economic incentive to cover needs for additional musicians with supernumerary hired labour. As Herbert noted, the membership of a chamber orchestra is dictated by the number of players required by its core repertoire. Similarly, contemporary music ensembles typically consist of a 16-member core that is made up of one player of each instrument from the main sections of a full orchestra plus two percussionists and a pianist. The basic activity of an orchestra or ensemble (i.e. performance of specific repertoire) thus influences its governance structure in ways generally not seen in sectors outside the performing arts.

The demand for musicians' labour in orchestras varies enormously, irrelevant of the governance system used. Some instrumentalists are required for practically every concert programme while, even in orchestras that perform almost every week, others may only be required for every second or third programme. In a freelance PGO, members who play less frequently required instruments are thus incentivised to advocate for the programming of works that require their instruments. By doing so they stand to increase their income. As Herbert noted, even if membership in a PGO does not typically come with a contractually agreed number of hours per week, month, or year, enfranchised members would normally expect a certain minimum number of hours. Moreover, as an enfranchised member they would have the right to protest to their colleagues who are responsible for programming if they felt consistently disadvantaged by their decisions. Likewise, the relatively low demand for the services of some instrumentalists would be expected to further hinder any desire on the part of existing members to offer enfranchised membership to such musicians.

The engagement of such players as supernumeraries is, then, less a sign of degeneration in the player-governance ethos than a response to the parameters of the sector. The engagement over time of increasingly large numbers of frequently required instrumentalists—such as the violinists Maria referred to—as supernumeraries would, nevertheless, be a symptom of such degeneration. The theoretical incentive to engage all post-foundation players as supernumeraries—including those whom the repertoire requires on a frequent basis—thus remains a challenge for the PGOs considered.

In this section, I looked at some of the key challenges facing PGOs as they establish a player-governed structure. During this process, important decisions are made about the balance between the number of members and the number of supernumerary musicians and how this balance can shift. These decisions go to the heart of player-governance. If imbalances result, a PGO may prove unsustainable as governance tensions create friction, inefficiency, or degeneration in the ethos of player-governance. The result can be artistic and then business failure[4] or a move towards a hierarchical, non-participatory organisation. The interviews highlighted the delicate aligning of interests and drivers at the heart of a PGO, a balance that is critical to the operationalisation and sustainability of player-governance. I firstly identified the challenges and balancing involved in achieving a sustainable membership. I then argued that while acknowledging concerns that the employment of unenfranchised, hired labour can lead to the degeneration of labour-management, the different labour market dynamics among management staff and musicians mean that PGOs are more efficient and sustainable if they engage management staff as hired labour. Those are the central elements of creating governance structures in these PGOs.

[4] Members of one orchestra in the study cohort—the London Mozart Players—were faced with the dissolution of their orchestra in 2014 after it lost all its public funding and its major sponsor (Hewett, 2014). It was at this point that the players took control of the orchestra and introduced player-governance.

4.5 The Role of Models

PGOs are possible sources of pooled experience, knowledge, and expertise for each other. Existing PGOs can serve as governance models for later entrants. In particular, musicians who work with more than one PGO increase the potential for knowledge sharing among these firms. Dow (2003) argued that the tendency of "traditional workers' cooperatives" to "congregate in certain industries, regions, and time periods" (p. 230) might be explained by the presence of a "template firm whose organizational structure was imitated when other coops were created in the same industry" (ibid. p. 231). My research suggested that the challenges facing PGOs, even when they share similar governance structures, show such diversity that in most cases founding members sought to find their own way. Mario's comments in this regard were particularly clear:

> It can sometimes be helpful to know that an orchestra has faced the same challenges, but it does not necessarily lead to solutions for the same problems in your own structure. A child has to fall five times before it learns to walk, even when, at least theoretically, you can tell someone how to walk without falling. So, you need to make certain mistakes yourself.

Walter recalled that as he and his colleagues set out to establish a PGO:

> There were a couple of ready-made suggestions on how to run and govern the orchestra, proposed by someone within the orchestra and someone closely connected on the outside. But we rejected that. We wanted to do it all ourselves and democratically.

Susanna said of information sharing:

> We do ask around. If we are on the committee and something comes up, we might ask someone who works for the Mahler Chamber Orchestra about how they do that. We do have players who work in other groups and who might come back and say, "This is how they do it, can we think about it?" Not that we have systematically gone out and researched or looked for this or that.

Alex partly concurred when she said that "we have, indeed, talked to people in other orchestras, the LSO for example, we have spoken to them … It is slightly different from our orchestra. No, we have actually done most of this on our own". The usefulness of these PGOs' pooled governance experience is limited by the diversity of their disparate operating contexts, backgrounds, and governance rules.

The research for this book revealed that the exchange between PGOs of experience, insights, and possible solutions to common problems mostly takes place on an ad hoc basis. In some cases, it is, as Susanna noted in her statement above, most effectively furthered by individual players who work with more than one PGO. Such players act as conduits for information sharing, but usually in an informal capacity. There is, then, nothing like an easily transferrable template among the PGOs in the research, but they are aware of the developments and practices that the firms have in common.

4.6 Conclusion: Defining Elements of a New PGO

This chapter investigated the rationales, interests, drivers, and limitations that came together to erect the three key structural pillars in the PGOs studied—members' artistic control, job security, and governance structures. The focus on the processes and activity of governance realisation and operationalisation, rather than on structures, emphasised the dynamic, creative but contested nature of player-governance, particularly during a PGO's early setup phase.

The vast majority of the writing on LMFs approaches these firms from the perspective of economics and, by so doing, overlooks many other factors that come into play. In the case of PGOs, such omissions are especially problematic. While orchestras can be studied from a purely economic perspective, doing so neglects other factors, foremost of which are artistic factors that have a role in player-governance. The PGOs in the research are quintessentially hybrid organisations that combine artistic motivations with economic rationales. This chapter reflects and illuminates that duality.

I began the chapter by considering the artistic motivations and interests that shape PGOs. The interviewees were clear about the centrality of taking control of artistic planning and programming. Walter highlighted "artistic motivation" as the "core idea" without which a PGO is "going to be flawed from the beginning". Martin felt that taking artistic control was "the defining element of self-governance". Alex said that, "certainly [among] all the people I know who are on the programming or artistic team there is this real desire and belief in wanting to play with *this* orchestra". These artistic motivations constitute a strong foundational resource that can help establish and sustain player-governance.

The challenge, however, is to ensure that PGOs remain able to counter any opportunistic interests among members to pursue unsustainable artistic planning and programming and ensure that, in Alvis' words, "it's not just players being idealistic and saying 'we're going to play this piece, why hasn't anybody come?'" If, as Martin said of his PGO, "effectively, the player membership is the music director", then members also need to take on the responsibility for commercial sustainability that is a key element of successful artistic planning. The interviewees indicated that this is indeed the case as they described the processes through which they ensure, as Alvis, put it, "it's not just a bunch of musicians being all artistic". The balancing of competing logics is, once again, the key element of sustaining player-governance.

Here there are parallels with the desire to improve job security for player members. Governance sustainability cannot be neatly separated from long-term commercial viability. PGO members that opportunistically give themselves more job security than the financial realities of their firm allow endanger the sustainability of the firm and, in turn, the sustainability of player-governance. From these conflicting imperatives emerged PGOs that were only partly able to realise their members' desire for improved employment security. This might be perceived as disappointing, but at the same time, it is evidence of the ability of PGO members to balance competing drivers in the interest of governance sustainability. Protection from being "thrown out at the whim of a conductor", a key element of improved job security, is only possible as a result of members' taking artistic control.

The chapter also mapped the interviewees' thinking on key questions around the right to participate in decision-making in their PGOs. Susanna described how "terribly messy" the setting of the necessary divisions between enfranchised and unenfranchised stakeholders can become. Determining membership numbers also calls for structural responses that do justice to the needs for optimal decision-making, to the artistic logics of labour demand in orchestras and ensembles, and to the ethos of player-governance. Here, too, the sustainability of player-governance is dependent on the ability of the PGOs studied to achieve a flexible, responsive, and dynamic balance between competing logics.

The next chapter turns to questions of hierarchy in PGOs. Orchestras have long been built around vertical hierarchies. Decision-making structures are clear and efficient. PGOs, however, seek to flatten hierarchies and need to find ways of sharing decision-making while preserving the effectiveness associated with traditional systems. Observations on how the case study PGOS do this form one primary focus of the chapter. The other spotlight falls on the sense of engagement, responsibility, and commitment that musicians report in connection with their work in the PGOs at the heart of this book.

References

Bathurst, R., Lloyd Williams, & Anne Rodda. (2007). Letting go of the reins: Paradoxes and puzzles in leading an artistic enterprise. *International Journal of Arts Management, 9*(2), 29–38. https://www.jstor.org/stable/41798995

Batstone, E. (1983). Organization and orientation: A life cycle model of French co-operatives. *Economic & Industrial Democracy, 4*(2), 139–161. https://doi.org/10.1177/0143831X8342002

Ben-Ner, A. (1988). The life cycle of worker-owned firms in market economies. *Journal of Economic Behavior & Organization, 10*(3), 287–313. https://doi.org/10.1016/0167-2681(88)90052-2

Bonin, J., Jones, D. C., & Putterman, L. (1993). Theoretical and empirical studies of producer cooperatives: Will ever the twain meet? *Journal of Economic Literature, 31*(3), 1290–1320. https://www.jstor.org/stable/pdf/2728242.pdf

Bonin, J., & Putterman, L. (1987). *Economics of cooperation and the labor-managed economy*. Harwood Academic Publishers.

Bowles, S., & Gintis, H. (1993). A political and economic case for the democratic enterprise. *Economics and Philosophy, 9*(1), 75–100. https://doi.org/10.1017/S0266267100005125

Cornforth, C. (2004). The governance of cooperatives and mutual associations: A paradox perspective. *Annals of Public and Cooperative Economics, 75*(1), 11–32. http://onlinelibrary.wiley.com/journal/10.1111/%28ISSN%291467-8292/issues

Dow, G. (2003). *Governing the firm: Workers' control in theory and practice*. Cambridge University Press.

Dow, G. (2018). *The labor-managed firm: Theoretical foundations*. Cambridge University Press.

Hesmondhalgh, D., & Baker, S. (2011). *Creative labour: Media work in three cultural industries*. Routledge. https://doi.org/10.4324/9780203855881

Hewett, I. (2014). London Mozart players: The ultimate comeback kids. *The Telegraph*. 28 May, Accessed 19 October 2025. https://www.telegraph.co.uk/culture/music/classicalmusic/10858384/London-Mozart-Players-the-ultimate-comeback-kids.html.

Jensen, A. (2013). The labor managed firm? A theoretical model explaining emergence and behavior. Chapter 11. In D. Kruse (Ed.), *Sharing ownership, profits, and decision-making in the 21st century*. Emerald. https://doi.org/10.1108/S0885-3339(2013)0000014020

Jensen, M. (2000). *A theory of the firm, governance, residual claims, and organizational forms*. Harvard University Press.

Lichtenstein, P. M. (1986). The concept of the firm in the economic theory of 'Alternative' organizations: Appraisal and reformulation. In S. Jansson & A.-B. Hellmark (Eds.), *Labor-owned firms and workers' cooperatives*. Gower Publishing.

Luksetich, W., & Lange, M. (1995). A simultaneous model of nonprofit symphony orchestra behavior. *Journal of Cultural Economics, 19*(1), 49–68. http://www.jstor.org/stable/41810532

Meade, J. E. (1972). The theory of labour-managed firms and of profit sharing. *The Economic Journal, 82*(325), 402–428. https://doi.org/10.2307/2229945

Murat, R. S. (1987). Workers' enterprises are not perverse. *European Economic Review, 31*(8), 1619–1125.

Olsen, E. K. (2013). The Relative Survival of Worker Cooperatives and Barriers to Their Creation. Chapter 4. In D. Kruse, (Ed.), *Sharing Ownership Profits and Decision-Making in the 21st Century*, Emerald. https://doi.org/10.1108/S0885-3339(2013)0000014005

Pencavel, J. (2013). The economics of worker cooperatives. In *Elgar research reviews in economics*. Edward Elgar. https://doi.org/10.4337/9781784710545

Rothschild, J., & Whitt, J. A. (1986). *The cooperative workplace: Potentials and dilemmas of organisational democracy and participation*. Cambridge University Press.

Stryjan, Y. (1989). *Impossible organizations: Self-management and organizational reproduction*. Greenwood Press.

Vanek, J. (1970). *The general theory of labor-managed market economies*. Cornell University Press.

Chapter 5
Democratic Orchestras in Action

5.1 Of Hierarchies, Engagement, and Virtuous Circles

Player-governed orchestras (PGOs) aspire to minimise hierarchies and maximise participatory decision-making in governance. However, performing—the productive work of orchestras and ensembles—is strongly hierarchical and has long been so. Practically all the critical decisions are entrusted to a conductor, with limited input from the leaders of instrumental sections (Atik, 1994; Logie, 2012). In the PGOs studied for this book, what has long been a hierarchically organised activity takes place within a governance structure that aspires to minimise hierarchy. Nonetheless, hierarchy in music performance appears to increase efficiency and can still be desired by the members of a PGO.

In this chapter's opening section, I consider the balancing of hierarchy and participation. I highlight how PGOs manage the conflicting imperatives of "intrinsic" music performance hierarchies and the anti-hierarchical desire for participatory decision-making at the heart of player-governance. This tension is most clearly manifested in the crucial relationship between players and conductors or performance leaders. The PGOs in this study, by allocating decisions about the hiring of conductors to member musicians, reverse the traditional relationship between players and conductors, but rather than simply turning the tables, their models recast the relationship as one of collaboration and partnership.

In the second section, the focus shifts to the challenges inherent in making participation work in these PGOs. The task of maximising decision-making efficiency while protecting the rights of members is familiar to many labour-managed firms (LMFs). For the PGOs studied, an additional challenge arises as they try to ensure that any political or personal tensions that may arise in governance fora do not spill over into and impinge on the spirit of cooperation, teamwork, and collegiality that orchestras and ensembles seek when on stage (Allmendinger et al., 1996; Boerner & Freiherr von Streit, 2005; Gaunt & Dobson, 2014; Lipton, 1987). Failing to do so

B. Long, *Democratising Orchestras*, Music Business Research,
https://doi.org/10.1007/978-3-032-17399-7_5

risks turning rehearsals and even performances into politically fraught battlegrounds, rather than an environment for creativity, artistic exploration, and a product for which the public wants to pay.

In the third section, the links between player-governance and engagement, commitment, and a sense of shared responsibility move to the foreground. An essential element in the sustainability of player-governance is the extent to which members respond to shared responsibility. The ways in which people relate to their work and its structures are key factors in their professional performance and wellbeing (Callan & Lawrence, 2009; Stanley & Meyer, 2016). High-quality performance among workers is, in turn, an important part of enterprise success and sustainability (Macey et al., 2009). Researchers use an array of terms to delineate and describe the ways in which people relate to and experience their jobs and the organisational contexts in which they work (Albrecht, 2010; Denunzio, 2016; Kahn, 1990; Meyer, 2016). Engagement, commitment, involvement, and job satisfaction are constructs at the heart of this conceptual array (Albrecht & Dineen, 2016; Callan & Lawrence, 2009; Judge et al., 2012; Kahn, 1990; Mogelof & Rohrer, 2005). The interviews for this book highlighted how and to what extent player-governance fosters such responses. The argument in this section is that the sustainability of player-governance is enhanced by its ability to create a virtuous circle: participation builds engagement, commitment, and shared responsibility, which, in turn, sustain player-governance. Sustained player-governance thus both results from and produces engagement, commitment, and a sense of responsibility in PGOs. Harnessing governance participation and exploiting its self-reinforcing ability to build engagement, commitment and shared responsibility are central to the sustainability of player-governance. A central focus of this section is on the ways in which engagement and commitment among musicians are facilitated in the PGOs studied.

5.2 Rethinking Artistic Hierarchies

Orchestral performance has traditionally been built on hierarchy. Conductors have practically unrestricted power over questions of interpretation.[1] PGOs, on the other hand, are built on a desire to reduce hierarchy and realise participatory and democratic decision-making. What results is a tension between the performance-related hierarchies found in the orchestral model and the relatively flat organisational structures and operating processes that exist in PGOs. Achieving and sustaining a balance between these two structures is at the heart of the long-term viability of PGOs.

One of the most important manifestations of player-governance in the PGOs is the reversal of the contractual relationship between conductors and musicians. The conductor of yore had the power to "hire and fire" players. Orchestral musicians

[1] See, however, Koivunen and Wennes (2011), who described "an ongoing relational process between the conductor and the musicians" (p. 51).

now enjoy more employment protection (Ayer, 2005; Long, 2015) but conductors continue to exercise great musical authority (Boerner & Freiherr von Streit, 2007; Hunt et al., 2004; Lewis, 2012). Their judgements of a player's proficiency can still have employment repercussions (Koivunen & Wennes, 2011).

The player-governance structures at the heart of this book enable enfranchised musicians to choose whether to work with a conductor at all, and if so, which conductor they want to work with. Conductors and performance leaders are hired because of decisions made by musicians. Repeated engagements depend on conductors enjoying continued support among the majority of members. This type of relationship represents a far-reaching reversal of the hierarchies found in customary orchestral operations.

Choosing the conductors with whom they work is, then, a central element of governance in the PGOs in this study. For Sophie, it is "the most important discussion we can have with each other if you are making music: what do you want to play, who do you want to play with, and how do you want to play?" Martin similarly noted that "we spend a long, long time talking about conductors,, and was of the view that at least some autocracy was important. In his view, the orchestra–conductor relationship is crucial and involves a delicate power balance:

> You have got to be really careful about it. That is a big challenge. It's art. It's a funny relationship. Everything else is a metaphor for the conductor and the orchestra. Because in a really good conductor–orchestra relationship the players do want a little bit of autocracy, they do want that. But they don't want it at the expense of everything. They just need someone who is going to say, "Look, we can't have a vote on this. You just have to do that." … So they do want that kind of leadership very much.

Comments made by Maria made clear both the degree of control democratic governance gives players in their dealings with conductors and the process involved:

> When someone comes and says, "I have seen this conductor who was great, we should give him a try" and the general feeling is "why not?", then [name of general manager omitted] gets in contact and they have a chat. … If an agreement is reached … then he will do a project with us and after that we meet here and discuss whether it was good and whether we want to work together again. And then the group decides whether we want to do something with him again. And there have been some where the group has said, "no, we could do without repeating that."

While musicians in PGOs have, then, considerable power when it comes to engaging conductors, Robert was keen to emphasise that this was not a matter of simply reversing semi-dictatorial powers, but rather of transforming a unidirectional power regime into one of partnership:

> One shouldn't have the idea that we try to separate ourselves from the conductors or principal artists, who, when you are talking about Baroque music, might be a violinist. We want to have a relationship with these people. We don't want them to dictate to us, but neither do we want to dictate to them. We want to work and collaborate with them. The whole enterprise is just one huge collaboration from start to finish. Everywhere you look, it is collaboration, collaboration, collaboration. It is working together.

In a similar vein, Martin said that

> When you are working with people like [names of conductors omitted], it is not always going to be the most fruitful relationship if you just say, "we want to do this, you do it." … There has to be give and take. In a way what is good about [name of orchestra omitted] is that when it's at its best, it's just being cooperative and it is receptive to ideas, and it doesn't really matter whose idea it was.

Later, Robert expanded on the vision of collaboration by highlighting the central questions involved:

> How can we do this? How can we make this happen? I hope that is how the conductors feel with us: "I want to do this piece, how can I make it happen? How can I encourage this orchestra to bring my artistic vision to life?" I respect them for that.

In response to a question about whether some conductors might not be suited to working with the ethos and artistic principles of his orchestra, Martin agreed, adding:

> Yes, and some don't want it either. It doesn't work with the [name of orchestra omitted]. It's not so much a problem with Classical and the Baroque, it can be a challenge, even then, but it is less likely. But when you start getting into the Romantic repertoire there is a temptation, if you work with a name conductor, what will happen is that they will turn up and just treat it like a symphonic orchestral job, and they will do two rehearsals and then one on the day and then do the program. That is a disaster with the [name of orchestra omitted]. It doesn't work.

Alvis offered a compact overview of how his orchestra's thinking on conductors evolved. He described how at the outset

> We thought we ought to have a principal conductor, because that's what orchestras do. So we continued with [name of conductor omitted], who was very supportive. But then, what we felt was, hang on a minute, this is a … Classical chamber orchestra, our core repertoire is Classical music, why do we need a conductor? … If we are empowering ourselves, why do we need a kind of dictatorial figure telling us what to do for that kind of repertoire? So, then we sat down and really thought about this and then we really made the decision that this would be a leader-led orchestra, player-directed orchestra. … We now have conductors who we bring in, in the expectation that they have got something to offer us. If a conductor is not going to bring something to the table, other than a beat, there's no point. And that was a very empowering decision to make.

On the question of musical leaders, be it a conductor or an instrumentalist, Angela sounded a warning and highlighted leadership as a key element in creating an efficient structure in the rehearsal room or on stage. For her, any absence of leadership resulted in "a free-for-all among the players … when we start having fights, arguments and mutiny in different pockets, because the directors had not got control and no one respects them".

In a statement quoted in the discussion about taking artistic control, Martin said that

> The really significant, defining element of self-governance is actually artistic. It's playing without a conductor, working with a conductor at its own discretion, not having an autocratic artistic director but actually taking artistic matters into their own purview and consideration.

5.2.1 *A Virtuous Circle*

The PGO–conductor dynamic is unusual among LMFs. As Martin pointed out, the first decision for the members of a PGO is whether to engage a conductor at all. When conductors are engaged by these PGOs, they are asked to take on leadership roles for discrete projects and provide "a little bit of autocracy" (Martin). Guest conductors (as distinct from musical or artistic directors) are not members of the PGOs they conduct and are contracted on a fee-for-service basis. Thus, for the duration of a project with a conductor, the musicians of a PGO transfer a considerable amount of their artistic control to an external, non-member leader who, while filling a leadership role, is in turn ultimately answerable to the membership, who will decide if he or she is engaged again for further projects. In the case of instrumental performance directors, such players are external to the organisations, while in other cases they may be members of the orchestra or ensemble who have been granted a leadership role and interpretative control by their colleagues.

Figure 5.1 visualises the circular control structure adopted by most of the PGOs studied. At the top of the diagram, player members have ultimate authority that they delegate to committees that, in turn, make decisions about the hiring of conductors or performance leaders. At the bottom and to the left, the work of players is directed by conductors and performance leaders to whom the players have delegated authority. The PGOs studied transform the vertical and hierarchical structure of the traditional orchestral model into a circular flow of control. Balancing the forces and dynamics of this organisational constellation is essential to the success and sustainability of the PGOs studied for the book.

The question remains, however, as to why PGOs continue to work with conductors at all. The circular model outlined above can be largely avoided if players decide against hiring conductors and take control of all artistic decisions, not just those of programming. Richard described the effort to reduce hierarchy in his orchestra as "not as extreme as in Orpheus"—a New York orchestra that badges itself as "the world's only conductorless orchestra"[2] (Seifter & Economy, 2001). While noting that "we used to have concerts on occasion when the section leaders changed positions", he felt that the hierarchy between solo and tutti players that has evolved in his orchestra was a question of "quality assurance" and "there is no alternative, because not everyone is the type of person who makes a section leader". Maria had a similar position: "I am one of these people who likes to play along. I like to react, but I am not keen on standing at the front." Angela observed that "some people are good at giving instructions, some people are good at receiving

[2] Other orchestras and ensembles, including some of those studied for my research, now also routinely perform without conductors. Orpheus has, though, more experience rehearsing and performing without conductors than any other orchestra. It has turned this experience into what it calls the Orpheus Process; a structured approach to rehearsal and performance without conductors (Seifter & Economy, 2001).

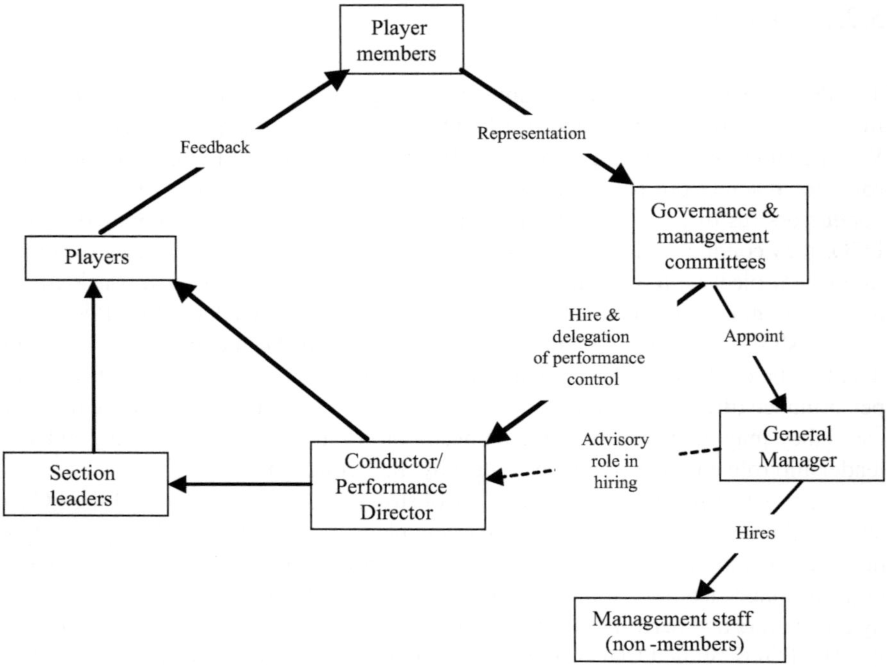

Fig. 5.1 Circular distribution of control in PGOs

instructions. Some play better when they are in a support role. Put them in a leading role and they go to pieces". In the same interview, she recalled that

> One of the biggest lessons that I had an instinctive feeling about at the very beginning was that everyone was a leader and everyone was equal. And, I think that was very optimistic, what's the word, slightly naive … we were all paid the same, there was no hierarchy, everyone was equal. I thought that was not realistic, because not everyone is a leader.

The orchestras and ensemble studied have been able to achieve a far-reaching and sustainable realignment of control. In particular, they have instituted a model of hired leadership in which a traditional authority figure, such as an orchestral conductor, is engaged by musicians and granted a collaborative leadership role rather than dictatorial power. Collaboration, along with "being cooperative and … receptive to ideas" (Martin) characterises the relationships with conductors sought by the musicians interviewed. The dynamics of the conductor–orchestra relationship have been well documented (Boerner & Freiherr von Streit, 2007; Hunt et al., 2004; Lewis, 2012), and it has often been described as akin to a dictatorship, in which conductors have all the power or what Alvis described as a "kind of dictatorial figure telling us what to do". Robert stressed that the realignment of this relationship realised by PGOs was not simply a matter of reversing the tables. Rather, members "don't want them to dictate to us, but neither do we want to dictate to them".

The relationship achieved between conductors and musicians in these PGOs represents a rebalancing of a key axis of power and authority. Players approach the conductor–orchestra relationship from a position that is rooted in self-assurance and the authority derived from having "set up our own orchestra, that belongs to us" (Sophie). They now have "conductors who we bring in, in the expectation that they have got something to offer us" (Alvis). Players want to "have a relationship with these people …. to work and collaborate with them" (Robert). This axial realignment is central to the mission of PGOs, their vision, and their contribution to the understanding of labour-management more widely.

The PGOs balance the continued exploitation of decision-making hierarchies in the rehearsal and performance context with a desire to reduce hierarchy as far as possible in their governance structures. There is a recognition that the artistic decision-making hierarchies in the traditional orchestral model can serve a valuable purpose. Conductors, instrumental leaders (usually lead violinists or keyboard players), and section leaders play a role in enhancing decision-making efficiency, but the power they exercise is delegated to them by members, who retain ultimate governance control. Robert spoke of "collaboration" and "working together" being the essential characteristics of the relationship between players in PGOs and their conductors. Alvis, when he spoke of engaging conductors "in the expectation that they have got something to offer us", was similarly clear about the essentially partner-like quality between conductors and PGOs. The PGOs studied have thus radically realigned the orchestra–conductor relationship, but without rejecting outright the hierarchy involved. Musical leadership continues to play a part, and there is an understanding that an approach that assumes every musician is equally skilled as a leader is unrealistic, unless players are recruited with such roles explicitly in mind.

Sophie made a statement that serves well to close this section and its emphasis on balancing hierarchy and player control. Asked about the decision to found a PGO, she was clear about the sense of developing an identity and orchestra that was led by the musicians and about the related desire to minimise hierarchy:

> I don't think there was ever an alternative. The idea that we would set up something hierarchical seemed so strange that we never even discussed it. It was totally clear. … We did have support from [name of conductor omitted] … but it was totally clear that we didn't want to be dependent on one person, but rather we wanted to find our own way. That was as clear as day, so that, as I said, we didn't even discuss it: that we wanted to set up our own orchestra that belongs to us.

5.3 Democracy in Action: Decision-Making

5.3.1 Speed and Deliberation

The spotlight now moves to the development, refinement, and optimisation of participation in the governance of the PGOs studied. PGOs pursue two key objectives in their governance processes: reaching the best decisions (using various understandings of decision quality) and sustaining the democratic legitimacy of player-governance by maximising the opportunities for members to take part in decision-making. PGOs need to ensure that any conflict from governance decision-making does not weaken the sense of cooperation and synergy at the core of high-level musical performance. The interviewees revealed how their PGOs have adapted democratic structures to fit their requirements as firms working in professional music performance. They made it clear that the benefits and sustainability of player-governance in the orchestras and ensemble in the research were a function of the continuous balancing of decision-making efficiency and the optimisation of enfranchisement and "voice" among members. In this section, the interviews foreground the ability to adapt democratic thinking to these PGOs' specific contexts and practices is a key element in their governance sustainability. Making democracy and participatory decision-making work in these PGOs requires reflexivity, an openness to evolution, and the ability to reach shared understandings of governance.

The section details the interviewees' experience of making democracy in PGOs work. Their views showed that the oft-repeated trope of democratic decision-making being inefficient and excessively time-consuming was too simplistic. These voices argued that, at times, the quality of decisions was more important than the speed with which they were reached. For Alvis, the emphasis lay on the quality of decisions and on the deliberation required:

> We don't make fast decisions; we really reflect on them. When we first took over the orchestra we felt that we had to make decisions quickly, but actually we are much more reflective. So, the idea of panicking; we don't do that anymore. That might sound a bit glib, but it's absolutely crucial to making really good, confident decisions. … I think we take our time with difficult decisions, we don't rush them, and, if we have to … we'd literally move the project back until we are all confident that this is the decision, as a unit, we are going to make. So, we try to get rid of those tensions, so that we can go and play and still get on with each other.

Leo spoke about balancing democracy and the need for quick decisions:

> That was the big discussion over the last two years: how can we rebalance it? Sometimes the democratic process is too slow, and sometimes there are issues that make you want to decide immediately … There is this split: should we wait or if we wait, what will happen to this project?

Daniel likewise thought that the essential concern was

> A question of balance. Who makes the decisions? There are critical decisions and there are less critical decisions which have to do with long periods of time. There are decisions that have to do with one hour on the concert stage. All of these decisions need the right kind of balance. They have got to be made in a way that is satisfying for all of the … musicians plus the members of the office who have to carry out the administration of all of this.

Alvis described a specific decision that benefited from a deliberative approach and spoke about the importance of getting "everybody on side":

> There were two very … different ideas … the two sides … were quite entrenched in their views. So, we just took our time … and … now that we've stepped back from it just a little bit … I'm more comfortable … just literally by … not making rapid decisions that people

> are going to resent. … When you do a big project, everybody has got to agree. You've got to get everybody on side.

These interviewees thus acknowledge the efficiency challenges of democratic decision-making in their organisations. They have developed strategies to address them and reach a balance between efficient decision-making and democratic participation. The PGOs in the study use committees and working groups that investigate problems and develop a range of possible solutions that can expedite decision-making. The range of solutions can subsequently be put to the wider membership. In other cases, decision-making is delegated. Mario said that

> I think the orchestra and the way we operate is a good reflection of society. There are elected representatives of the musicians, which means one does not need to be active in every role and can delegate responsibility. The representatives who have that mandate can direct things while one remains one's own boss, because at the end of the day you can influence the processes used to make decisions. That is representative democracy.

Leo was, likewise, aware of the balance between direct and representative democracy when he said that

> On our website, it says we are organised as a basic democracy, which is [only] partly true, because I think it is more of a representative democracy. Nevertheless, the musicians have a meeting every month, at which general matters and special questions are discussed as well as what has happened in the last few months, what will happen in coming months, and criticism about how things have worked out in the end. … But these large meetings are, I think, not the right forum for reaching decisions quickly. Therefore, the ensemble elects three representatives to an artistic committee.

Richard was also clear about the trade-offs between speed and consensus:

> The timespan between when a problem arose and when a solution was found was extremely long, when you always need to have everybody on board. This preparatory work in smaller groups expedites it. It does, however, restrict the diversity in some respects. Not everyone is then really close to the decisions from the start. Many only come to the problem later and hear about it at a later stage. There are pros and cons to that. At the moment it is important for us to prioritise speed a little.

The interviewees describe how this adoption of representative democracy brings in other elements. Some members may have lower levels of commitment to democratic ideals or may not want to devote high levels of energy to the governance of their organisation. For Maria, this meant acknowledging that governance structures do not assume a uniform level of organisational engagement:

> Meanwhile it is no longer the case, as it used to be, that we're all required to sit here when there is a meeting. There are a few that are compulsory, but there are many that are voluntary. And, of course, it's always the same people that come. That's human nature, and it is also right in a group of this size. It took us a while to accept it. But I think, on the other hand, we would go crazy if all of us joined in the discussion. That would be terrible. It's good that a few simply say, "We trust you, you do that, and I'm happy to play along."

The various trade-offs involved in player-governance generally, and the different forms of democracy in particular, were central to comments made by Martin:

> Self-governance has this kind of utopian perspective that it is going to be a sort of social contract and that people come to it equally and there is an equal share in power along with this sort of democratic process. All of that is wonderful and it is reasonably achievable, but it does bring with it quite an administrative burden.

Balancing the desire to make good decisions with that of maximising the level of participation in the attendant processes and thus the democratic legitimacy of an organisation's governance and management is a central priority in the sustainability of player-governance in the PGOs studied. At the same time, decision-making occurs in an environment in which tension from management or governance decision-making fora can spill over into the rehearsal room and onto the performance stage. Such spillage can be detrimental to the cooperation, synergy, and relationships that are conducive to high-level music performance (Boerner, 2006; Dobson & Gaunt, 2013; Gaunt & Dobson, 2014). This risk can be exacerbated when, as is frequently the case, governance hierarchies and those within an orchestra or ensemble as a team of performers do not align. There is no reason why senior players in the music-performance hierarchy, such as section leaders, should be elected to similarly senior roles within the governance structure. Indeed, one interviewee thought this was difficult to achieve. Richard said that,

> Time and again you notice that it is difficult for more highly exposed players to also have highly exposed positions on committees. But you see that in all orchestras. In my experience, it is quite rare for a solo oboe or solo cellist to be on the board. Quite often that is because someone on a committee makes themselves vulnerable to attack. And when you sense the collective hostility of 20 people, it is easier to survive as a tutti player than when you, as a solo cellist, are dependent on support. You need the positive energy. It is simply difficult to play a solo when you have just come from a discussion that went pear-shaped. Of course, that is not always so, but I think there is a tendency there.

Walter observed that

> There is, I think, pretty good separation between the administrative, the committees, the general meetings, and then playing together. I am not saying it is always easy, of course. On the whole, I think we are able to separate these things. If the most important thing is to play together, if that is always there, it is possible to overcome the rest.

Governance and administrative work is not always disruptive and a source of friction for players. Daniel made this clear when he said that

> To a certain extent, the structure does, for me, have something to do with the collegiality, the cementing together of the ensemble, because we do work together a lot, but most of the time it is not on stage. What happens on stage, then, is actually, because of the working together that we do in the background — the preparation for a concert, the rehearsal period and the performance itself — is, then, different because we know these people very well.

Later in the same interview, he put it more forcefully:

> That is part of the background which does come out on stage: this feeling that the experience of working together even in that situation where the project manager has to say, "No, we can't do it the way you would like, we have to do it another way," and you have to be prepared for that and you have to say, "That's OK. I understand the difficulty, please go ahead, I will deal with it." That is part of the cementing of the whole ensemble that gives me the power that I need, the joy in life that I need to go out and play that fucking instrument on that stage for the audience.

5.3.2 *Direct and Representative Democracy*

The interviews provided many insights into the challenges of making democracy work in the player-governed context. Concerns about the risk of governance conflicts infiltrating orchestras' musical performance highlighted the essential task of balancing various possible forms of democratic organisation and participation. I became aware of the tensions between decision-making efficiency and the maximisation of enfranchisement and "voice" (Mantouvalou, 2014; Wilkinson et al., 2014) among members. Other writers acknowledge that the achievement and sustenance of a balance between these outcomes are challenging (Kruse, 2013; Leach, 2016; Putterman, 1982). One of the most common complaints about democratic decision-making concerns the extra time it can require, especially if unanimity or consensus is needed. Many commentators on LMFs have argued that they are inefficient because of their inability to make quick decisions (Hansmann, 1996; Leach, 2016). Much of the literature on group decision-making posits that in a democratic system, large groups require more time and resources to decide than do small ones (Dow, 2003; Hansmann, 1996; Putterman, 1982). Finding a middle way between direct and representative democracy is a central challenge to these PGOs.

Representative democracy using committees elected from the membership can expedite decision-making, but at the cost of alienating members if they feel marginalised from the deliberative processes of such committees. The PGOs studied have all implemented governance systems that go some way towards representative democracy. In particular, they have instituted artistic committees to optimise decision-making in this essential area. At the same time, the companies are conscious of the need to ensure that all enfranchised members continue to have a voice in critical decisions. Introducing such representative democracy is a common method of increasing the efficiency of democratic decision-making within organisations.

In a system of direct democracy, each enfranchised voter is entitled to vote on a proposal without having to consider the interests of anyone else, and all enfranchised members are entitled to vote on a proposal. In a system of representative democracy, members elect peers to committees that are charged with making decisions on behalf of and in the interests of the electorate as a whole. These representatives are expected to represent the interests of the people who voted for them and to vote accordingly. Voters can elect a different representative or stand for election at the next opportunity, if they feel that their representatives have failed to protect the interests of voters.

As governance moves towards representative democracy, a separation opens up between an organisation's enfranchised members and decision-making fora. Members may feel that they are no longer directly involved in or informed about decisions, or as Richard noted, the result can be that "not everyone is then really close to the decisions from the start". There is, then, a trade-off between direct and representative forms of democracy. Direct democracy promises a high level of participation, voice, and transparency, but at the price of decisions that take longer to reach than in other systems. These problems are heightened when unanimity or consensus is required. As Sebastian said of his PGO: "the ensemble has sixteen voices and getting them all to agree, unless the question is a very obvious one, is quite unlikely. The likelihood that the CEO is going to be of the same opinion is trivial." The greater the number of enfranchised members, the more time-consuming direct democracy is likely to become.

By relieving members from taking part in all decisions, representative democracy can expedite decision-making. This form of governance delegates control in areas of specialised knowledge such as financial or legal matters to those who have relevant skills or are prepared to acquire them. Delegation to representatives may, though, lead to a sense of alienation among members who feel less well informed about the factors influencing decisions. If members become less engaged, there is a risk of losing one of the essential strengths of player-governance that "participation may result in better decisions" (Strauss, 1998, p. 10). The challenge for player-governance is to foster its potential for effective decision-making by achieving a balance between decision-making efficiency and members' sense of enfranchisement.

As they deal with this delicate balance between high-participation decision-making and efficiency, PGOs also run the risk of democratic decision-making being counterproductive if any political tensions that arise in management and governance meetings involving players disturb the sense of teamwork that is thought to exist in high-performing orchestra and ensembles (Boerner, 2006; Gilboa & Tal-Shmotkin, 2012; Murnighan & Conlon, 1991; Tal-Shmotkin & Gilboa, 2013). It is essential for the success of a PGO that in the presence of the tensions that may arise in a participatory governance and management system, players remain able to, in the words of Alvis, "go and play and still get on with each other". However, the interviews throw light on the risk of tensions arising when players are required to deal with complex governance and management matters in decision-making fora that subsequently spill over into the team-based music-making context.

This is exacerbated in the case of section leaders, for whom, as Richard observed, "it is simply difficult to play a solo when you have just come from a discussion that went pear-shaped". Much to the same effect, Patrick described the challenges experienced by section leaders when they are expected to deal with concerns about performance quality. To reiterate:

> We are trying to get the leaders and the principals to do that. But that is not easy, because some of these people want to be able to just play and don't want to be one of the people in the firing line having to go and have that hard conversation with whoever.

Martin, likewise, highlighted the "enormous burden" put on section leaders;

> Because it is not just that they turn up and they lead their section, but they have got this sort of political issue as well, they have to manage the team, they don't have an HR person, there isn't an artistic director looking over them, there isn't a [famous conductor like Georg] Solti saying, 'you're fired, you're fired'. It is sort of down to them and they have this very immediate, very difficult role with the people around them.

5.3.3 *Parallel Hierarchies*

A further feature of player-governance that emerged from the interviews was the way in which PGOs overlay the hierarchies and power dynamics of a music performance team with those of the organisational structure. The two hierarchies—no matter how flat they may be—overlap, and this has the potential to create various tensions and challenges. The research for this chapter highlighted that the musical skills and abilities required of a section leader in an orchestra are not necessarily those that make the same individual a competent member of a governing board or management team. Indeed, the artistic demands made of players who are required to play solo passages may hinder them from also taking on leadership roles in the governance structure. Richard was clear about this when he noted that, for example, solo oboists and solo cellists seldom held important decision-making positions in the governance structure of PGOs.[3]

This risk of excluding musical leaders from governance leadership can, in turn, lead to friction when committees, such as artistic planning committees, make decisions about playing personnel in which section leaders feel they should be consulted. Angela described being notified about "something that is simply an outrageous decision that [the artistic committee] have made. I totally disagree with it. I was totally not consulted, and I'm a principal player. Things are happening that even principals don't even know are happening".

Speaking of the artistic committee, Angela also noted that "there are some ruthless decisions being made in there where they are not even having a wider discussion with the principal players", before asking:

> How can my number two [name of instrument omitted] player make a decision about a principal player over my head as a principal player? I think that is wrong. I'm more qualified, in the orchestra, because I'm a principal player. But they are making some radical decisions, which I think needs to be done, but I'm not sure we are doing it in the right way.

The tensions that can result from this duality of decision-making structures inherent in a PGO are clearly deserving of attention. The interviewees make it clear that player-governance is not a panacea for the tensions, rivalries, and conflicting interests that arise in many professional contexts. Instead, player-governance requires organisations to be aware that a delicate balance between management and artistic responsibilities is required and needs to be constantly maintained and sustained. Interpersonal rivalries, tensions, and conflicts arise in many professional contexts, yet may be particularly dangerous in organisations that have creativity at the heart of their operation. As Alvis noted, "if you've got one person who absolutely still thinks it's a stupid idea, that's going to create a lot of tension." Orchestras and ensembles, irrelevant of their governance systems, experience such interpersonal dynamics (Kemp, 1996; Kenny & Ackermann, 2009). However, in PGOs they are potentially more damaging because musicians in such organisations work

[3] Young's (2017) research produced a similar finding about the willingness of section leaders to take on non-performance roles.

together in multiple contexts. They need to collaborate and achieve balances in committee and board meetings as much as they do on stage.

5.4 Engagement, Commitment, and Shared Responsibility

Participation fosters and sustains player-governance by enhancing engagement, commitment, and a sense of responsibility among members in the PGOs. Speaking with the interviewees showed that high levels of these three phenomena—engagement, commitment, and a sense of responsibility—were, indeed, associated with player-governance and the participation it allows. However, the three terms are understood and used in many ways, so before considering the interviews, I will establish some working definitions for the key terms by surveying and synthesising thinking on engagement and commitment. I also examine how the interviewees use the terms, and the role engagement, commitment, and responsibility play in the PGOs studied.

I argue that participation contributes to the sustainability of player-governance to the extent that it can be harnessed to grow engagement, commitment, and shared responsibility. All three elements play important roles in the success and sustainability of the PGO models found in the cohort. Harnessing participation and exploiting its power to cultivate engagement, commitment, and shared responsibility are central to the sustainability of player-governance.

5.4.1 Definitions

In organisational and occupational psychology, the range of terms used to describe how workers relate to their work and their work contexts includes "commitment" (Albrecht & Dineen, 2016), "engagement", "disengagement", and "burnout" (Callan & Lawrence, 2009; Denunzio, 2016; Iddagoda et al., 2016; Kahn, 1990; Macey et al., 2009; Schaufeli et al., 2002), "job satisfaction" (Callan & Lawrence, 2009; Johansson & Theorell, 2003; Judge et al., 2012; Mogelof & Rohrer, 2005; Olbertz, 2006), and "flow" (Csikszentmihalyi, 2008; Kirchner et al., 2008). I begin by exploring how concepts such as engagement and commitment are understood by writers in the field.

According to Albrecht and Dineen (2016), "traditionally, job satisfaction, organizational commitment, and job involvement have been considered the three 'classic' or core barometers of the individual–organization relationship" (p. 70). The literature, moreover, divides this relationship between task-focused responses that manifest themselves when workers "lose themselves in their work, and experience a sense of engrossment when doing their work" (Fleck & Inceoglu, 2010, p. 36), and a further set of responses that relate to the organisation in which tasks are performed, to relationships with co-workers, employers, or clients, and to the legal and organisational structures within which people work (Albrecht, 2010; Albrecht & Dineen, 2016; Denunzio, 2016). Fleck and Inceoglu (2010) labelled this group of cognitions and psychological states "organizational engagement" (p. 36). Making sense of this conceptual miscellany and charting its relevance to PGOs poses this section's first task.

Engagement was the idea most often mentioned by the interviewees. Contemporary thinking about engagement in the work context began with a seminal article written in 1990 by Kahn. He defined engagement as the "harnessing of organization members' selves to their work roles; in engagement, people employ and express themselves physically, cognitively, and emotionally during role performances" (Kahn, 1990, p. 694). As he elaborated the concept, Kahn (1990) isolated three central elements that constitute engagement:

1. "employment and expression of a person's 'preferred self' in task behaviors that promote connections to work and to others,"
2. "personal presence (physical, cognitive, and emotional)" and
3. "active, full role performances". (p. 700)

"Vigor, dedication, and absorption" form the pillars of engagement as understood by Schaufeli et al. (2002, p. 75). They characterised vigour as "high levels of energy and mental resilience while working, the willingness to invest effort in one's work, and persistence even in the face of difficulties" (ibid.). Dedication they described as a "sense of significance, enthusiasm, inspiration, pride, and challenge" (ibid.). The third element in their definition, absorption, is described as "being fully concentrated and deeply engrossed in one's work, whereby time passes quickly and one has difficulties with detaching oneself from work" (ibid.). For Denunzio (2016), engagement was characterised by "high-energy positive emotions such as vigor and enthusiasm, as well as a deep level of focus on and attention to one's work" (p. 400). Macey et al. (2009) defined engagement as "an individual's sense of purpose and focused energy, evident to others in the display of personal initiative, adaptability, effort, and persistence directed toward organizational goals" (p. 7). For a comprehensive comparison of ways in which engagement is conceptualised, see Iddagoda et al. (2016). Table 5.1 presents the terminologies for "engagement" of four key authors and author groups in the field.

Interest in engagement as a concept extends beyond the definitional. The conditions under which it may emerge are an additional area of inquiry. Kahn (1990) posited three "psychological conditions" that had to be fulfilled before workers could experience engagement: "meaningfulness, safety, and availability" (p. 703). Macey et al. (2009) found that "engagement follows when: employees have the capacity to engage; employees have a reason or the motivation to engage; employees have the freedom to engage; and employees know how to engage" (p. 10). Table 5.2 summarises these conditions.

Macey et al. (2009) conceived of engagement, its antecedents, and consequences as a "value chain" that leads from a "high performance work environment" to "shareholder value" (p. 8). In Fig. 5.2, I have adapted this model to reflect the specific consequences of engagement in music performance. In particular, I have replaced the ultimate consequence in Macey et al.'s model—shareholder

Table 5.1 Overview of selected descriptions of engagement

Author(s)	Understandings of "engagement"
Kahn (1990)	"Employment and expression of a person's 'preferred self' in task behaviors that promote connections to work and to others" "Organization members display 'personal presence (physical, cognitive, and emotional)'", "Organization members display 'active, full role performances'"
Schaufeli et al. (2002)	Vigour: "high levels of energy and mental resilience while working, the willingness to invest effort in one's work, and persistence even in the face of difficulties" Dedication: "sense of significance, enthusiasm, inspiration, pride, and challenge" Absorption: "being fully concentrated and deeply engrossed in one's work, whereby time passes quickly and one has difficulties with detaching oneself from work"
Denunzio (2016)	"This experience includes high-energy positive emotions such as vigor and enthusiasm, as well as a deep level of focus on and attention to one's work" "Engagement connotes action — engaged employees immerse themselves in their work, expend high levels of effort, and are generally considered to be highly productive members of the organization"
Macey et al. (2009)	"An individual's sense of purpose and focused energy, evident to others in the display of personal initiative, adaptability, effort, and persistence directed toward organizational goals"

Table 5.2 Overview of selected conditions for engagement

Author(s)	Conditions for "engagement"
Kahn (1990)	**Meaningfulness**: "sense of return of self in role performances" **Safety**: "sense of being able to show and employ self without fear of negative consequences to self-image, status or career" **Availability**: "sense of possessing the physical, emotional, and psychological resources necessary for investing self in role performances"
Macey et al. (2009)	"Employees have the **capacity to engage** … Engagement requires a work environment that does not just demand 'more' but promotes information sharing, provides learning opportunities, and fosters a balance in people's lives, thereby creating the bases for sustained energy and personal initiative" "Employees have a reason or the **motivation to engage** … Engagement happens when (a) employees have work that interests them and aligns with their values; and (b) employees are treated in a way that reinforces the natural tendency to reciprocate in kind" "Employees have the **freedom to engage** … Engagement happens when people feel safe to take action on their own initiative. Consequently, trust matters most under conditions of adversity, ambiguity, and the need for change — precisely when employee engagement is most important" "Employees **know how to engage** … Strategic engagement happens when people know what the organization's strategic priorities are and why, and when the organization aligns its processes and practices — its culture — with attainment of those goals"

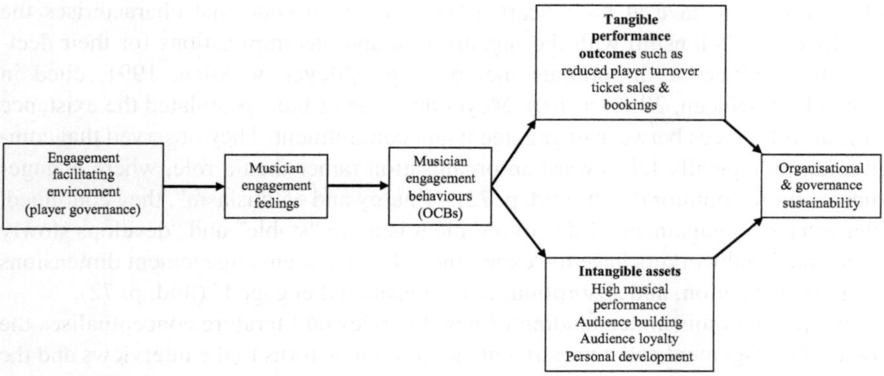

Fig. 5.2 Adapted representation of Macey et al.'s (2009) employment engagement value chain

value—with organisational sustainability, a more relevant goal for not-for-profit companies such as PGOs. Similarly, the intangible assets that orchestras and ensembles might hope to accrue as a result of heightened engagement are different from those that Macey et al. (2009) listed in their more broadly applicable model "brand equity, customer satisfaction and loyalty, innovation, lower risk" (p. 8). These outcomes are still relevant to orchestras and ensembles but are less so than those I have included in the revised model. The details of specific goals vary between industries and sectors; the basic conceptualisation and direction of Macey et al.'s model remain valid, nevertheless.

Macey et al.'s (2009) discussion of engagement-facilitating environments guided my consideration of whether player-governance and the participation it facilitates serve as such an environment. Various researchers suggest that worker participation and empowerment of the type embodied in player-governance is, indeed, conducive to high levels of engagement and commitment that, in turn, help sustain player-governance as a virtuous and self-sustaining circle emerges. In their study of health-care workers, Laschinger et al. (2016) found that "empowerment appears to be an important driver of commitment, both directly and indirectly. Structural empowerment is a leadership strategy that can influence psychological empowerment and ultimately organizational commitment" (p. 326). In particular, empowerment in the form of player-governance is an example of what Kahn (1990) described as a "sense of being able to show and employ self without fear of negative consequences to self-image, status or career" (p. 703).

In addition to talking about engagement, the interviewees used the word "commitment" when describing the relationships they develop with their PGOs. In workplace conversations and even among some commentators (Albrecht & Dineen, 2016; Iddagoda et al., 2016), the concept is often used interchangeably with that of engagement. However, a range of researchers in the field draw boundaries between the commitment and engagement. Albrecht and Dineen (2016) observed that while "the constructs are similar in that they both refer to positive psychological states that are adaptive for employee wellbeing and performance" (p. 72), most understandings of commitment have at their heart a "psychological state that characterises the employee's relationship with the organization and has implications for their decision to continue or discontinue membership" (Meyer & Allen, 1991, cited in Albrecht & Dineen, 2016 (p. 70)). Meyer and Allen (ibid.) postulated the existence of four differences between engagement and commitment. They observed that commitment is typically felt toward an organisation rather than a role, where engagement is more commonly felt (ibid. p. 72). "Energy and enthusiasm", they continued, characterise engagement while commitment is more "stable" and "develops slowly over time" and workers have to "experience all constituent engagement dimensions (vigour, dedication, and absorption) to be considered engaged" (ibid. p. 72).

Armed with this understanding of how the relevant literature conceptualises the ideas of engagement and commitment, attention now turns to the interviews and the roles these ideas—along with that of responsibility—play in sustaining player-governance.

5.4.2 *Engagement, Commitment, and Responsibility in PGOs*

Interviewees often used the terms "engagement" and "commitment" as they talked about their responses to player-governance. Their comments in this area were some of the most voluminous in the interviews. Many interviewees were vocal about the connection between player-governance and engagement, commitment, and a sense of responsibility for the organisation. Susanna said that player-governance was

> An element in having players feel more engaged. A lot of our success, and a piece of feedback that keeps coming back to us, is that we seem really energised on stage. … there is an energy and communication, a sense of wanting to be there. I think that partly comes from having the opportunity to be involved. … I certainly think it's an element.

Richard maintained that though "democracy is not an end in itself … it makes another musical dimension possible", while Simon felt that it "generates more energy among individuals because they identify with it more. The willingness to go the extra yard, so to speak, is greater, the engagement is greater, and that produces different musical results". Patrick said of his decision to join the orchestra that "I realised that there was a different kind of energy or a different kind of engagement, a higher level of engagement that came with … the fact that it was self-governing and self-run".

Other interviewees spoke of the satisfaction afforded by the opportunities for participation that player-governance provided. Robert highlighted the particular satisfaction that came with involvement in artistic planning and programming and linked this with a sense of ownership:

> I was responsible for planning and curating the current season … So, recently I have had a great sense of satisfaction of playing in a concert that I helped to plan, and for which I chose particular pieces. There is a great pleasure in playing a piece that I picked out and was quite unknown … and to hear the feedback from people: "That's a really good piece." And I feel, "Yes, and I chose that," and I was really pleased that it went well. There is a great sense of

> ownership in that respect. There are those moments when self-governing makes a real difference.

In a related vein, he described the sense of satisfaction from another opportunity to undertake artistic planning and programming:

> I was responsible for devising a whole education project based on [name of musical work removed]. Here, too, I had a huge sense of ownership of that project because I devised it. In many small ways, and sometimes not so small ways, self-governing works really well. If it wasn't a self-governing orchestra, they might well have gone to someone outside the orchestra altogether and asked them to devise an education project for us. But in the [name of orchestra omitted], they said "so-and-so could run this project, let's get them to do it."

Richard has a similar role and likewise spoke of the satisfaction that came with the engagement involved:

> At the moment, I am very engaged in the contemporary music series that we have … and I see that as a field that interests me a lot and is satisfying, and where I think I want to contribute a lot. That is the kind of thing that we ourselves structure in-house, we come up with the programs, we think about how we realise it.

For Sophie, the sense of engagement that appears to be fostered by player-governance went hand in hand with a feeling of being important to the organisation: "the artistic side must, without question, be outstanding, but I also do think that it is so good because everyone identifies with it more strongly. No one feels so dispensable as might be the case elsewhere." Patrick had a particularly evocative take on questions of engagement and stressed the importance of the self-directed nature of the process in a player-governed organisation:

> It's the difference between going to a restaurant and eating a wonderful three-course meal — and you do that every day, and that's fine — or you can go shopping, go to the markets, buy your own produce, cook it all up at home and eat something equally good, or maybe less good. If food is your only concern, then you can eat in the restaurants. But it's not just about that, it's also about the fact that you are making it yourself.

Some of the interviewees clearly sought to understand their experience with PGOs through a lens shaped by their experience with other organisations. Susanna said:

> They are all led by the conductors, the ones I work for. They might ask for your suggestions, but you don't really have that same sense of engagement or that feeling that you can make a difference. It's about how you play and not very much else. Whereas here, there is room for all sorts of other ways of expression.

Sophie observed that

> Of course, freedom brings risks, but it also creates opportunities. I had a different job that was much better paid, but which I gave up because I didn't enjoy it. And I am far from being the only one who has responded to the so-called "meaning question" in that way.

From a manager's perspective, Martin was clear that

> All orchestras have their issues, they all have problems, it is not as if the [orchestra name omitted] is special in that respect, but it is an additional commitment and engagement that you get from players, which makes everything stand out in relief, I think. They will come

> back at you with a little more determination than perhaps anywhere else. They will very quickly respond to things if they're uncomfortable. That's good!

Most of the interviewees have experience working with other orchestras and ensembles. This gives musicians an awareness of other governance and management structures. Richard, for example, acknowledged the challenges that player-governance can create for individuals, but through a comparison with other structures also emphasised the high levels of engagement that come with managing them:

> It's a challenge that's worth taking on. It's got something to do with that presence thinking that you mentioned before. It is demanding, no question, and it costs nerves, but I think it's worse for a group or an ensemble when people withdraw, when they just perform a function while watching the clock and are unsatisfied, start a hobby and somehow transfer their whole life outside the orchestra. That is why for many of us here it's a strong life focus, and it's accepted that it's a life focus. I know that from other orchestras where you have to withdraw and what actually enlivens you is your hobby, gardening and pets, or travel, where you always try to get more engaged in your leisure time and much less in what you actually work at. A lot of that's to do with the space that people are allowed.

This engagement, identification with the organisation, and "willingness to go the extra yard" were allied with ideas of responsibility that several interviewees raised. Walter made a clear connection between player-governance and a sense of responsibility for the orchestra or ensemble:

> We are shareholders and we are all equally responsible. I think that shows in performance. You can see that we are very engaged. There are no leaders, followers and passengers. Everyone feels totally responsible, active. … All the members, not just the board, have to take responsibility.

Angela echoed these sentiments:

> I think it is because it is a sort of personal feeling of responsibility, the fact that we think that the organisation is going to listen to us. Which is the opposite to [name of conductor omitted] orchestra, or [name of orchestra omitted] or [name of orchestra omitted], which are all governed by one person. You think, "Oh, they're going to listen to my opinion about this. I've got a say." That's attractive in itself because it makes you feel valued. And I felt valued.

Responsibility for the public face of the orchestra was at the heart of Simon's reflections on how the orchestra changed after becoming player managed:

> I think what it has done, is it has galvanised the players because they have to behave very responsibly, have to really take on the role of being advocates for the orchestra. That might seem an unusual thing to say, but you get tenured musicians who are very negative. Not that they are particularly negative people, but they feel a disconnect with the direction the orchestra wants to go. And what we are just doing is, basically, we are saying "OK, it's up to us now, it's up to you."

Mario emphasised the importance of player-governance more broadly: "I think that this very self-determined way of making music, of having lots of free space, operating in a very flat hierarchy, wanting to be involved in decision-making, taking on responsibility, operating very internationally, that is becoming increasingly relevant."

Kahn (1990) included in his description of engagement the "expression of a person's 'preferred self' in task behaviors that promote connections to work and to others" (p. 700). This inclusion of co-workers manifested itself in the interviews. Several interviewees made analogies between their organisations and families, while also stressing the importance of friendship among players. Maria stated that "in essence we are like a big family. We all have faith in each other's performance and in our togetherness. And that crosses over into the music-making". Walter said that

> We are a group, we are not alone. We support each other. We are human, with highs and less highs. It's also a strength to be able to provide support to the others in the group. That's a beautiful thing. A bit like in a family.

Later in the interview he added that "there is another element that is important beyond the artistic quality: we are an orchestra of friends. We started out as a group of friends and I think that it's still mostly true that people enjoy being together".

Several interviewees' statements suggest that the involvement of PGO musicians in the governance and management of their organisations creates potential for self-development and learning. Patrick claimed that

> The kind of people who are attracted to a self-run orchestra are people who are keen to evolve personally and musically. So they are willing to look out for the next thing and they are a bit more open-minded because you don't have that mentality of "This is my job, this is what I'm going to be doing for the next forty years. This is my work time."

In a similar vein, Richard highlighted the potential for players to invest themselves beyond their musical roles:

> That someone's personality is active and present, and that there is also room for someone as a person. Not only in a function, I am a member of the first violins, for example, that is a function, but when you are allowed to be present as a personality: what do you bring to the table? What are your strengths? Is there a place in which you can positively contribute these strengths? Then it is also musically noticeable.

Sophie raised learning, too:

> It is also a big learning process. You learn how to lead discussions, you learn how to run votes, you learn how not to run votes. You learn which things should be discussed and for which things it is simply not worth it because you get tangled up in trivialities and don't get any further with the important things. An ongoing, very, very big learning process for everyone who is involved.

Mario stressed the personal development derived from involvement with a democratic structure that brings together different personalities:

> That was a real learning process. I am also someone who is relatively rational, and then dealing with emotionality and taking emotional arguments just as seriously as rational ones, and that emotional arguments, that from a rational perspective might appear wrong, can be just as valid and correct. That is something that you have to learn to deal with. And that being right, or being proven right is not the only criterion for success.

Player involvement in governance and management extends, in some instances, to the conceptualisation, development, and planning of professional development programmes and offers a further chance for players to expand their professional activities and skills. Susanna described how

> I've also become involved in the education program. … as well as all the playing, I now can lead workshops and I get to devise the under-fives concerts and present some of those … I am heading up the nursery project that I visited today, for example. So there is a whole area of life that I didn't have any ambition in that has opened up to me and I have had training. It's a great other asset.

These reflections about the opportunities for personal development afforded by player-governance resonate with Kahn's (1990) description of engagement as "expression of a person's 'preferred self' in task behaviors that promote connections to work and to others" (p. 700). Writers on the "learning organisation" idea (Senge, 2006) emphasise the importance of learning for human well-being. Senge includes in his seminal book *The Fifth Discipline* (2006) a memorable quote from Edward Hall: "humans are the learning organism par excellence. The drive to learn is as strong as the sexual drive — it begins earlier and last longer" (cited in Senge, 2006, p. 14). The opportunity to develop and learn at work is thus closely aligned with the building of engagement. I discuss the importance of this and of theories of the learning organisation below.

The interviews, while overwhelmingly positive about the opportunities for engagement and commitment presented by player-governance, also revealed that complications can arise. The relationships in family-like groups and among friends can, for example, be inappropriate to a professional context. Angela felt that

> We have got ourselves into trouble in some places because we've allowed people to stay in because of friends and family. … We don't tell each other "That's not working." And that's where we are not doing our homework. If we are a self-governing orchestra, we need to govern ourselves honestly. I want to be told it's not good enough … If I can't take it, that's my problem. I know that doesn't mean you don't love me. We're here to make the [name of orchestra omitted] good. I don't care whether you're my best friend or not.

Other interviewees suggested that high levels of engagement, commitment, and a sense of responsibility in their PGOs might be off-putting for some musicians. Walter said that

> There are also musicians who are not cut out for it, and we have seen that. Right from the beginning, some of our members said, after a year or two "No, this is not for me, I would prefer something else where I don't have that commitment."

Much to the same effect, Daniel said that "someone from the back of the second violins probably wouldn't know where to start in this kind of ensemble. It's a huge engagement that's required from each individual musician". High levels of engagement, commitment, and responsibility may be challenging to some musicians. If this is the case, then caution is required in the face of any attempt at extrapolating to other organisations. If musicians with higher personal and individual propensity to engagement and commitment are attracted by the opportunities afforded by PGOs and others are put off and choose to work in other organisations, a "selection effect"

(Weltmann et al., 2015, p. 270) may result. Such selection effects may represent an example of sorting that contributes to the sustainability of player-governance by boosting the homogeneity of interests and attitudes to work among members (Dow, 2018).

5.4.3 "Everyone Feels Totally Responsible, Active"

The interviews illustrate the richness of professional experience offered by PGOs. Players generally embrace opportunities to engage broadly and deeply with their organisations. They welcome chances to develop skills in addition to those related directly to music performance. There is a consensus among the interviewees that high levels of commitment, engagement, and responsibility manifest themselves in high-quality performance outcomes and make "another musical dimension possible" (Richard). Such perceptions cannot, though, be objectively measured. Nonetheless, my research strongly suggests that player-governance and the sense of engagement and commitment it embodies have a positive impact on artistic quality in the organisations studied.

The interviews strongly suggest that giving musicians the opportunity for participation in governance creates an organisational environment in which engagement and commitment can develop, while also acting as a sorting mechanism that increases the homogeneity of interests among members and, as a result, helps sustain player-governance. In the terms proposed by Macey et al. (2009), player-governance creates the "freedom to engage" (p. 10). The interviews indicate that player-governance and the opportunity for involvement in management decision-making create a framework in which high levels of engagement can be achieved. Several interviewees made this connection explicitly. Susanna made it in reverse by noting that in other orchestras that are led by conductors rather than their musicians, "you don't really have that same sense of engagement or that feeling that you can make a difference." Governance participation and player engagement go hand in hand.

Kahn's (1990) "safety" prerequisite—"the sense of being able to show and employ self without fear of negative consequences to self-image, status or career" (p. 703)—is clearly reflected by Susanna when she observes that "here, there is room for all sorts of other ways of expression". In Richard's view, PGOs provide a structure in which personalities are "active and present", and members were valued for more than simply performing a musical function. Likewise, Angela described responding to the opportunities for involvement in a PGO in terms reminiscent of Macey et al.'s "freedom to engage" (2009, p. 10): "You think, 'Oh, they're going to listen to my opinion about this. I've got a say." For her, this contributed to a sense of being valued. Maria voiced similar early impressions of player-governance when she spoke of the excitement she felt on finding that "I was able to channel my energy into creating something, things were moving. That was very attractive".

Various benefits accrue to firms with high levels of worker engagement (Albrecht et al., 2015; Böckerman et al., 2012). Creating an environment in the PGOs that provides opportunities for personal development is an important result of player-governance, member participation, and engagement. Adaptability is a further organisational attribute that results from engaged workers (Reeves & Deimler, 2011). The musicians in the PGOs in the cohort are "willing to look out for the next thing" (Patrick), but more importantly, they feel that they can make use of such insights to help ensure the future and the sustainability of their organisations. Susanna spoke of "feeling that you can make a difference" in a PGO, while Richard spoke of being "allowed to be present as a personality". In Kahn's (1990) terms, player-governance provides the "safety" to engage or the "sense of being able to show and employ self without fear of negative consequences to self-image, status or career" (p. 708).

The perception that player-governance provides greater scope for personal development, the acquisition of skills that complement musical proficiency, and the exercising of extra-musical abilities and knowledge may be a particularly important factor in the music performance sector. The core work of orchestral musicians—rehearsing and performing—provides only limited scope for professional development and promotion. Players typically end their careers in the same role in which they started. Even "promotion" within a section of the orchestra—say, from second clarinet to principal clarinet, or from the second violin section to the firsts—is rare. Schulz (1981) surveyed orchestral musicians in Vienna and found that 23 per cent of string players agreed with the statement that "I suffer from the fact that in the orchestra my chances of promotion are limited" (p. 41). By allowing musicians to be involved in the governance and management of their organisations, PGOs create a valuable opportunity for musicians to undertake professional development, or be rewarded with a sense of career progression.

Alongside engagement and the opportunity for learning and development, the interviewees pointed to a connection between player-governance, via increased engagement and commitment. Many of the sentiments described by interviewees are consistent with what have been described as organisational citizenship behaviours (Poutsma et al., 2015). Poutsma et al. (2015) defined organisational citizenship behaviours (OCBs) as "behaviors that may result in employee contributions that exceed formal job expectations" (p. 224). OCBs are viewed as results of high levels of engagement. Fleck and Inceoglu (2010) reported that

> Engaged employees are also more likely to "go the extra mile" for the organization and show behaviors that go beyond the requirements of their job, such as taking the initiative to solve problems, or offering help to co-workers before being asked for it. (p. 39)

Alvis, for example, spoke of player management having "galvanised the players", meaning that they "have to really take on the role of being advocates for the orchestra". Being an advocate for the orchestra is the sort of organisational citizenship behaviour highlighted by Fleck and Inceoglu (2010), who found that "engaged employees are more likely to act as positive advocates for the organization when interacting with people external to the organization" (p. 39). Walter emphasised ideas of ownership when saying that "we are shareholders and we are all equally responsible. I think that shows in performance. You can see that we are very engaged. There are no leaders, followers and passengers. everyone feels totally responsible, active". These views align with the literature. Pierce and Furo (1990), for example, found that "employee ownership can have a positive effect on a work group's norms, cohesiveness, and cooperative behaviors; on an employee's work-related attitudes, motivation, and behavior; and on an organization's performance and profitability" (p. 42). The interviews and the literature both highlight the promise of engagement generated by player-governance and the boost to sustainability from the resulting OCBs.

It is, though, important to recall the cautionary words of some interviewees that not all musicians are "cut out for" (Walter) membership of an organisation in which levels of commitment and engagement are usually so high. Clearly there is an element of self-selection among the members of PGOs. This is, though, true of any organisation. Establishing "fit" between organisations and workers is a central part of human resource management in all enterprises (Albrecht et al., 2015).

Much research in the field focuses on employee-owned firms, often those that have introduced employee stock ownership schemes (Buchko, 1993). As noted, the PGOs I consider in this book do not, though, provide any opportunity for financial dividends or the acquisition of tradable shares in their companies. The high levels of engagement, commitment, the acceptance of responsibility, and other forms of OCB reported by the interviewees indicate that these features can develop in freelance organisations and in the absence of financial incentives such as dividend payments or the acquisition of tradable entitlements. This aligns with the findings of Pendleton et al. (1998) that

Participation in decisions accompanying employee ownership has a more powerful impact on feelings of ownership than levels of shareholding per se. Employees feel like owners if they perceive that they have been involved in the process of transition. An assessment that participation in work organization decisions … has increased also has a clear positive impact on feelings of ownership. (p. 112)

Ultimately, for an orchestra or ensemble, the most important benefit from greater engagement and commitment is the achievement of the highest possible standard of performance. Susanna spoke of her orchestra being "really energised on stage" and she traced this, at least in part, back to opportunities for engagement that PGOs provide. "Different musical results" were also something that Simon thought resulted from greater engagement. For Robert, being involved in the artistic planning of a concert season produced a "great sense of satisfaction" and a "great sense of ownership". Caution is called for, though. A wide range of factors is involved in achieving high standards of musical performance (Dobson & Gaunt, 2013; Koivunen, 2003; Koivunen & Wennes, 2011; Langendörfer et al., 2006). The optimisation of performance and its connection to governance sustainability are the central focus of the next chapter.

Other research suggests that worker empowerment can play a role in boosting engagement with task performance. Albrecht et al. (2015) posited that "organizations that create the conditions that support, enhance and sustain employee engagement will have higher levels of job, unit and organizational performance, and therefore competitive advantage" (p. 13). In a similar vein, Laschinger et al. (2016) find that "workplace empowerment is a logical driving force behind employee commitment" (p. 320). Concepts such as engagement, commitment, and responsibility clearly resonate with the members of the PGOs studied.

5.5 Conclusion: PGOs as a "Strong Life Focus"

The themes that emerged from the interviews in this chapter congeal around the idea of participation and its role in achieving the sustainability of player-governance in orchestras and ensembles. The participation of playing members in decision-making is the essence of player-governance, but the interviews make it clear that participation also needs to be facilitated, channelled, and harnessed. The modern orchestra evolved around rigid hierarchies with conductors at the pinnacle and section leaders in a supporting role. Player-governance, however, challenges these hierarchies because it seeks to distribute authority across the membership. Nonetheless, the interviewees spoke in terms of a rebalancing and realigning of artistic decision-making hierarchies, rather than a wholesale rejection. The PGOs in the study continue to work with conductors and other performance leaders, but on players' terms. The shift is from a hierarchy to a collaboration in which leadership still plays a role (Ternier, 2025), though a circumscribed role which might be understood as the leader as collaborator.

The perennial challenges inherent in optimising and sustaining workplace democracy formed the central theme of the interviews. The interviewees were conscious of the trade-offs between the efficiency of representative democracy and the participatory and democratic legitimacy of direct democracy. Their thinking also revealed less clear-cut concerns. The optimal balance between direct, high-participation democracy and its representative form emerged as contextual. Quick decisions were, in some situations, less important than those founded on thorough consultation and high levels of participatory decision-making. Sustaining the participatory and democratic core of player-governance is, then, a matter of continuing adaptability, responsiveness, and negotiation. This process also needed to shield the collaborative and team-oriented music performance space from any tensions that might arise during participatory governance decision-making. This separation was further complicated when the PGOs in the research had two parallel decision-making structures, one for governance, and the other for music performance. Musical leaders within these PGOs are not necessarily governance officers, and this creates a potential for conflict that needs to be managed if it is not to weaken and threaten player-governance.

The participation of players in the governance of their orchestras and ensembles creates an environment in which organisational engagement, commitment, and a sense of responsibility can flourish. This clearly emerged from the experience of the interviewees. They spoke of feeling "galvanised", of "everyone feel[ing] totally responsible", and of a willingness among players to "go the extra yard". These responses are central to the sustainability of player-governance. To have long-term viability, the model needs to be embraced by members, it needs to add value and meaning to the working lives of players, thus giving them a “strong life focus” (Richard). When this happens, the result is a virtuous circle that builds commitment to and support for player-governance among members. This dynamic is crucial to the sustainability of player-governance. In the next chapter, the focus shifts to the optimising of performance, perhaps the ultimate test for the value and sustainability of player-governance. A governance model that does not support or facilitate high-level musical performance is unlikely to survive for long.

References

Albrecht, S. L. (Ed.). (2010). *Handbook of employee engagement*. Edward Elgar Publishing.

Albrecht, S. L., Bakker, A. B., Gruman, J. A., Macey, W. H., & Saks, A. M. (2015). Employee engagement, human resource management practices and competitive advantage: An integrated approach. *Journal of Organizational Effectiveness: People and Performance, 2*(1), 7–35. https://doi.org/10.1108/JOEPP-08-2014-0042

Albrecht, S. L., & Dineen, O. J. (2016). Organizational commitment and employee engagement: Ten key questions. In J. B. Meyer (Ed.), *Handbook of employee commitment*. Edward Elgar.

Allmendinger, J., Richard Hackman, J., & Lehman, E. V. (1996). Life and work in symphony orchestras. *The Musical Quarterly, 80*(2), 194–219. https://doi.org/10.2307/742362

Atik, Y. (1994). The conductor and the orchestra: Interactive aspects of the leadership process. *Leadership & Organization Development Journal, 15*(1), 22–28. https://doi.org/10.1108/01437739410050123

Ayer, J. (2005). *More than meets the ear: How symphony musicians made labor history*. Syren Book Company.

Böckerman, P., Bryson, A., & Ilmakunnas, P. (2012). Does high involvement management improve worker wellbeing? *Journal of Economic Behavior and Organization, 84*, 660–680. https://doi.org/10.1016/j.jebo.2012.09.005

Boerner, S. (2006). Creating cooperative climate in an orchestra: The role of the musicians’ flow and the conductor’s leadership style. *Musicae Scientiae, 10*(2), 245–263.

Boerner, S., & Freiherr von Streit, C. (2005). Transformational leadership and group climate—empirical results from symphony orchestras. *Journal of Leadership & Organizational Studies, 12*(2), 31–41. https://doi.org/10.1177/107179190501200203

Boerner, S., & Freiherr von Streit, C. (2007). Promoting orchestral performance: The interplay between musicians’ mood and a conductor’s leadership style. *Psychology of Music, 35*(1), 132–143. https://doi.org/10.1177/0305735607068891

Buchko, A. A. (1993). The effects of employee ownership on employee attitudes: An integrated causal model and path analysis. *Journal of Management Studies, 30*(4), 633–657. https://doi.org/10.1111/j.1467-6486.1993.tb00319.x

Callan, V. J., & Lawrence, S. A. (2009). Building employee engagement, job satisfaction, health, and retention. In S. Cartwright, and C. L. Cooper (Eds.), *The Oxford handbook of organizational well being*. Oxford University Press. https://doi.org/10.1093/oxfordhb/9780199211913.003.0017.

Csikszentmihalyi, M. (2008). *Flow: The psychology of optimal experience*. Harper Perennial.

Denunzio, M. (2016). Engagement. In S. G. Rogelberg (Ed.), *The Sage Encyclopedia of industrial and organizational psychology*. Sage. https://doi.org/10.4135/9781483386874

Dobson, M. C., & Gaunt, H. F. (2013). Musical and social communication in expert orchestral performance. *Psychology of Music, 0*(0), 1–19. https://doi.org/10.1177/0305735613491998

Dow, G. (2003). *Governing the firm: Workers' control in theory and practice*. Cambridge University Press.
Dow, G. (2018). *The labor-managed firm: Theoretical foundations*. Cambridge University Press.
Fleck, S., & Inceoglu, I. (2010) A comprehensive framework for understanding and predicting engagement. In *Handbook of employee engagement*. Edward Elgar. https://doi.org/10.4337/9781849806374.00009.
Gaunt, H., & Dobson, M. C. (2014). Orchestras as "Ensembles of Possibility": Understanding the experience of orchestral musicians through the lens of communities of practice. *Mind, Culture & Activity, 21*(4), 298–317. https://doi.org/10.1080/10749039.2014.951900
Gilboa, A., & Tal-Shmotkin, M. (2012). String quartets as self-managed teams: An interdisciplinary perspective. *Psychology of Music, 40*(1), 19–41. https://doi.org/10.1177/0305735610377593
Hansmann, H.. (1996). *The ownership of enterprise*. The Belknap Press of Harvard University Press.
Hunt, J., Stelluto, G., & Hooijberg, R. (2004). Toward new-wave organization creativity: Beyond romance and analogy in the relationship between orchestra-conductor leadership and musician creativity. *Leadership Quarterly, 15*(1), 145–162. https://doi.org/10.1016/j.leaqua.2003.12.009
Iddagoda, Y. A., Opatha, H. H. D. N. P., & Gunawardana, K. D. (2016). Towards a conceptualization and an operationalization of the construct of employee engagement. *International Business Research, 9*(2), 85–98. https://doi.org/10.5539/ibr.v9n2p85
Johansson, Y. L., & Theorell, T. (2003). Satisfaction with work task quality correlates with employee health. *Medical Problems of Performing Artists, 18*(4), 141–149. https://www.jstor.org/stable/48710968
Judge, T. A., Charles, L. H., & Reeshad, S. D. (2012). Job satisfaction and job affect. In Kozlowski, S. W. J. (Ed.). *The Oxford handbook of organizational psychology*. Oxford University Press.
Kahn, W. A. (1990). Psychological conditions of personal engagement and disengagement at work. *Academy of Management Journal, 33*(4), 692–724. https://doi.org/10.2307/256287
Kemp, A. (1996). *The musical temperament: Psychology and personality of musicians*. Oxford University Press. https://doi.org/10.1093/acprof:oso/9780198523628.001.0001.
Kenny, D. T., & Ackermann, B. (2009). Optimizing physical and psychological health in performing musicians. Chap. 36. In S. Hallam, I. Cross, & M. Thaut (Eds.), *The Oxford handbook of music psychology*. Oxford University Press.
Kirchner, J. M., Bloom, A. J., & Skutnick-Henley, P. (2008). The relationship between performance anxiety and flow. *Medical problems of performing artists, 23*(2), 59–65. https://www.jstor.org/stable/48710835
Koivunen, N. (2003). *Leadership in symphony orchestras, discursive and aesthetic practices*. (Doctoral dissertation). University of Tampere, https://trepo.tuni.fi/handle/10024/67230
Koivunen, N., & Wennes, G. (2011). Show us the sound! Aesthetic leadership of symphony orchestra conductors. *Leadership, 7*(1), 51–71. https://doi.org/10.1177/1742715010386865
Kruse, D. (Ed.). (2013). *Sharing ownership, profits, and decision-making in the 21st century*. Emerald.
Langendörfer, F., Hodapp, V., Kreutz, G., & Bongard, S. (2006). Personality and performance anxiety among professional orchestra musicians. *Journal of Individual Differences, 27*(3), 162–171. https://doi.org/10.1027/1614-0001.27.3.162
Laschinger, H. K., Read, E., & Zhu, J. (2016). Employee empowerment and organizational commitment. In J. B. Meyer (Ed.), *Handbook of employment commitment*. Edward Elgar.
Leach, D. K. (2016). When freedom is not an endless meeting: A new look at efficiency in consensus-based decision making. *Sociological Quarterly, 57*(1), 36–70. https://doi.org/10.1111/tsq.12137
Lewis, L. (2012) *The incomplete conductor: Theorizing the conductor's role in orchestral interpretation in the light of shared leadership practices* (Doctoral dissertation). Royal Holloway, University of London. https://pure.royalholloway.ac.uk/portal/files/11821983/2012lewislaphd.pdf
Lipton, J. P. (1987). Stereotypes concerning musicians within symphony orchestras. *The Journal of Psychology, 121*(1), 85–93. https://doi.org/10.1080/00223980.1987.9712647

Logie, N. (2012) *The role of leadership in conducting orchestras* (Doctoral dissertation). The Open University, http://oro.open.ac.uk/id/eprint/38069.

Long, B. (2015). Forms of precarity and the orchestral musician. *The Asia Pacific Journal of Arts and Cultural Management, 12*(1), 3–13. http://apjacm.arts.unimelb.edu.au/article/view/207/0

Macey, W. H., Schneider, W., Barbera, K. M., & Young, S. A. (Eds.). (2009). *Employee engagement: Tools for analysis, practice, and competitive advantage*. Wiley.

Mantouvalou, V. (2014). Democratic theory and voices at work. In A. Bogg & T. Novitz (Eds.), *Voices at work: Continuity and change in the common law world*. Oxford University Press.

Meyer, J. P., & Allen, N. J. (1991). 'A three- component conceptualization of organizational commitment'. *Human Resource Management Review, 1*(1), 61–89.

Meyer, J. P. (Ed.). (2016). *Handbook of employee commitment*. Edward Elgar.

Mogelof, J. P., & Rohrer, L. H. (2005). Rewards and sacrifices in elite and non-elite organizations: Participation in valued activities and job satisfaction in two symphony orchestras. *International Journal of Manpower, 26*(1), 93–109. https://doi.org/10.1108/01437720510587307

Murnighan, J. K., & Conlon, D. E. (1991). The dynamics of intense work groups: A study of British string quartets. *Administrative Science Quarterly, 36*(2), 165–186. https://psycnet.apa.org/doi/10.2307/2393352

Olbertz, F. (2006). Job satisfaction of professional orchestra musicians. In H. Gembris (Ed.), *Musical development from a lifespan perspective*. Lang.

Pendleton, A., Wilson, N., & Wright, M. (1998). The perception and effects of share ownership: Empirical evidence from employee buy-outs. *British Journal of Industrial Relations, 36*(1), 99–123. https://doi.org/10.1111/1467-8543.00082

Pierce, J. L., & Furo, C. A. (1990). Employee ownership: Implications for management. *Organizational Dynamics, 18*(3), 32–43. https://doi.org/10.1016/0090-2616(90)90062-T

Poutsma, E., Coen, v. E., & Paul Ligthart, E. M. (2015). Employee ownership and organizational citizenship behavior: High performance ownership systems and the mediating role of psychological ownership. Chap. 8. In *Advances in the economic analysis of participatory & labor-managed firms*. Emerald. https://doi.org/10.1108/S0885-333920150000016015

Putterman, L. (1982). Some behavioral perspectives on the dominance of hierarchical over democratic forms of enterprise. *Journal of Economic Behavior & Organization, 3*(2–3), 139–160. https://doi.org/10.1016/0167-2681(82)90015-4

Reeves, M., & Deimler, M. (2011). Adaptability: The new competitive advantage. *Harvard Business Review, 7-8*, 134–141.

Schaufeli, W. B., Salanova, M., González-Romá, V., & Bakker, A. (2002). The measurement of engagement and burnout: A two sample confirmatory factor analytic approach. *Journal of Happiness Studies, 3*(1), 71–92. https://psycnet.apa.org/doi/10.1023/A:1015630930326

Schulz, W. (1981). Analysis of a symphony orchestra (sociological and sociopsychological aspects). In M. Piperek (Ed.), *Stress and music, medical, psychological, sociological and legal strain factors in a symphony orchestra musician's profession*. Braumüller.

Seifter, H., & Economy, P. (2001). *Leadership ensemble, lessons in collaborative management from the world's only conductorless orchestra*. Times Books.

Senge, P. (2006). *The fifth discipline: The art and practice of the learning organization*. Doubleday.

Stanley, D. J., & Meyer, J. B. (2016). Employee commitment and performance. In J. B. Meyer (Ed.), *Handbook of employee commitment*. Edward Elgar.

Strauss, G. (1998). An overview. In F. Heller, E. Pusić, G. Strauss, & B. Wilpert (Eds.), *Organizational participation, myth and reality*. Oxford University Press.

Tal-Shmotkin, M., & Gilboa, A. (2013). Do behaviors of string quartet ensembles represent self-managed teams? *Team performance management: An international journal, 19*(1/2), 57–71. https://doi.org/10.1108/13527591311312097

Ternier, C. (2025). Workplace democracy democratized: The case for participative and elected management. *Analyse & Kritik, 47*(1), 79–105. https://doi.org/10.1515/auk-2025-2003

Weltmann, D., Blasi Joseph, R., & Kruse Douglas, L. (2015). Does employee ownership affect attitudes and behaviors? The role of selection, status, and size of stake. In *Advances in the economic analysis of participatory & labor-managed firms*. Emerald. https://doi.org/10.1108/S0885-333920150000016016

Wilkinson, A., Donaghey, J., & Dundon, T. (2014). In R. Freeman (Ed.), *Handbook of research on employee voice*. Edward Elgar.

Young, A. (2017). *Job satisfaction of orchestral musicians: The effects of non-performance organizational roles* (Doctoral dissertation). University of Miami. https://scholarlyrepository.miami.edu/oa_dissertations/1825

Chapter 6
Optimising Performance

6.1 The Challenges: Monitoring, Recruitment, Generational Change

Performing at the highest possible level is at the heart of every orchestra and ensemble's mission. Optimising performance is central to governance and management activity. Players and managers who took part in this research highlighted the essential role that high performance standards have in their player-governed orchestras (PGOs). The interviewees were, however, also aware of what Maria called the "explosive" impact of the peer-to-peer monitoring required by player-governance. They described a friction between the traditionally hierarchical nature of performance monitoring in orchestras and the demands of shared responsibility for maintaining standards that result when players take control of artistic decision-making. Susanna sketched the dilemma: "when you work in other orchestras, it is so much easier, in lots of ways, to work for a dictator and all hate the dictator together. It's so much easier. You are all looking in the same direction." Such dynamics are familiar to orchestral musicians (Prinz, 1993), but Susanna felt that "you can't do that in a self-governing orchestra. You absolutely can't do it". The need to maintain high performance standards produces a tension between hierarchical monitoring's relative ease and the demands that mutual monitoring makes. Optimising performance in orchestras involves three main tasks: monitoring, managing generational change, and recruiting the best players.

Mixing player-governance and performance optimisation results in an intensified process that brings strengths and challenges. As in other areas of governance and artistic decision-making discussed earlier, performance optimisation throws into sharp relief the tensions between the competing hierarchical and horizontal logics at the heart of the PGOs in the research cohort. Monitoring performance is built on an implicit hierarchy. From an early age, musicians are socialised into proficiency hierarchies in which the authority to monitor and assess another player's performance

B. Long, *Democratising Orchestras*, Music Business Research,
https://doi.org/10.1007/978-3-032-17399-7_6

assumes superior skills on the part of the monitor. The relatively flat hierarchies of player-governance challenge these monitoring hierarchies. As Susanna said of peer monitoring, "players do question it and say, 'Who has got the right to question a colleague's playing?' None of us have got that right. But we haven't given anybody else that right either." This short quote lays bare the dilemma. Optimising performance is essential. The players assume artistic control and along with it the collective responsibility for performance optimisation, but they find it difficult to deal with situations in which colleagues are not performing at the desired level. This dilemma is at the heart of this chapter, and addressing it is essential to governance sustainability among the cohort of PGOs. A failure to optimise and maintain performance poses an existential threat.

The literature generally argues that mutual monitoring among workers is a strength of labour-management (Bowles & Gintis, 1993; Dow, 2018; McCain, 2007). Hansmann (1996) observed that when workers monitor each other, each has "an incentive to monitor her fellow employees and to apply pressure on them not to shirk, an incentive largely lacking in an investor-owned firm" (p. 70). Such writing mostly leaves unexplored the tension between the quintessentially hierarchical nature of monitoring and the anti-hierarchical logic of peer monitoring that comes through in Susanna's statement above.[1] The work practices and cultures of orchestras are, on the other hand, particularly well suited to exploring this tension. Performance deficiencies in orchestras and ensembles are usually clear to most (if not all) players, and even a single minor problem can seriously detract from the overall performance. Monitoring of artistic performance is, though, often controversial, and objective measures are largely absent. Mutual monitoring is a key element of labour-managed firms (LMFs), and the PGOs studied represent an ideal real-world laboratory in which to observe its operation.

Mutual monitoring and the allied questions of generational transition and recruitment in the PGOs I looked at involve considerable complexity, as well as bringing their own risks and challenges that range much wider than "improving the productivity of the firm" (Hansmann, 1996, p. 70). Recruitment is more multifaceted because new players and members must be able to flourish in a player-governed structure as well as performing at a very high standard. The management of generational change is particularly challenging when founding members are experiencing age-related declines in proficiency. Questions of generational change also give rise to discussions about organisational identity because founding and long-term members realise that, to be sustainable, their PGOs must become "institutionalised". Underlying these themes is the problem of monitoring performance in an artistic context, where objective measures are generally not available, authority structures are diversified and horizontal, and no one has the "right to question a colleague's playing", but nor have members "given anybody else that right either". The essence of the argument in this chapter is that to achieve and sustain peak performance, the PGOs in the study need to balance the conflicting demands of performance

[1] See, however, Bowles and Gintis (1993).

monitoring, maintain recruitment processes that are efficient but thorough in establishing the suitability of members from multiple perspectives and ensure that generational change is dealt with sensitively. The chapter devotes sections to each of these sub-themes: (1) monitoring and maintaining performance quality, (2) recruiting musicians, and (3) managing generational change.

6.2 Peer Monitoring and Performance: "A Totally Difficult Subject"

The musicians and management staff in this study outlined a dilemma at the heart of their organisations: maintaining the highest possible performance standards is an essential element of organisational sustainability, but the mechanics and politics of mutual monitoring are fraught with potentially destructive energies. Musicians who as members share control of their organisations have an incentive to monitor the performance of their peers. Not doing so exposes their orchestras or ensembles to the consequences of falling performance standards. In competitive marketplaces, these results include reduced revenue from ticket sales and recordings, less hiring by promoters, and the loss of opportunities to engage with high-profile conductors and soloists.

On the other hand, musicians' monitoring of peers may foster high levels of awareness for their own performance. In the PGOs studied, there are, however, risks that, in the absence of agreed performance measures, responsibilities for making decisions about the work of members dissipate in a sea of personal loyalties and rivalries.

Writers on mutual monitoring in LMFs suggest that it is one of their key strengths because it is supposed to minimise shirking, build engagement, and foster collegiality (Alchian & Demsetz, 1972; Ben-Ner, 1988; Bowles & Gintis, 1993; Hansmann, 1996). As Lehman (2002) noted, mutual monitoring is far from being simple, straightforward, or an unalloyed strength of player-governance (p. 146). Nonetheless, monitoring performance is an essential prerequisite for optimising player-governance, and the research for this chapter showed that these PGOs worked hard to address the dilemmas involved and balance the inherent tensions.

Mutual monitoring in a sector that lacks clear and widely agreed performance measures is more difficult and demanding than the LMF literature allows. To ensure their sustainability, PGOs must be able to balance the need for effective performance monitoring with the lack of objective measures and the resulting potential for conflict and tension. Martin highlighted the stakes and tensions involved in peer monitoring among musicians:

> If person A, sitting next to person B, starts playing sharp, and they may have been playing together for fifteen years or twenty years, since day one … when … they hadn't considered that fifteen years down the line they may be sitting next to a peer who is underperforming and they'd have to do something about it, and if they didn't do something about it, then the orchestra would simply become a band of brothers who gradually age and decay together

> and fall entirely into decline and into obscurity, where the audience ceases to be fee-paying and becomes friends and family who turn up on a social basis. And the orchestra does not want that. The orchestra wants to play at Salzburg … it wants its donors and its support and it wants its international touring.

Patrick added to the list of challenges and highlighted the contradictions:

> We are all one level, it's democratic. … This then leads to the problem that you need some kind of body with a mandate to be able to say, "look, if someone is slipping" — you don't have to throw someone out — but you have to be able to talk to them before it gets too late. That is contradictory in our structure, because we need someone, or a group of people, with that mandate, but on the other hand we are democratic and we decide everything.

Susanna highlighted the inherent dilemma and raised the first of the key themes in this section when she said of peer monitoring that "players do question it and say 'who has got the right to question a colleague's playing?' None of us have got that right. But we haven't given anybody else that right either". Thus the stakes are high, and there is a fundamental tension between the hierarchical nature of monitoring and the democratic logic of player-governance.

The thoughts of several interviewees congealed to form the second important theme of this section: the emotional and social burden of mutual monitoring. Sophie described the discussions involved as "extremely contentious", and Mario called the process "super painful". Maria described dealing with a case of unsatisfactory performance as a "totally difficult subject" that was "brutal" and "really awful" while "cost(ing) us very much discussion, energy and nerves". Susanna felt it was "absolutely the hardest thing we have to do" and thought that "for some outsiders, that is a great reason not to be in the [name of orchestra omitted], because they see the difficulty of that". Simon also noted that

> Politically, it is very difficult to speak with colleagues and to find a way of saying, "your artistic quality is not sufficient for this thing at the moment, we need to rotate," or something like that. That is always a very sensitive point.

Various explanations for why mutual monitoring is so difficult emerged from the interviews.

The absence of objective measures in musical performance was one element. Martin spoke about this lack of objective measurements and performance indicators that might support mutual monitoring:

> If you are a footballer, people can really tell if you don't score goals. … But when someone's really not playing well in an ensemble, when they are a little bit out of tune, sometimes you get this leprechaun problem where it's fine one day and then it's a problem again. It's very difficult to take a measured, responsible approach to that and not be accused of gerrymandering or abusing the process, because the empirical data doesn't exist. You cannot refer to "facts" in artistic performance. You can only really refer to opinions.... And that is another reason why the burden of self-governance is so heavy.

Socialisation in a specific profession is a further challenge to mutual monitoring. It occurs during professional training and education and continues in the workplace and within firms. Mario said this of life in his PGO:

> The activities are very closely interwoven and that, "I turn up at work and go home at the end of the day and have my private life or an existence in addition to my job," that is much more difficult with this kind of music-making because the private and professional are much more interwoven. And when professional conflicts or challenges arise, through poor performance or the like, that is something that impacts your whole life.

Richard mentioned the difficulty of "all sitting together on stage and having an unpleasant discussion, for example about quality — who is playing how well". The result can be that "in the end we have to come together and play music, even though beforehand there was not a single point of agreement, no harmony, nothing. That is very, very difficult".

It is perhaps inevitable that in the face of such challenges, some of the interviewees longed for a more traditional and hierarchical model of performance monitoring. Richard observed that

> I think, we all wish that there was some external person who is neutral and makes a judgement call, where we can simply say, "He is to blame, he is evil, he is the bad guy." That would be a great relief for us. But on the other hand, that is simply part of it.

Walter spoke in similar terms:

> We have, of course, had to deal with these problems and it's very difficult. We don't have a fixed conductor, who often takes this role elsewhere, who can be the "bad guy" and then go. The orchestra members stay together for a longer time. It is very tricky.

In a statement quoted at the opening of this chapter, Susanna noted that while the "bad-guy" model was seductive, it was unworkable in a player-governed context. Working under dictatorial conductors was "so much easier" because it allowed players to "all hate the dictator together", but in a PGO, she thought that "you absolutely can't do it".

6.2.1 *Positives of Mutual Monitoring*

Mutual monitoring clearly presents considerable challenges, but some of the interviews showed that it also fostered positive attitudes, in particular, responsibility for performance quality and a culture of self-assessment and monitoring. Herbert noted that

> In an orchestra in which the musicians are all equal, every musician has a great responsibility to the others. That means always checking well, is the quality of the performance that I'm delivering sufficient and good for what we collectively want?

In the words of other interviewees, there was also a connection between this sense of responsibility and player-governance. Sophie said that "if something is not good, you have to do something about it yourself. Who else is going to do it?" This approach was reinforced by Mario, who said that "you can't delegate the responsibility and you can't put if off. You have to take responsibility yourself and you have to take responsibility in the context of friends or family-like surroundings". This, in turn, feeds into high levels of self-awareness and self-monitoring, as illustrated by this exchange between Leo and Daniel about quality review during monthly meetings:

> Leo: We discuss the concerts that have taken place and then people will say of a guest musician: "He was great, but I wouldn't ask him to do the other piece." There is also room for self-criticism and criticism among the members. One is definitely allowed to say, "you did not play well in this piece."
>
> Daniel: There has to be an internal forum for self-criticism. But the interesting thing for me is the way that this self-criticism works. In my experience, the self-criticism functions on a personal level and one uses one's colleagues as a model for one's own comparison and self-criticism. This, of course, works very, very well, because you deal with it all yourself and then you do your very best to give your colleagues no opportunity to criticise you about the standard and quality of your performance.
>
> Interviewer: So, performance maintenance is primarily based on self-reflection?
>
> Daniel: In terms of instrumental performance, yes. I think it is different in other areas. But certainly, in terms of instrumental performance, that is [the case].

This combination of responsibility for the organisation and rigorous self-monitoring promises benefits.

6.2.2 Processes for Monitoring

The final group of interview statements in this section attempts to deal with issues raised by the processes and procedures of maintaining performance standards. Susanna spoke of a need for such arrangements: "you have to work out strategies for who is deciding, how do you decide? Who has got that role? Otherwise you end up in terrible, muddy waters" .Walter commented that

> Over time, we have developed some procedures to cope with that. Everybody knows what they are, whether it's a behaviour problem or whether it's a playing problem. When that happens, we tell the musician they have some time to fix problems and if that's not the case they will eventually go back onto probation, there is a trial period and we all have to vote. It's very unpleasant. Fortunately, we haven't had to do it very often, partly because everyone understands that it's like being a chamber musician or a soloist, you can't just sit there and relax.

Documented processes are, nonetheless, unlikely to suffice when tackling such a complex and highly charged dilemma. They are not panaceas. Several interviewees pointed out the inevitable difficulties such processes may entail. Mario noted that, while

> There are written statutes with rules covering things such as breaches of conduct or artistic underperformance, … there is, on the one hand the abstract thinking of the rules, and then there is the emotional aspect, and finding the right balance, without causing enormous friction or other conflicts, that is a great challenge, as in any social mechanism.

Angela felt that her orchestra's documented performance maintenance procedures were "saying one thing and doing another". The anonymous nature of feedback in some procedures was also a source of friction that came through in comments she made, and that brought home the highly charged nature of mutual monitoring:

> You're invited to give feedback at the end of every project, and you can give anonymous feedback. You're being asked to grass on people and remain anonymous. I think that is despicable. … I will not write feedback and remain anonymous. I want to own every note that I play and own every word that I say. I don't need to be anonymous. … I work hard to keep my standards up. They can fire me tomorrow if my standards are not good enough. I want them to, I hope I recognise it before they do. I want people to tell me when I'm playing out of tune, or too fast, or too slow. Not to find out about it a month later through nasty letters from a little gang … who all want to remain anonymous. It's destructive. I also want to be told when I'm doing something really well. I want to be told immediately: "That's wonderful," as well as, "That didn't work." It's important. We need to express to each other with absolute honesty. I want tough love.

The interviews indicate that mutual monitoring among orchestral musicians is an important but contested element of player-governance that results from players' decision to take responsibility for artistic control, and with it, performance quality. Taking control of and responsibility for artistic decisions brings with it the responsibility to deal with its less enjoyable side: addressing problems of inadequate performance. At such moments, some of the players interviewed would welcome the opportunity to pass this responsibility back to a "bad-guy" music director, even when they acknowledged that this longing implies the reinstatement of a hierarchy that is antithetical to player-governance. The discussion now moves from performance monitoring to a focus on recruiting players, another essential element in optimising performance and building sustainability in a competitive marketplace.

6.3 Recruiting Players

Members of LMFs have an interest in ensuring that the work quality and productivity of recruits are at least as high as those of existing members. As Dow (2003) observed, "in their roles as decision-makers, residual claimants, and asset owners, LMF insiders have a keen interest in the characteristics of any new member" (p. 159). This interest is even greater in sectors that demand high levels of human capital, such as orchestral performance. Recruits must be excellent musicians. In PGOs, they must also be able and willing to work in player-led governance structures, to meaningfully contribute to decision-making, and, at a minimum, be open to the possibility of taking on a governance role. Hiring processes that deal with such a breadth of skills and attitudes are necessarily more comprehensive than those that assess little more than a musician's playing proficiency.

It is these interests and processes that are investigated in this section, where I argue that recruitment to PGOs is a more complex and time-consuming process than in externally governed orchestras; Lehman (2002) reached a similar conclusion. At the same time, this thorough, multifaceted recruitment is germane to sustaining player-governance. Recruitment to the PGOs studied plays a role in their governance sustainability by ensuring that potential new members are as committed to their governance model as were the founders.

Before turning to the organisational side of recruitment, I consider the process from the side of potential players and ask what motivates musicians to seek membership. Do musicians simply want to play with the best possible orchestra or ensemble, irrelevant of governance type? Or does governance play a role for musicians making career choices? Patrick reported being "happy to play with a good orchestra". He also felt that what made his "the most interesting orchestra" was "not directly the fact that it was self-governing and self-run, but the things that I realised came, consciously or subconsciously, from that". He surmised that "it appeals to a certain sort of person, regardless of the quality of music-making". Members described disparate motivations for seeking membership in these PGOs.

In contrast to Patrick, Herbert thought that it was "becoming more the case that the people are interested simply because it is a fantastic orchestra". He also highlighted the level of individual connection players may feel when he said that "as a musician, you always want to play with other fantastic players and to show the others that you can also play fantastically". Walter, similarly, felt that new players "sometimes … just want to join because it's artistically attractive", though he also noted that "people who stay are obviously interested in the artistic goals, but they will also fit in the spirit". For some members, the benefits of player-governance appear secondary to the search for work in a high-quality orchestra.

6.3.1 "The Most Important Decision of All"

I turn now to the organisational perspective on recruitment. The attitudes of the interviewees in the following quotes can be clustered around three themes: the importance of recruitment in PGOs, the attention paid to factors other than musical proficiency, and the resulting complexity when both of these considerations are combined.

The importance of recruitment was at the heart of comments made by Sophie, who explained that "it is important for us to get to know the people a little, how they tick, what they are like in such a community. That's why it takes so long, sometimes too long". This sense of community came through when she added that "who plays with us is the most important thing. That is the most important decision of all in the orchestra, and that's why it takes a while". The sociological dynamics of music performance make successful recruitment crucial in PGOs.

Walter concurred when he said that "partly the reason the orchestra has remained the way it is, is the very strong method of recruitment". Maria, speaking about the centrality of the democratic ethos in her PGO, also stressed the primacy of recruitment. She felt that it was "the most important [factor for success] of all", and "the reason why we have been successfully together for so long". She went on to explain that "from the start, we placed the greatest importance on the interpersonal. The musical was — it would be going too far to say it was of secondary importance — of equal importance". Her closing words highlighted the role of the personal: "We have never taken someone on who was fantastic but whom we didn't want as a person. … We don't take on people whom we don't already know." Herbert supported this line of thinking when he noted that

> We are a very special ensemble that works together a lot. We do a lot of concerts together and when we find someone, they also have to fit with us in many respects, need to have the right personality that complements the people who are already here, in the various groups and in the ensemble as a whole.

A third group of comments clustered around the idea that the recruitment processes in the PGOs studied were protracted. For some interviewees, this was a positive feature and a sign of thoroughness. Walter observed that "it's a long procedure to become a member. There are several stages and it's not just a straight audition and probation period as in most orchestras. … I think that makes a big difference". Herbert highlighted the time involved transitioning from supernumerary musician to member: "We don't hold auditions and a day later whoever won it is a partner, rather, we invite people to play with us." He went on to explain that "sometimes that lasts one, two years or perhaps longer" before members, having established that the player in question "fits in with us, … [we] have a vote, without [the player's] knowledge, and decide whether he or she can be a partner with us. It's only then that we speak to the musician and ask, 'Could you imagine it?'" Membership in these PGOs involves much more than instrumental proficiency. A thorough recruitment system, even when time-consuming, has a central role in making player-governance work.

Walter mentioned similar ideas about the familiarisation of potential new members with the orchestra: "When you spend a lot of time on the road in an orchestra, even if you are not a member, you participate in so much that you can feel if it's tense, or relaxed, whether it's happy or less happy." He also described how this familiarisation could extend to attending meetings in advance of becoming a member:

> The recruitment process lasts quite a while, so by the time people are members, they have already attended some of the meetings. We invite them to meetings when they are in the final stages of their trials so that they know what is going on.

Sebastian commented on the relative importance of the audition and the subsequent trial period during which suitability as a member is established: "What you learn about the player from the audition is really the prerequisite, and what the player then shows of themselves on trial is finally much more important than what they demonstrate in an audition."

Not everyone was approving of such lengthy recruitment processes, however. Patrick explained his dislike for it: "I think that it's bad. I don't think it's a good process. I don't think what we have is a 'process'. It's more like happenstance." He felt that it was "really difficult for us because we are touring and there are so many different types of program. This means that often members aren't there and it is very difficult to do". Martin was likewise concerned that "the decision-making activity associated with appointing people in an orchestra, on trial is really hard. It almost always ends up taking up a huge amount of time". Long member recruitment procedures can create friction and tension.

6.3.2 *Recruitment Processes*

Members make player recruitment decisions in the PGOs studied. In most cases, there are separate processes for auditions that precede engagement as a supernumerary and for subsequent acceptance as a member (when membership is an option). A probationary period of 12 months or more between these processes is common. In the smallest organisation I considered, a candidate for membership needs the unanimous approval of members. Among the others, the approval of two-thirds or three-quarters of the membership is typically required for membership. In the only orchestra with a music director in my cohort, only one vote is granted to the holder of that position.[2] In contrast, audition panels in externally governed orchestras normally consist of a much smaller group of players along with the music director, who may have a veto or a weighted vote (Lehman, 2002). In such cases, recruitment usually happens solely through an audition, which may be concluded in only an hour or two, though extended probation periods are also common.

As noted in Chap. 3, orchestras rely on high levels of human capital. An important area in which they can gain a marketplace advantage is the proficiency of their players and the performance of the collective. This is, though, true of all professional orchestras and ensembles, irrelevant of their governance structures. The extra challenge in PGOs is to ensure that new, enfranchised members are as committed to the democratic, player-governed ethos as were their founders. A failure to do so runs the risk of eroding the collective commitment to player-governance, and therefore a serious challenge to its sustainability.

When it comes to recruitment, the primary difference between PGOs and most other LMFs lies in the former's labour structures. The number of musicians engaged by an orchestra or ensemble is primarily determined by musical factors. For PGOs to be able to recruit members, a range of musical indicators must require it. It is not possible for PGOs to offer supernumerary players more-or-less automatic conversion to membership based solely on length of service or some economic indicator, as might be possible in other business partnerships. PGO models have similarities with the partnerships found in many legal, consulting, medical, and accounting firms; that is, sectors in which levels of human capital are high. However, PGOs differ from them because musical factors play such a decisive role. As previously discussed, membership numbers in the PGOs studied are determined by musical factors such as repertoire and programming choices. The PGOs researched for this

[2] The experience of the Auckland Philharmonia is salient to the question of music directors voting in a PGO. Considerable tension resulted when a revision of its constitution granted the music director a 33 per cent weighted vote in artistic decisions, and one disgruntled member even took legal action (Bathurst et al., 2007).

book have upper limits on their membership numbers that are dictated by the demand for musicians' labour. Exceeding these numbers only reduces the amount of work for existing members.

6.4 "A Potentially Very Dangerous Discussion to Have": Managing Generational Change

Managing generational change is a key sustainability problem for PGOs that are seeking to optimise performance. It challenges them to modify their identities from member-specific organisations to long-horizon firms that embody collective ideas above and beyond the interests and engagement of individual members. Generational change presents PGOs with two key challenges. The first is the added difficulty of mutual monitoring when it needs to respond to age-related declines in playing proficiency. The second is maintaining a commitment to player-governance as founding members leave, in some cases as a result of retirement.

Orchestral work demands high-level motor skills and psychological resilience (Halleland et al., 2009; Sternbach, 1995). Research shows that many musicians find manual dexterity difficult to sustain as they age (Brandfonbrener, 2003; Gembris & Heye, 2014; Manturzewska, 1990). Recent research by Brodsky (2025) found, however, that problems of ageing among orchestral musicians were primarily related to eyesight, general fatigue, and sitting and reported "no deteriorations among the Seasoned Musicians concerning their capacities to control fine motor movements" (p. 380). He concluded that "most Symphony Orchestra players, including the more Seasoned Musicians (above 55 years of age), perform at a more than acceptable level and retain their positions. Seasoned Musicians play very well!" (Brodsky, 2025, p. 374). Nevertheless, in 2014, the third international orchestra conference concluded that "a significant number of players can face psychological and physical impairments that adversely affect their ability to perform before they reach retirement age or can afford to retire" (International Federation of Musicians, 2014). The discussion required in dealing with end-of-career transitions is even more delicate when the organisations concerned have the flat structures of PGOs. Here, the decision to broach the subject of age-related proficiency decline must be made by peers who may be close, long-term colleagues and friends. In some cases, new players are former students of musicians whose skills may be waning as a result of ageing. Such conversations are even more challenging when the players concerned are founding members of their PGOs.

Kirsten highlighted the dilemma: "The inherent problem with being a young, pioneering orchestra is that we get old, and our playing ability decreases and no human being is very good at recognising that." Maria concurred: "At the moment we have a quite explosive issue: we are getting older and there will be cases when someone won't be able to deliver the performance that we are looking for." Patrick summarised the risks:

> If you look at other self-governing orchestras that have a similar provenance to us, they have often started like we did as a youth orchestra, idealistic, wanting to change things and then they have gone through together, so they have all been twenty to thirty [years old] and twenty years later they are all forty to fifty and then twenty-five years later it is difficult, even verging on impossible, to maintain artistic standards for that length of time. We have to find ways to think about how to do that. It is a potentially very dangerous discussion to have.

Susanna noted how generational change played a role in a recent revision of the organisation's governance:

> What drove that was a feeling of disjunction. It was around the time when the orchestra was twenty-five years old, so there were all sorts of questions to do with founding members hitting a certain age — a large group of people hitting similar ages at similar times — and what the impacts of that might be for the future. If they all decided to stop at the same time, you would suddenly have no orchestra.

Dealing with end-of-career transition among musicians is a problem that faces all orchestras. But the peer decision-making of player-governance adds extra challenges. Maria highlighted the difficulty of managing sensitive personnel decisions within a flat hierarchy:

> We don't have a retirement age, nor do we have a boss who tells you, "Now you are sixty you can keep playing for two years and that'll be it," or who might say to a first flute, "it might be better if you go back to second." Our hierarchies are too flat for that.

For Angela, the lack of adequate pensions made the problem of asking players to consider retirement more difficult:

> If, from day one … every player … had given a [small amount] of every fee into a pot for all of our pensions, we'd have a way to help people to leave, a very noble way, actually, a respectful way. I think we have not done that. We don't have that pot.

Other interviewees were conscious of the demands made by the profession and were open to the idea of pursuing other interests before retiring. Sophie said that

> I don't think that I want to be touring around the world until I retire. I can imagine that at a certain age many people start looking around to see if they can do something else, find a different orientation. It's quite good to have such a mix.

For Patrick, the chance to develop business skills within his PGO was an attractive way to create the "mix" Sophie referred to, build a second career, and a motivation to join:

> I don't think that I can be a performing musician my whole working life, I think it's too physically demanding. So, I thought it would be an opportunity to get a leadership role and see how the business side works and perhaps see that as springboard or pivot to something else.

Robert dealt with these challenges from both angles—as a member of the governance team responsible for dealing with end-of-career transitions and himself reaching the later stages of his career:

> I'm now at the stage at which my role in the [orchestra name omitted] is changing. I'm still a player member, but I'm now an associate principal. I'm not going to be the main principal

> player, I will be someone who they can call on to come and fill in when there are gaps. So, I'm very much in a transitional stage at the latter end of my playing career. I will carry on playing as a working musician for at least a good ten years, but not perhaps in the same way. … I've been on both sides of the table, discussing personnel issues for other player members and then having to have discussions with [name of general manager omitted] about my own future. I can see things from both sides.

The retirement of founding players can occasion debates about the identity of a PGO. Mario's thoughts highlight the issue:

> For the orchestra it is still a great challenge to determine to what extent the orchestra is defined through its members, i.e., through the individual members of the association, or to what extent the orchestra is an idea that extends beyond the individuals and is then an open container for new protagonists who then also have to find a meaningful place in it. … And to what extent [the orchestra] is a life form that works for everybody or only for a certain group of people, or also for those for whom it is a stage-of-life project, and for others again a project that is at the centre of their lives. That is something that is always fluid and that generates discussion.

The idea of a PGO as a flexible "container" that provides a framework within which there is room for evolution as new members join and make it their own is a subtle but important element in the sustainability of player-governance. Robert, a founding member of his PGO, spoke to the theme of bridging the generations from the perspectives of new members:

> They might look at us and say, "What right do we newcomers have to make decisions?" But we look at them and say, "Well, you have got every right to make decisions, because you are so good at what you do and it's going to be your future." This is an issue that we will be addressing in years to come. It's only coming to the fore as people are now starting to retire and create generational change. Now there is a significant number of younger members. In the past there were only a few. We have new members on [the artistic committee] who are helping make the decisions. [Name removed] is one of our leaders who was appointed four or five years ago and is now also on the board. There is certainly a willingness to pass on to the next generation and let them make of it what they will.

The interviewees were generally confident that it was possible to maintain the commitment to player-governance as founding members were replaced. Sophie said that "the people who join and stay are people for whom that [democratic ethos] is just as important. … When you find the right people, I can see that it extends quite wonderfully". Mario agreed:

> Interviewer: Can this spirit, this ethos, that special quality of the orchestra be retained? Is it passed on?
>
> Mario: Yes, I think so, simply because it is a particular way of working. … I think there are people in each generation who want to work in this way.

Ensuring that the best possible musicians are performing at any time is essential for the success of all orchestras and ensembles. Doing so requires the recruitment and retention of the best players possible, as discussed above. It also needs a respectful, supportive, and dignified process for assisting musicians who are no longer able to consistently perform at the required standard because of age-related loss of proficiency. Addressing retirement becomes challenging when players themselves are unable or unwilling to recognise and acknowledge that they are no longer playing at that level. As Kirsten observed of the recognition that playing proficiency usually declines with age, "no human being is very good at recognising that".

The risk for PGOs is that the difficult nature of a process that requires peers to manage each other's end-of-career transition invites procrastination in dealing with age-related performance decline. Indeed, the sustainability of player-governance is linked to the ability to successfully manage generational change. The interviewees were conscious that end-of-career transitions are rarely easy, and the challenges involved are heightened by the relatively flat hierarchies of PGOs. However, retirement is not the only element involved in successful generational change. Departing members need to be replaced by players who share their commitment to player-governance and who have the skills required to sustain and develop it during a future that will present new challenges and contexts. PGOs must create an environment that welcomes and facilitates governance engagement by new members.

The earlier discussion concerning founding logics made it clear that artistic motivations such as the desire to perform with specific colleagues, along with the economic rationale of minimising precarious work, were far more important than any idea of establishing a long-term enterprise. Interviewees' comments on the early years of their PGOs suggest that specific membership was a key element of organisational identity during the early years. The ability of the PGOs in the cohort to remain sustainable, as they continue into the second and third decades of their existence and beyond, indicates that in the intervening years they indeed do change into "open container[s] for new protagonists" that "extend beyond the individuals".

The PGOs studied are still struggling with the challenges and dilemmas of generational change and no simple, flexible, and painless approach to it emerged from the interviews. Managing change effectively is central to the operation and sustainability of these PGOs, particularly those that are grappling with the retirement of their founding members.

6.5 Conclusions: A Challenging but Vital Activity

In this chapter, I examined player-led activities that seek to maintain the highest possible standards of performance, namely the monitoring of performance and dealing with cases of deficiency, the managing of age-related declines in performance standards, and the recruitment of new members with the highest possible instrumental proficiency. All three are central to achieving the highest possible standards on stage.

In the second section, recruitment was put under the microscope, and a now familiar pattern emerged: recruitment is made more complex, but also more thorough, in a player-governed context. Taking on the most proficient musicians available is essential for any orchestra or ensemble. The PGOs studied also work hard to ensure that new recruits embrace, understand, and support player-governance. The recruitment of suitable new members is central to sustaining player-governance.

This chapter could have treated age-related decline in performance as just another type of proficiency loss, along with loss linked to physical or mental health problems, family-related problems, or substance abuse. I decided, however, to treat age-related decline and retirement separately for two reasons. Firstly, age-related proficiency declines are not usually reversible or "treatable" in the way that health problems may be. More importantly in the player-governed context, age-related declines in performance, especially when they are experienced by founding members, can have wider implications than simply an organisation's need to manage the retirement of an individual musician. In a PGO, such a player might also be a senior board member or other governance officer. Their retirement could have far-reaching implications for governance.

Here again, the existence of parallel decision-making structures in the PGOs studied can create difficulties. A member's governance skills, experience, and expertise might reach their zenith just as their instrumental proficiency begins to suffer from age-related decline. Separating the two structures—governance and performance—so that, for example, a senior board member might be allowed to continue in that role while retiring from performance, would pose a serious threat to the basic principle of player-governance. It would also considerably increase the risk of senior governance officers gradually becoming an oligarchy. The sustainability of player-governance is, then, dependent on a PGO's ability to successfully and sensitively regenerate membership, particularly when founding members retire.

Optimising performance is at the core of an orchestra's work. PGOs face particular challenges, but have also been able to take opportunities in this area. The chapter showed once again how the case study PGOs bring flexibility to the task and how they have managed to buttress the stability of their democratic governance. Player-governance calls for a unique ability to highlight and understand the risks while looking for and harnessing the positives. At the same time it is the engagement and commitment of players at the heart of player-governance that help these PGOS rise to the challenge and create performances.

References

Alchian, A. A., & Demsetz, H. (1972). Production, information costs, and economic organization. *The American Economic Review, 62*(5), 777–795. https://www.jstor.org/stable/1815199

Bathurst, R., Williams, L., & Rodda, A. (2007). Letting go of the reins: Paradoxes and puzzles in leading an artistic enterprise. *International Journal of Arts Management, 9*(2), 29–38. https://www.jstor.org/stable/41798995

Ben-Ner, A. (1988). The life cycle of worker-owned firms in market economies. *Journal of Economic Behavior & Organization, 10*(3), 287–313. https://doi.org/10.1016/0167-2681(88)90052-2

Bowles, S., & Gintis, H. (1993). A political and economic case for the democratic enterprise. *Economics and Philosophy, 9*(1), 75–100. https://doi.org/10.1017/S0266267100005125

Brandfonbrener, A. (2003). From the editor: Old musicians never die: Issues of aging in orchestral musicians. *Medical Problems of Performing Artists, 18*(4), 135–136. https://doi.org/10.21091/mppa.2003.4023

Brodsky, W. (2025). *Seasoned musicians playing beyond the 5th decade: A case study on symphony orchestra lifestyle and ageing*. Oxford University Press. https://doi.org/10.1093/9780198956501.001.0001

Dow, G. (2003). *Governing the firm: Workers' control in theory and practice*. Cambridge University Press.

Dow, G. (2018). *The labor-managed firm: Theoretical foundations*. Cambridge University Press.

Gembris, H., & Heye, A. (2014). Growing older in a symphony orchestra: The development of the age-related self-concept and the self-estimated performance of professional musicians in a lifespan perspective. *Musicae Scientiae, 18*(4), 371–391. https://doi.org/10.1177/1029864914548912

Halleland, H., Harris, A., Sørnes, S., Murison, R., & Ursin, H. (2009). Subjective health complaints, stress, and coping in orchestra musicians. *Medical Problems of Performing Artists, 24*(2), 58–62. https://www.jstor.org/stable/48710793

Hansmann, H. (1996). *The ownership of enterprise*. The Belknap Press of Harvard University Press.

International Federation of Musicians. (2014). *Conclusions of the 3rd international orchestra conference*. International Federation of Musicians.

Lehman, E. V. (2002). *Models of self-governance and workplace democracy: A comparison of select orchestras in Germany, the U.S. And U.K* (Doctoral dissertation). City University London. http://openaccess.city.ac.uk/7618/

Manturzewska, M. (1990). A biographical study of the life-span development of professional musicians. *Psychology of Music, 18*(2), 112–139. https://doi.org/10.1177/0305735690182002

McCain, R. (2007). Cooperation and effort, reciprocity and mutual supervision in worker cooperatives. In S. Novkovic & V. Sena (Eds.), *Cooperative firms in global markets: Incidence, viability and economic performance*. Emerald. https://doi.org/10.1016/S0885-3339(06)10007-1

Prinz, M. (1993). Wenn Ich Die 7. Beethoven-Symphonie Nicht Mehr Spiele, Ist Es Noch Immer Zu Viel: Kreativität Im Großen Orchester. *International review of the aesthetics and sociology of music, 24*(1), 69–76. https://doi.org/10.2307/836989

Sternbach, D. J. (1995). Musicians: A neglected working population in crisis. In S. L. Sauter & L. R. Murphy (Eds.), *Organizational risk factors for job stress*. American Psychological Association. https://psycnet.apa.org/doi/10.1037/10173-018

Chapter 7
Combining Theory and Practice: Voting Rights, Incentives, Authority

7.1 Voting Rights, Incentives, Remodelling Authority

It is now time to bring together the earlier theoretical discussion (Chap. 2) and the empirical, case study observations from Chaps. 4–6. The current chapter paints a portrait of player-governed orchestras (PGOs) as a type of labour-managed firm (LMF). The analysis incorporates the labour-management viability conditions proposed by Dow (2003) and Jensen and Meckling (1979) (see Chap. 2) and relates these to the features and operations of PGOs. The chapter foregrounds the essential features of PGOs as a type of LMF. Writers on labour-management have said little about not-for-profit firms [see Borzaga & Sacchetti, 2015 and Taylor, 2015 for two exceptions]. PGOs' focus on utilities other than profit sharing sets them apart from the LMFs typically considered in the literature. Similarly, the work of orchestral musicians, like that of many other cultural industries workers (Hesmondhalgh & Baker, 2011), differs in important ways from that of other workers (Allmendinger et al., 1996; Bennett, 2008; Cottrell, 2004). Orchestral players have unique proclivities for labour-management in the abstract and face specific challenges when actually establishing and running PGOs. These firms represent special examples of labour-management in practice, and studying them enriches the literature on LMFs.

The contexts and parameters of orchestras' operations set PGOs apart from most other LMFs. Orchestras display a clear division between two groups of workers—players and administrators—that challenges some theoretical positions about membership and voting rights in LMFs. Orchestras' not-for-profit status is a further important characteristic of the firms studied, whereas the distribution of profits to members is a crucial element in most theoretical LMF models. Section 7.2 investigates the alternative utility, incentives, and responsibilities partners have through their membership of a PGO. Artistic control and employment security emerge as the most salient alternatives to profit-share. In Sect. 7.3, I consider the renegotiation of authority in PGOs. Vertical authority structures are deeply rooted in orchestras and

B. Long, *Democratising Orchestras*, Music Business Research, https://doi.org/10.1007/978-3-032-17399-7_7

at first glance such firms might appear to be unsuitable sites for worker control. Yet the PGOs I studied have developed pragmatic solutions to the realignment and renegotiation of the authority systems inherent in orchestral music-making. These three features—deciding who votes in PGOs, mapping the incentives and utility that shape their operations and structures, and the renegotiating of authority—are the essential features of PGOs that encapsulate these firms' specific contribution to the practice of labour-management.

7.2 Who Should Vote in a PGO? A Boundary Problem

Workers who establish and seek to sustain control of their organisations must agree on the best voting franchises for their firms. Defining voting rights is easier when a firm's workers have relatively homogeneous interests (Dow, 2003). For Benham and Keefer (1991), "homogeneity of voter interests … reduces disagreement and eases voter fears that firm policies will diverge a great deal from their own interests" (p. 709). In the PGOs studied, however, musicians and management staff constitute distinct groups and a boundary problem arises. Voting rights must accommodate the different interests of various groups within these organisations, and possibly even outside (González-Ricoy & Magaña, 2024; Stehr, 2022).

Patrick outlined some of the questions involved in delineating a franchise when he mentioned some of the possible voting groups: players, "the office", and non-members who regularly play with the orchestra. Various combinations of these three groups might constitute a voting franchise in a PGO. Which possible franchises exist in a PGO, then, and does one of them promise greater governance sustainability than the others? The following discussion responds to these questions, based on an analysis of how the PGOs in this study sustain control by workers despite having to deal with divergent worker constituencies. Understanding the dynamics of voting and membership in the context of varied worker interests provides a valuable empirical contribution to the labour-management literature.

Giving all workers membership and voting rights seems the most straightforward way to create a franchise. Orchestras have various worker constituencies, including musicians and management, full and part-time workers, new recruits, and old hands. A franchise could include or exclude any of these groups. Voting rights might reflect an orchestra's division of labour between players and management staff. Other criteria could further subdivide these groups. Years of service, for instance, could serve as an eligibility criterion; voting rights would then be restricted to workers who have completed a probation period.[1] Already, various possible franchises start to emerge.

[1] Musicians seeking membership in the Vienna Philharmonic, for instance, must have completed at least three years of service in the Vienna State Opera orchestra (Vienna Philharmonic, n.d.).

A franchise that differentiates between workers who work a lot and those who work less frequently might also make sense. For office staff, for example, a division between full-time and part-time workers could be appropriate. In the case of players, voting might be restricted to those who work more than a specified fraction of whatever counts as full commitment. In the following discussion of franchises, the terms "sufficient-hours players" or "sufficient-hours managers" describe players and managing staff who meet time-fraction requirements.

Combining the musicians/management and hours-worked categories produces four potential voter groups: sufficient-hours players/insufficient-hours players and sufficient-hours managers/insufficient-hours managers. Additional franchises result from combining these groups in various ways, but in the PGOs studied, only five qualify as realistic and deserving of further consideration. The following analysis excludes combinations that involve musicians disenfranchising themselves. Such franchises are unrealistic because musicians founded all the firms studied and in normal circumstances would have little interest in giving up their voting rights.[2] Five groupings remain and appear in Table 7.1. A discussion of them forms the basis of this section.

In practice, all the orchestras studied have adopted the last of the franchises in Table 7.1 (LP/NM). They all restrict membership and voting rights to players—thereby excluding management staff, unless they are also players—while engaging some players as unenfranchised supernumeraries, thus limiting membership to a subset of all their musicians. The basic principle holds that musicians who perform more than a certain amount of the PGO's total work may qualify for membership and voting rights. In reality, the process of setting such dividing lines is complex. Susanna made this clear when she described her PGO's governance restructuring and its attempt to "make a demarcation" between enfranchised and unenfranchised musicians. The result was "[an] area around the line [that] gets terribly messy". In this case, some players were excluded from the franchise "because of where they are on the fixing lists". The choices involved in establishing a franchise have important implications for the sustainability of player-governance. In the remainder of this section, I explore the rationales involved.

Comparing the literature on voting rights in LMFs to the practices of the PGOs studied reveals essential differences. Much of such writing warns that dividing an LMF's workforce into members with voting rights and hired labour without the same entitlements leads to degeneration in labour-management. Pencavel's (2013) overview of the literature highlighted how "the worker co-op has been described as an impermanent production unit that changes its participatory qualities over time" because its "incentive is to replace departing member-workers with hired workers

[2] Players have, however, given up their voting rights in at least two cases. In 1908 the musicians of the New York Philharmonic voted to accept a funding package from a group of philanthropists who required that the players give up the orchestra's cooperative governance and institute a board controlled by the financiers (Aldrich, 1908; New York Philharmonic, 1909). In 2005, the members of the Auckland Philharmonia voted for a similar transition from cooperative to corporate structure after operating for 25 years as a PGO (Bathurst et al., 2007; Bathurst & Monin, 2010).

Table 7.1 Possible voting franchises in PGOs

Franchise type	Franchise name and code	Summary	Comments
Unlimited	All players/all management AP/AM	Players in/ management in	All management staff and players are granted membership and are enfranchised
Limited by working hours	Limited players/ limited management LP/LM	Sufficient-hours players in/ insufficient-hours players out Sufficient-hours management in/ insufficient-hours management out	Management staff and players who work more than a defined share of total commitment are granted membership and are enfranchised
Limited by type of work	All players/no management AP/NM	Players in/ management out	Membership and enfranchisement are granted to players but not management staff
Limited by type of work and working hours	Limited players/ no management LP/NM	Sufficient-hours players in/ insufficient-hours players out Sufficient-hours management out/ insufficient-hours management out	Only players who work more than a defined number of hours per year are granted membership and are enfranchised. Management staff are not enfranchised

(wage employees)" (online article, no page). He warned that "over time, an organization that starts with all workers being members and all members being workers becomes one in which most workers are hired employees and only a remnant of worker-members remains" (ibid.).

Ben-Ner (1984), writing about stability in producer cooperatives (PCs), cautioned that "the only sure way to void the transformation of a PC into a capitalist firm appears to be prohibition on hiring wage-laborers" (p. 259). Dow (2018) was more cautious, concluding that "the general temptation" to "replace departing members with hired employees" was "real, but in practice it can be (and often is) restrained through institutional mechanisms" (pp. 107–08). The widespread use of hired labour is common in professional partnerships (Leblebici & Sherer, 2015) and medical practice (Hansmann, 1990), where it does not seem to cause degeneration.

7.2.1 Should Management Get Votes?

An orchestra's handling of players and the management team is the first feature requiring attention when considering franchises (AP/NM and LP/NM in Table 7.1). Operating staff and musicians both depend on the success and sustainability of their firms, but in the firms studied, only players have the right to vote. The way orchestras are established helps explain the difference. The initial idea to set up any ensemble or orchestra almost invariably comes from a conductor, a group of players, or an individual musician. Management staff may have roles from the start, but they do not provide the impetus. The founding members in the PGOs studied were almost all players.[3] Being present at the outset does not, however, count as a criterion for enfranchisement because sufficient-hours musicians taken on later are also granted membership and voting rights. Other factors must be considered.

The statements I collected from the interviewees shed light on how a limited franchise might be more sustainable than extending voting rights to all the employees of an orchestra. Musicians' and management workers' diverging interests in artistic control and insecure work soon come into focus. Patrick, Susanna, Claudia, and Angela made this clear. Patrick highlighted the desire of musicians to retain artistic control in the face of others wanting to "call the artistic shots". Angela emphasised the primacy of controlling musicians' "musical destiny".

For management staff, having artistic control is, though, not as critical. They do have an interest in programming, to the extent to which it shapes an orchestra's earning potential and continuing commercial success, and thus their long-run employment security. Programming that leads to what Susanna called "box-office death" can imperil an orchestra's survival as a firm and endanger the jobs of management staff and players alike. Marketing, development, or financial managers do not, however, work with conductors or performance leaders in the way that players do, and nor do they have the corresponding desire to recast the orchestra–conductor relationships that emerged in Chap. 4.

The second significant divergence in the interests of players and management staff concerns job security. For musicians in the orchestras studied, the search for improved security is a crucial factor, one that reflects the labour market for musicians and the fluctuating demand for their work. On the other hand, sectors such as marketing, accounting, or project managing generally offer higher security than musicians have. Therefore, two broadly similar yet distinct interest groups emerge and create a dilemma for orchestras seeking to implement control by workers. Combining players and office workers in a single, all-worker franchise risks creating a fractious control structure that struggles to accommodate the diverging interests of the two constituencies and eventually proves unsustainable. On the other hand, a franchise excluding management staff because their interests differ from those of players may reduce a labour-managed orchestra to what Dow (2003)—writing about LMFs in general—called a "pale imitation of democratic procedures" (p. 201). In the face of such a dilemma, a focus on governance sustainability and stability suggests that a franchise preferring musicians is most likely to succeed.

The PGOs I studied give voting rights to players but withhold them from management staff. Such a differing treatment of workers in the same firm supports governance survival by mirroring the division of labour, divergent labour markets, and

[3] In one case, a musician in an early incarnation of one of the PGOs in my study subsequently stopped playing and became the chief executive.

the resulting differences in the interests of the two groups. The literature supports this conclusion. Dow (2003) observed how "when workers do not have uniform tasks or skills, voting rights in LMFs are often confined to a subset of the workforce, with others being hired as employees or contractors" (p. 204). Restricting the number of voters may also expedite and simplify decision-making—a goal that democratic control may struggle to realise (Benham & Keefer, 1991; Shipper, 2014; Jensen & Meckling, 1979). Dow (2001) noted that such efficiency gains might result from "disenfranchising groups such as clerical workers whose interests diverge from those of the dominant coalition" (p. 208). Restricting voting rights to musicians, as the PGOs in this study do, appears to bolster labour-management.

The exclusion of management staff from membership may be viewed by LMF theorists as counter to the participatory principle at the heart of labour-management, but it might actually protect player-governance against oligarchic forms of degeneration when a small leadership team emerges and increasingly takes control without meaningful reference to the wider membership. Among the PGOs studied, managers accrue control by virtue of their centrality to their organisations, their access to information, or their specialist leadership and management skills. These skills are necessary for the success of a PGO, but such specialisation clearly poses a threat of "oligarchisation" (Diefenbach, 2018, p. 3). Some LMFs have sought to address this risk by rotating members through leadership and management positions or imposing term limits on member-managers (Cornforth, 1995).

Engaging management as hired labour, as all but one of the PGOs in the research do, is an alternative bulwark against the risk of oligarchic management castes. This approach treats managers as hired specialists, akin to consultants, who provide specific services to the membership but who can be more easily removed and thus controlled because they are not members and do not have voting rights. In a similar way, engaging conductors on a project basis and at the discretion of members prevents their accretion of excessive control. Conductors, too, are engaged as specialists who bring performance efficiency and artistic profiles but who are subject to ultimate governance control by members.

This section concentrated on the balances between the two key stakeholder groups in PGOs. In it, I argued that the engagement of management staff as hired labour with no voting rights was a rational response to the division of labour within the PGOs studied and to the ways in which labour markets for musicians and management workers differ. The PGOs of this research consistently restrict membership, and with it voting rights, to the musician segment of their workforce, while engaging management staff as hired labour. The latter do not enjoy the same rights and powers to shape their PGOs that enfranchised players do. This flies in the face of traditional labour-management thinking, which argues that the contracting of hired labour threatens the sustainability of the participatory ethos if the share of unenfranchised workers grows (Dow, 2018). In the case of this research cohort, however, I argue that in their accommodation of the divergent labour-market dynamics between musicians and management workers, these PGOs represent a successful and sustainable model of labour-management.

7.3 The Benefits of Work in a PGO

Members enjoy various benefits from working in PGOs. The desire to maximise them creates incentives to pursue some strategies rather than others. The interaction of these incentives with the parameters of orchestral work and its organisation creates a framework that is atypical among LMFs. Maximising monetary returns to members typically counts as a paramount goal for LMFs (Furubotn, 1976; Kruse, 2013; Meade, 1972; Pencavel et al., 2006). In his overview of the literature, Pencavel (2013) identified a "dividend maximization hypothesis" (online article, no page). Workers' sharing in profits is usually a key rationale behind labour-management.

The writing of other theorists is more circumspect. Dow (2003) cautioned that "from the standpoint of the modern theory of the firm, it is not obvious that LMFs maximize anything" (p. 142). Instead, he observed that

> Firms are complicated coalitions in which each agent has her own preferences, information, and feasible actions. These coalitions face difficult coordination, bargaining, and incentive problems. Whether the strategic actions of individual labor and capital suppliers translate into the pursuit of some objective by the coalition as a whole is very much open to debate. (Dow, 2003, p. 142)

Jossa (2017) pursued similar thinking when he proposed benefits beyond maximising monetary returns and concluded that "the guiding principle of the cooperative firm is the criterion of maximising the well-being [of] workers, i.e. a compound of wages per worker, job stability and a number of additional non-pecuniary benefits such as pleasant working conditions" (p. 42). This refocusing on a broader concept of "utility" (Jossa, 2018, p. 33) is pivotal to understanding incentives in not-for-profit LMFs, such as orchestras.

The study of PGOs as LMFs would be curtailed without the prospect of understanding control by musicians in the broader terms of utility rather than financial returns. In PGOs, other types of utility replace the maximising of pecuniary returns. Non-monetary benefits, including the right to exercise artistic control and increasing job security—the two most salient ideas to emerge from the case studies—act as alternative forms of utility in orchestras. The chance to maximise artistic control and employment security provides the members of the PGOs studied with real incentives for participation. In what follows, I explore artistic control and job security as forms of utility in PGOs, while remaining wary of projecting onto members a "pursuit of some objective by the coalition as a whole" (Dow, 2003, p. 142). The insights presented enrich ideas about LMFs by exploring alternative forms of utility and incentives in not-for-profit LMFs, a neglected field of labour-management studies.

7.3.1 Benefits of Artistic Control

The fundamental role of members in making artistic decisions in PGOs clearly emerged from the interviews. Artistic planning and programming are two of an orchestra's pivotal management activities (Herman, 2022; Pompe et al., 2013) and members' control of artistic matters is at the heart of PGOs. Other research has shown that musicians have a strong desire to be involved in artistic decisions. Schulz (1981) found that 83 per cent of the Vienna Symphony musicians he interviewed were "in favour of participation" in decision-making (p. 54). Rickert et al. (2013) investigated well-being among cellists in an Australian orchestra and found that "lack of creative input" led players to feel like "note producers" working in a "note factory" (p. 226). Other researchers have highlighted the stress and damage to health that can result when musicians feel excluded from artistic control (Johansson & Theorell, 2003; Parasuraman & Purohit, 2000). Creation of a framework through which PGO members can take control of artistic decision-making is, then, a response to desires that are widely held among orchestral musicians.

The interviewees similarly described how important it was for members to control artistic decisions in PGOs. Martin and Walter thought that members having such control was the essential element of player-governance, while Sophie spoke of it being the "core of everything". Leo highlighted how responsibility for artistic planning and programming flowed through into greater motivation for players to give their best on stage. Satisfying the desire of players to control some of the most important decisions made in managing an orchestra is, nonetheless, not the whole story. Allocating artistic authority to musicians also boosts efficiency and may reduce alienation, with the result that members have a heightened sense of engagement and commitment.

The reduction of information asymmetries between workers and management is hailed as one of the advantages of labour-management (Dow, 2003; Hansmann, 1996). Strauss observed that worker participation in decision-making "may result in better decisions" (1998, p. 10) because "employees often have information which senior management lacks" (ibid.). Such participation, he argued, also allowed "different views to be aired" (ibid.) so that "groupthink is reduced" (ibid.). Player-governance takes artistic decision-making away from an artistic director and a small group of senior managers. Members' control brings artistic decisions into a broader forum of player representatives. Information is shared more widely, and the collective knowledge and experience of all members has the potential to shape the orchestra.

The potential for greater information sharing is an essential strength of member-led artistic control in the PGOs I studied. The intellectual and artistic capital in an orchestra of 30, 40, or more highly trained musicians is considerable. Facilitating opportunities for members to share their experience, insights, and perspectives is a crucial strength of these PGOs. The conversations balancing the idealism of players with the challenges of economically sustainable programming that Susanna described go to the heart of the PGO model. Robert likewise highlighted the shared understanding between players and board members. The taking control of artistic decision-making, the rejection of autocracy from conductors, and musicians having a sense that they can influence their professional futures are also central. Equally important are the conversations and understanding that are facilitated by the information exchange at the heart of player-governance.

Decisions on artistic questions must, however, balance competing factors (Herman, 2023; Pompe et al., 2011), some of which are beyond the control or influence of decision-makers, in particular, the varying demands for musicians made by different composers and works. Taking artistic control does not free PGO members from addressing the dilemmas of programming and artistic decision-making. These challenges involve creating programs and projects that build long-term audience loyalty and willingness to purchase tickets and recordings, while balancing production costs such as conductor, soloist, and players' fees. These challenges exist independently of the governance structure an orchestra adopts.

The interviewees were, nevertheless, aware of the risks and conflicts that might arise through opportunistic and short-term artistic planning and programming by musicians. There is a risk that players develop programs that primarily appeal to their interests with little concern for budgetary repercussions or marketing challenges. Robert spoke of the risk that player-governance would lead to musicians planning projects with little regard for financial considerations. However, the interviews also indicated that players were conscious of such risks and introduced governance and management systems to ensure that programming and artistic planning consider financial implications. Susanna noted that in practice members understood the compromises required. Robert spoke of checks and balances between the artistic ambitions of musicians and the concerns of marketing and fundraising professionals. The risk of members' substituting their artistic and economic interests for those of audience development appears manageable.

To further understand the importance of artistic control in orchestras as a form of member utility, it also helps to consider its potential for reducing alienation. As part of their study of creative labour, Hesmondhalgh and Baker (2011) developed a "model of good and bad work" (p. 25) that rests in part on ideas of worker alienation and responses to it. Their analysis is rooted in Karl Marx's thinking and Blauner's (1964) book on "alienation and freedom" in particular. Like Blauner, Hesmondhalgh and Baker (2011) steered away from granting power to workers as a means to address powerlessness as an ingredient of alienation (p. 28). Instead, their work mainly focused on autonomy, which they characterised as "self-determination" (ibid., p. 40). LMFs show, nonetheless, that workers controlling high-level decisions beyond their "immediate job and work load" (Blauner, 1964, p. 18) is feasible. As the interviews undertaken for this research show, exercising collective control is also a response to powerlessness and alienation. The levels of commitment, engagement, and identification with their orchestras that interviewees highlighted amply demonstrate the utility and broader positive outcomes that PGOs derive when musicians take artistic control.

7.3.2 Employment Security

After taking artistic control, improving job security is the second critical form of utility for PGO members that emerged during this research. The firms studied do not provide the level of employment security offered by some orchestras, but they do reduce the precariousness of freelancing. By doing so, PGOs at least partly address and fulfil an interest among players who are acutely aware of perils such as being dependent on the goodwill of conductors for work. The interviews undertaken as part of this study revealed that the crucial economic incentive for PGO members was the belief that establishing and running their respective firms would improve their employment security, even if only modestly. Despite the interviewees' desire to improve job security by founding or joining a PGO, the reality is that all the firms considered offer their members only a slightly more secure form of what is, in essence, freelance work. Improved job security is a significant form of utility in PGOs.

Nonetheless, increasing job security is not straightforward. The interviewees described approaches that illuminate the dilemmas of organisational sustainability and responsible decision-making in a labour-management context. Job security in PGOs poses far-reaching challenges for decision-makers and requires that they balance competing demands. Orchestras with large enough financial reserves, public funding, sponsorship, or philanthropy can offer musicians full security. Such contracts offer players tenure and regular salaries even when they do not play all calls. Orchestras without similar resources cannot be so generous; they offer less security in order to remain financially viable. In a PGO, balancing the demands of players and the firm's commercial viability is the responsibility of members. They must steward their firm's governance and economic sustainability while also seeking to maximise their own job security.

Decision-makers in a PGO must balance three factors: players' desire for maximal job security, fluctuating demand for musicians' services, and the firm's ability to attract non-ticket income. One of the musicians' key rationales for membership disappears if PGOs cannot offer members a modicum of job security. At a minimum, PGOs need to offer members a regulated and transparent player-booking system. Without such an arrangement, members have little incentive to support the governance work necessary to enable control by players. The absence of a player-booking system would result in a drift towards increased market-based and ad hoc contracting of players while members seek opportunities for greater job security elsewhere. An orchestra would be left to recruit players from an expanding pool of musicians who felt little commitment to the firm. The result could be increased costs and uncertainty of contracting coupled with less efficient production (in particular, rehearsals) if the continuity of musicians involved from project to project withered.

PGOs that lack the financial reserves or non-ticket funding to allow them to offer tenured positions must, nevertheless, ensure that musician contracting tightly mirrors programming-related variability in demand for players. Offering higher levels of employment security by, for example, paying members when they are not playing a particular project could jeopardise the firm's financial future. Dealing with players' interests in improving job security can create tension between governance sustainability and economic survival. PGOs must be able to balance the competing demands highlighted above, and, perhaps most importantly, their members need to resist the temptation to pursue opportunistic strategies. The ability to achieve a sustainable balance between the desire for employment security and financial rigour demonstrates that the PGOs studied do not fall victim to opportunistic behaviours. These firms do not provide employment security beyond the point at which it ignores the variability of demand for players and thus threatens their financial viability.

High levels of job security for orchestral musicians depend on an orchestra's ability to secure sufficiently high levels of funding from non-ticket sources such as public funding bodies, philanthropists, or sponsors (Flanagan, 2012). Player-governance does not relieve PGOs from having to address the entangled economics of programming, demand for musicians, and the desire for the highest possible levels of job security for members. The essential element is that the power to make the relevant decisions is vested in the players, who are also the crucial interest group. A conflict of interest arises, and the sustainability of governance is at risk if the player decision-makers cannot get the balance right.

Before leaving the subject of improved job security as a type of utility in freelance PGOs, it is worth briefly considering the differences between financial returns and the search for better job security as motivations. One of the weaknesses of profit sharing as a form of utility in LMFs is a free-rider problem that arises because founders must share the financial benefits of membership with others. As Dow (2018) wrote:

> Even if an LMF would have substantial productivity advantages, it may not be in the interest of a single individual or small group to incur the cost of creating one, because other agents will appropriate most of the resulting benefits. This is true both for creation of new firms and the conversion of conventional firms into LMFs. (p. 387)

The utility derived from job security differs from that of profit sharing because it is less clearly finite and it more closely approximates a non-rival good.[4] Secure work remains a non-rival good as an orchestra or ensemble expands up to the point at which a PGO takes on more members than it needs for its core repertoire. Only, for example, after an orchestra that usually plays with ten violins recruits an eleventh does rivalry in the form of positions on hierarchical fixing lists become a concern. The division of labour within an orchestra is also a consideration. The recruitment of an eleventh or twelfth violinist to a PGO that regularly needs ten has little impact on the employment security of other instrumentalists, such as trumpet players or cellists. For these players, improved job security remains a non-rival good if, as in the example, violinist members join. The barrier to the formation of

[4] A non-rival good can be used or consumed by one beneficiary without reducing its amount or utility to others.

freelance PGOs or the conversion of conventional orchestras may, then, be lower than is the case among profit-sharing LMFs. It may also mean that the ongoing risk of post-establishment free-riding in PGOs is reduced and, as such, suggests that LMFs that do not distribute surpluses have more sustainable governance structures than do their profit-sharing peers.

Showing how members of not-for-profit firms and those in the creative and cultural industries experience utility represents this section's contribution to the understanding of labour-management. The PGOs in the study demonstrate that intangible, non-pecuniary forms of utility, such as taking control of artistic decisions, can provide powerful motivations for labour-management. The presence of two incentives—taking artistic control and boosting job security—additionally illustrates Dow's (2003) observation quoted above concerning the complexity of interest coalitions in firms. The balancing act involved in lifting job security without making firms unsustainable further exemplifies the "difficult coordination, bargaining, and incentive problems" (ibid., p. 142) LMFs face. Taken together, these two forms of utility provide the primary motivation for the engagement of PGO members, and in so doing, provide a solid basis for the sustainability of player-governance structures.

7.4 Strengths of Renegotiated Authority and Leadership

Redefining internal authority and leadership is a hallmark of LMFs and PGOs. Jossa (2017) suggested that LMFs' "reversed capital-labour relationship" (p. 97) helps make them part of a "new mode of production" (ibid.). Dow (2003) observed how in LMFs "it is clear to everyone that authority is an instrumental, utilitarian social arrangement serving the interests of the subordinates, chosen by them, and continuing only with their consent" (p. 36). In his book on Orpheus, a PGO based in New York, the orchestra's then executive director, Seifter (and his co-author, Economy), observed that "in Orpheus, we stand the traditional model of fixed organisational leadership on its head" (2001, p. 90). Joyce Rothschild-Whitt has written extensively on the sociology of "collectivist organizations" (1979) and "co-operative workplaces" (2012) while contrasting them with "bureaucratic organizations" (Rothschild & Russell, 1986; Rothschild & Allen Whitt, 1986). For her, "perhaps more than anything else, it is the basis of authority that distinguishes the collectivist organization from any variant of bureaucracy" (Rothschild-Whitt, 1979, p. 511). The following analysis highlights how PGOs renegotiate authority structures, including the subtleties and balancing involved.

The essential feature of authority in LMFs is its foundation in shared decision-making. The principle underlying such collective authority is simple: "all those who would be affected by a decision have a right to be invited to take part in making it" (Rothschild & Stephenson, 2009, p. 801). The negotiation of authority in LMFs is, then, not about simply rejecting authority or leadership, but rather subjecting both elements to collective decision-making and oversight. Delegating authority to leaders remains possible in LMFs, but at the discretion of members and on their terms.

The primacy of the collective's authority, along with its task of ensuring that all members can take part in decision-making, are the two central features of player-governance that emerge from my case studies.

Hierarchical authority and leadership structures in orchestras are long-established and often rigid. Holoman (2012) described them as "not far removed from feudal ways" (p. 18) while, for Cahn (1992), the symphony orchestra was "one of the last bastions of authoritarian rule in the industrialized world" (p. 28). Commentators often focus on the "god-like" (Cottrell, 2004, p. 127) and charismatic nature of conductors' work (Atik, 1994; Boerner et al., 2004). But musicians' work with conductors is often problematic (Ladkin & Bathurst, 2012). As Faulkner (1973) observed, "an occupational lore develops around performers' problems and work adventures with conductors" (p. 149). Players routinely describe some of them as "dictatorial" (Cottrell, 2004, p. 108) and complain about the lack of opportunities for input (Bennett, 2008; Brodsky, 2006; Cottrell, 2004; Parasuraman & Purohit, 2000; Schulz, 1981). The renegotiation of authority within PGOs begins with conductors.

The authority of conductors does not neatly square with that of decision-makers in other enterprises. In some respects, conductors are like chief executives or production managers (Mintzberg, 1998), but elements of the conductor–orchestra relationship are unusual among corporate authority structures (Atik, 1994; Glynn, 2008). Unless a conductor also has a position such as an artistic or music director post with an orchestra, their authority is temporally circumscribed. They may have almost unchallenged authority over practically every aspect of a performance, but such power is only exercised within the bounds of the project for which they are contracted, and such an engagement may last as little as a few days or a week. Nevertheless, even when an orchestra works with multiple conductors over a year and none has the role of a music director, the interviewees who took part in this research placed great importance on members' controlling who conducts.

The right to choose whom musicians collaborate with is particularly important in PGOs. In some cases, such choices start with consideration of whether to engage a conductor at all for a particular project. Performing without a conductor is increasingly common, particularly among chamber orchestras of the type studied for this book (Carnicer et al., 2015). When orchestras play without a conductor, leadership and authority typically come from the concertmaster (the most senior violinist) (Beau, 2014). Nevertheless, the experiences of the PGOs studied show that working with a conductor remains the default arrangement.

The orchestras I studied have renegotiated conductor–orchestra authority but have not rejected it. The Orpheus model that allows an orchestra to always perform without a conductor (Khodyakov, 2007; Lehman, 2002; Seifter & Economy, 2001) has not been widely adopted by other PGOs. In the orchestras studied for this book, conductors are instead engaged for their specialist skills, the rehearsal efficiency they can bring, and the marketing/branding advantages the best of them contribute. The interviewees' comments made this clear, particularly those of Alvis, who described his orchestra's journey away from engaging conductors because that was the customary mode, to bringing in conductors only when they have something to contribute. PGOs thus reassess and renegotiate authority. As Robert described it, this renegotiation serves not so much to reverse power and authority structures as to redefine and reinvent them. It is not about players dictating to conductors. Rather, these PGOs delegate decision-making to conductor/leaders when doing so creates efficiency, but on terms that are ultimately controlled by members.

Conductors are, nonetheless, not the only authority figures in orchestras. General managers also wield power. Here too, research suggests that orchestral musicians and senior managers often have conflicted relationships (Allmendinger et al., 1996). When attention turns to executives in PGOs, a crucial debate arises: should they be members of the firm, or hired labour drawn from outside it and denied voting rights? One school of thought insists that all workers in a PGO must be members: "The only sure way to void the transformation of a PC [producer cooperative] into a capitalist firm appears to be prohibition on hiring wage-laborers" (Ben-Ner, 1984, p. 259). The primary risk of deviating from this stance, the argument goes, arises if the labour-management principle becomes compromised and "over the long run, the proportion of members in the PC workforce decreases and the organization is transformed gradually into a capitalist firm" (ibid., p. 248). Whether chief executives are selected from the membership or come from outside thus shapes the authority they exercise and may have broader implications such as threatening an LMF's democratic ethos.

A second school of thought displays more pragmatism concerning the possibility of recruiting chief executives from outside an LMF's membership and paying them as hired hands. Dow (2003) acknowledged that "any reasonably large worker-controlled firm will … have an administrative system with professional managers" (p. 276). How much, though, should the powers of such managers be circumscribed by members? One answer to that question involves a board of LMF members restricting its own role to engaging and supervising managers before delegating more or less all decisions to them. Such an extreme case engenders debate about the "extent to which democracy must be sacrificed on the altar of managerial authority in order to make workers' control a viable governance structure" (ibid., p. 278). The PGOs in the current study embody one response to this trade-off. Their members retain control over the basic elements of orchestral operations, including programming, selection of artistic personnel, and performance monitoring. These PGOs thus restrict the scope of the general managers they engage, typically to the management of external relations, marketing, legal affairs, and financial controlling, plus the oversight of non-playing staff. Executives answer to members, while specific—mostly artistic—areas of these firms' operations remain under the direct control of members, with managers supplying, at most, advice.

The experience with authority of the PGOs in this study is nuanced and complex. For its first six years, the Orchestra of the Age of Enlightenment had general managers who were also player members (Wallace, 2006). The London Mozart Players adopted player-governance only in 2014 and initially its executive team consisted mostly of players (London Mozart Players, 2015, 2014), though the arrangement proved temporary (London Mozart Players, 2021). The other PGOs studied all have externally recruited chief executives. Pragmatism drove the choice in some cases.

As new orchestras evolved and grew, the position of chief executive became too time-consuming for musicians who wanted to continue working as players. Benefits and efficiencies also arose from uniting disparate areas of control in the hands of a manager from beyond the membership. This was particularly true when members' desire to continue working on the artistic side of the enterprise meant they were reluctant to take on full-time management roles.

The psychology and sociology of orchestral musicians also play a crucial role in the way they approach conductor and management authority in their firms. Even when the study of orchestral music-making often highlights the collective nature of such work, players continue to identify as artists with a sense of individuality and personal sovereignty (Bennett, 2008). The pre-professional training that musicians undertake is germane to this self-image (Dobson & Gaunt, 2013). In writing about the orchestral musicians he interviewed, Cottrell (2004) observed how they were "intensively trained to develop their inner world and to have strong conceptions of themselves as self conscious individuals" (p. 117). Such individualism was reflected by the interviewees in my research, particularly Martin, who spoke of how members "come back at you with a little more determination than perhaps anywhere else" when they feel uncomfortable with decisions made in his orchestra.

The daily individual practice that players undertake, usually at home and self-directed, strengthens this understanding. Musicians thus perform part of their routine work—on average, seven hours a week, according to research by Krampe and Ericsson (1995)—away from the orchestra. Moreover, such practice work primarily serves to maintain basic proficiency that is not connected to any specific employer. It develops and fosters individual and transferable human capital that exists independently of employers and is transferred between engagements. Musicians' ownership of their instruments may also give them an atypical sense of professional independence and sovereignty. Orchestral players remain economically dependent on their employers, but their creativity and productive capability exist separately, giving them a sense of individuality that is atypical among most workers.

Amongst such individualistic workers, it is likely that, as Cottrell (2004) observed, "frustrations arise … when in certain situations the final shape of the object of the creation — their musical performances — are not entirely in their own hands" (p. 117). Throughout the interviews undertaken for this book, underlying demand for self-determination as a means to minimise such frustrations was apparent. Sophie felt that there had never been an alternative to player-governance in her orchestra, and Walter was similarly resolute about the desire among his playing colleagues to take control of their orchestra from the start. Robert and Martin likewise underlined the desire of musicians to collaborate and cooperate with conductors, but not to dictate to them.

A tension thus emerges in the work and self-awareness of orchestral musicians, one that seems particularly conducive to the establishment and running of PGOs. Players' training and work create and nurture professional independence that is bolstered by the freelance contracts offered by firms such as those in this study. Orchestral work, nonetheless, remains essentially collective and collaborative, with interpersonal relationships taking on central importance. As Dobson and Gaunt (2013) noted:

> It is possible that greater emphasis is placed on working relationships in this context than in other professions, relating to a team effort for a distinct common goal (the performance) in which the majority of one's working hours are spent in the direct presence of – and in constant collaboration with – one's colleagues. (p. 12)

This tension mirrors and indeed feeds the adaptive and blended approaches to renegotiating the authority of conductors and chief executives in PGOs. Members of the PGOs I studied are pragmatic about power and control in their firms. Player-governance ensures that members retain ultimate control, but they are prepared to delegate limited situational authority to appropriately skilled specialists such as chief executives and conductors on the basis that such an arrangement benefits the firms and its members.

7.5 Key Elements of PGO Viability

By highlighting PGOs' three constitutive components, this chapter contributes to the labour-management literature. These firms show that labour-management remains feasible in contexts characterised by disparate interests among a firm's workers. Establishing pragmatic voting franchises that mirror the exigencies of orchestral work gives PGOs solid footings for their governance structures. In all the firms studied, the founding musicians have restricted voting rights to a subset of players. Much of the LMF literature warns that restricting membership and voting rights to some workers while engaging others as hired hands threatens the longevity of labour-management. However, the firms in my study show how aligning membership with a firm's operational and structural dynamics can become an overriding consideration. The conditions and parameters specific to individual LMFs or, indeed, whole sectors, can tip ideas on membership toward restricted franchises despite theoretical concerns about possible dilution of a firm's democratic ethos. Restricting voting rights can boost the viability of labour-management.

The core LMF literature has, moreover, said little concerning labour-management in non-profit firms. This chapter showed that forms of utility other than monetary returns take centre stage in not-for-profit firms. Particularly noteworthy was the desire among freelance musicians to increase job security by exercising governance control. However, funding in the PGOs studied circumscribes the extent to which job security can be ensured. These firms show how PGO members counteract any incentives for opportunistic decision-making, and instead reach commercially sustainable arrangements that enhance job security as far as is prudent.

The renegotiation of authority in the PGOs considered is the third cornerstone of these firms and their unique embodiments of labour-management. With their centuries-old hierarchies, orchestras are prime candidates for investigations and realignments of authority. The primary message from this research is, nevertheless, that such renegotiation redirects authority rather than rejecting it. Vertical control continues to play a role, as do leaders such as conductors and executives. Nonetheless, the PGOs of this study have instrumentalised authority, taking control of it and turning it to members' advantage. Authority thus becomes an efficiency tool that members can delegate to specialists whom they engage for their ability to further the goals of the collective. PGOs retain the traditional hierarchies of orchestral music-making when such structures serve musicians' interests. The results are flexible and responsive authority and leadership structures that adapt to the challenges these PGOs face, giving them a resilience that stands them in good stead for continuing viability.

The next chapter returns to the topic of how PGOs sustain their democratic structures and processes. The chapter begins with a discussion of the oft-theorised degenerative potential of labour-management, before it highlights the ways in which the orchestras achieve governance sustainability.

References

Aldrich, R. (1908). Future of the Philharmonic Society: The organization at a critical stage of its career after sixty-seven years. *New York Times*, 20 December.

Allmendinger, J., Richard Hackman, J., & Lehman, E. V. (1996). Life and work in symphony orchestras. *The Musical Quarterly, 80*(2), 194–219. https://doi.org/10.2307/742362

Atik, Y. (1994). The conductor and the orchestra: Interactive aspects of the leadership process. *Leadership & Organization Development Journal, 15*(1), 22–28. https://doi.org/10.1108/01437739410050123

Bathurst, R., & Monin, N. (2010). Finding myth and motive in language: A narrative of organizational change. *Journal of Management Inquiry, 19*(3), 262–272. https://doi.org/10.1177/1056492610362917

Bathurst, R., Williams, L., & Rodda, A. (2007). Letting go of the reins: Paradoxes and puzzles in leading an artistic enterprise. *International Journal of Arts Management, 9*(2), 29–38. https://www.jstor.org/stable/41798995

Beau, G. (2014). Beyond the leader-centric approach: Leadership phenomena and aesthetics in a conductorless orchestra. *Society and Business Review, 11*(1), 62–79. https://doi.org/10.1108/SBR-10-2015-0060

Benham, L., & Keefer, P. (1991). Voting in firms: The role of agenda control, size and voter homogeneity. *Economic Inquiry, 29*(4), 706–719. https://EconPapers.repec.org/RePEc:oup:ecinqu:v:29:y:1991:i:4:p:706-19

Ben-Ner, A. (1984). On the stability of the cooperative type of organization. *Journal of Comparative Economics, 8*(3), 247–260. https://doi.org/10.1016/0147-5967(84)90055-6

Bennett, D. (2008). *Understanding the classical music profession: The past, the present and strategies for the future*. Ashgate.

Blauner, R. (1964). *Alienation and freedom; The factory worker and his industry*. University of Chicago Press.

Boerner, S., Krause, D., & Gebert, D. (2004). Leadership and co-operation in orchestras. *Human Resource Development International, 7*(4), 465–479. https://doi.org/10.1080/1367886042000246030

Borzaga, C., & Sacchetti, S. (2015). *Inclusive Governance in Non-Profit Organisations*. Paper presented at ICA Conference Paris 2015.

Brodsky, W. (2006). In the wings of British Orchestras: A multi-episode interview study among symphony players. *Journal of Occupational & Organizational Psychology, 79*(4), 673–690. https://doi.org/10.1348/096317905X68213

Cahn, W. L. (1992). Authority and motivation in the symphony orchestra: A symphony musician's point of view. *Contemporary Music Review, 7*(1), 27–38. https://doi.org/10.1080/07494469200640211

Carnicer, J. G., Garrido, D. C., & Requena, S. O. (2015). Music and leadership: The role of the conductor. *International Journal of Music and Performing Arts, 3*(1), 84–88. https://doi.org/10.15640/ijmpa.v3n1a8

Cornforth, C. (1995). Patterns of cooperative management: Beyond the degeneration thesis. *Economic and Industrial Democracy, 16*(4), 487–523. https://doi.org/10.1177/0143831X95164002

Cottrell, S. (2004). *Professional music-making in London: Ethnography and experience*. Ashgate.

Diefenbach, T. (2018). Why Michels' 'Iron Law of Oligarchy' is not an iron law – and how democratic organisations can stay 'Oligarchy-Free'. *Organization Studies, 40*(4), 545–562. https://doi.org/10.1177/0170840617751007

Dobson, M. C., & Gaunt, H. F. (2013). Musical and social communication in expert orchestral performance. *Psychology of Music, 0*(0), 1–19. https://doi.org/10.1177/0305735613491998

Dow, G. (2001). Allocating control over firms: Stock markets versus membership markets. *Review of Industrial Organization, 1*(2), 201–218. https://www.jstor.org/stable/41798995

Dow, G. (2003). *Governing the firm: Workers' control in theory and practice*. Cambridge University Press.

Dow, G. (2018). *The labor-managed firm: Theoretical foundations*. Cambridge University Press.

Faulkner, R. (1973). Orchestra interaction: Some features of communication and authority in an artistic organization. *The Sociological Quarterly, 14*(2), 147–157. https://www.jstor.org/stable/4105966

Flanagan, R. (2012). *The perilous life of symphony orchestras: Artistic triumphs and economic challenges*. Yale University Press.

Furubotn, E. G. (1976). The long-run analysis of the labor-managed firm: An alternative interpretation. *American Economic Review, 66*(1), 104–123. http://www.jstor.org/stable/1804949

Glynn, M. (2008). Maestro or manager? Examining the role of the music director in a symphony orchestra. In J. Lampel, J. Shamsie, & T. Lant (Eds.), *The business of culture: Strategic perspectives on entertainment and media*. Taylor & Francis.

González-Ricoy, I., & Magaña, P. (2024). The demos of the democratic firm. *Politics, Philosophy & Economics, 23*(4), 346–367. https://doi.org/10.1177/1470594X241239986

Hansmann, H. (1990). When does worker ownership work? ESOPs, law firms, codetermination, and economic democracy. *Yale Law Journal, 99*(8), 1749–1816. https://doi.org/10.2307/796676

Hansmann, H. (1996). *The ownership of enterprise*. The Belknap Press of Harvard University Press.

Herman, A. (2022). *Orchestra management: Models and repertoires for the symphony orchestra* (1st ed.). Routledge.

Herman, A. (2023). *Orchestra management: Models and repertoires for the symphony orchestra*. Routledge.

Hesmondhalgh, D., & Baker, S. (2011). *Creative labour: Media work in three cultural industries*. Routledge. https://doi.org/10.4324/9780203855881

Holoman, D. K. (2012). *The orchestra: A very short introduction*. Oxford University Press.

Jensen, M., & Meckling, W. (1979). Rights and production functions: An application to labor-managed firms and codetermination. *Journal of Business, 52*(4), 469–506. https://www.jstor.org/stable/2352442

Johansson, Y. L., & Theorell, T. (2003). Satisfaction with work task quality correlates with employee health. *Medical Problems of Performing Artists, 18*(4), 141–149. https://www.jstor.org/stable/48710968

Jossa, B. (2017). *Labour managed firms and post-capitalism*. Routledge. https://doi.org/10.4324/9781315299518

Jossa, B. (2018). *A new model of socialism: Democratising economic production*. Edward Elgar. https://doi.org/10.4337/9781788117838

Khodyakov, D. (2007). The complexity of trust-control relationships in creative organizations: Insights from a qualitative analysis of a conductorless orchestra. *Social Forces, 86*(1), 1–22. https://www.jstor.org/stable/4495025

Krampe, R. T., & Ericsson, K. A. (1995). Deliberate practice and elite musical performance. In J. Rink (Ed.), *The practice of performance: Studies in musical interpretation*. Cambridge University Press. https://doi.org/10.1017/CBO9780511552366.005

Kruse, D. (Ed.). (2013). *Sharing ownership, profits, and decision-making in the 21st century*. Emerald.

Ladkin, D., & Bathurst, R. (2012). Performing leadership: Observations from the world of music. *Administrative Sciences, 2*(1), 99–119. https://doi.org/10.3390/admsci2010099

Leblebici, H., & Sherer, P. D. (2015). Governance in professional service firms, from structural and cultural to legal normative views. In L. Empson, D. Muzio, & J. Broschak (Eds.), *The Oxford handbook of professional service firms*. Oxford University Press.

Lehman, E. V. (2002). *Models of self-governance and workplace democracy: A comparison of select orchestras in Germany, the U.S. and U.K* (Doctoral dissertation). City University London. http://openaccess.city.ac.uk/7618/

London Mozart Players. (2014). *Press Release February 12th 2014 - "A Renaissance for the London Mozart Players!"*. London Mozart Players. Accessed 21 October 2025 http://london-mozartplayers.com/press-release-february-12th-2014/

London Mozart Players. (2015). *London Mozart Players - a new management structure*. London Mozart Players. Accessed 21 October 2025. https://www.londonmozartplayers.com/london-mozart-players-a-new-management-structure/

London Mozart Players. (2021). *Introducing our new chief executive*. London Mozart Players. https://www.londonmozartplayers.com/wp-content/uploads/2021/10/LMP-Flynn-Le-Brocq-press-release.pdf

Meade, J. E. (1972). The theory of labour-managed firms and of profit sharing. *The Economic Journal, 82*(325), 402–428. https://doi.org/10.2307/2229945

Mintzberg, H. (1998). Covert leadership: Notes on managing professionals. *Harvard Business Review, 97*(6), 140–147. https://hbr.org/1998/11/covert-leadership-notes-on-managing-professionals

New York Philharmonic. (1909). *Meeting of the Philharmonic Society February 12 1909*. New York Philharmonic. https://archives.nyphil.org/index.php/artifact/d1c98238-4c2d-4487-9043-e0666edf90de-0.1/fullview#page/92/mode/2up

Parasuraman, S., & Purohit, Y. S. (2000). Distress and boredom among orchestra musicians: The two faces of stress. *Journal of Occupational Health Psychology, 5*(1), 74–83.

Pencavel, J. (2013). The economics of worker cooperatives. In *Elgar research reviews in economics*. Edward Elgar. https://doi.org/10.4337/9781784710545

Pencavel, J., Pistaferri, L., & Schivardi, F. (2006). Wages, employment, and capital in capitalist and worker-owned firms. *Industrial and Labor Relations Review, 60*(1), 23–44. http://www.jstor.org/stable/25067573

Pompe, J., Tamburri, L., & Munn, J. (2011). Factors that influence programming decisions of us symphony orchestras. *Journal of Cultural Economics, 35*(3), 167–184.

Pompe, J., Tamburri, L., & Munn, J. (2013). Symphony concert demand: Does programming matter? *Journal of Arts Management, Law & Society, 43*(4), 215–228. https://doi.org/10.1080/10632921.2013.818085

Rickert, D. L., Barrett, M. S., & Ackermann, B. J. (2013). Injury and the orchestral environment: Part I. The role of work organisation and psychosocial factors in injury risk. *Medical Problems of Performing Artists, 28*(4), 219–229.

Rothschild, J. (2012). Co-operative workplaces, collaborative communities: An introduction to economic self-help and mutual aid. *International Journal of Self Help & Self Care, 6*(2), 121. https://doi.org/10.2190/SH.6.2.b

Rothschild, J., & Allen Whitt, J. (1986). *The cooperative workplace: Potentials and dilemmas of organisational democracy and participation*. Cambridge University Press.
Rothschild, J., & Russell, R. (1986). Alternatives to bureaucracy: Democratic participation in the economy. *Annual Review of Sociology, 12*, 307. https://doi.org/10.1146/annurev.so.12.080186.001515
Rothschild, J., & Stephenson, M. (2009). The meaning of democracy in non-profit and community organizations. *American Behavioral Scientist, 52*(7), 800–806. https://doi.org/10.1177/0002764208328734
Rothschild-Whitt, J. (1979). The collectivist organization: An alternative to rational-bureaucratic models. *American Sociological Review, 44*(4), 509–527. https://doi.org/10.2307/2094585
Schulz, W. (1981). Analysis of a symphony orchestra (Sociological and Sociopsychological Aspects). In M. Piperek (Ed.), *Stress and Music, Medical, Psychological, Sociological and Legal Strain Factors in a Symphony Orchestra Musician's Profession*. Braumüller.
Seifter, H., & Economy, P. (2001). *Leadership ensemble, lessons in collaborative management from the world's only conductorless orchestra*. Times Books.
Shipper, F. (Ed.). (2014). *Shared entrepreneurship; A path to engaged employee ownership*. Palgrave Macmillan.
Stehr, P. (2022). The boundary problem in workplace democracy: Who constitutes the corporate demos? *Political Theory, 51*(3), 507–529. https://doi.org/10.1177/00905917221131821
Strauss, G. (1998). An overview. In F. Heller, E. Pusić, G. Strauss, & B. Wilpert (Eds.), *Organizational participation, myth and reality*. Oxford University Press.
Taylor, K. (2015). Learning from the co-operative institutional model: How to enhance organizational robustness of third sector organizations with more pluralistic forms of governance. *Administrative Sciences, 5*(3), 148–164. https://doi.org/10.3390/admsci5030148
Vienna Philharmonic. (n.d.) *A Symbiotic Relationship: Vienna State Opera/Vienna Philharmonic*. Accessed 20 October 2025. https://www.wienerphilharmoniker.at/en/orchestra/tradition
Wallace, H. R. (2006). *Spirit of the orchestra*. Orchestra of the Age of Enlightenment.

Chapter 8
Sustaining Democracy in an Orchestra

8.1 Adaptability, Social Energy, Organisational Identity

At the heart of this book sits the question about whether an LMF's control by its workers is sustainable or contains the seeds of its own degeneration. How do player-governed orchestras sustain their governance structures? Is labour-management a transitory or immature arrangement that either withers or "ripens" into control by a small subset of workers, capital owners, or a board of external directors? To conclude the book, the following three sections collect the research findings on how my cohort of PGOs sustain player-governance under a trio of rubrics. These focus on the roles played by adaptability, social interaction, and the energies it produces, and the fostering of musical quality in a player-governed context. The chapter is central to the book's contribution to our understanding of labour-management as it draws on my empirical research to demonstrate how player-governance can be sustained and the threat of degeneration can be countered. It extends the understanding of labour-management in the context of not-for-profit creative firms and highlights the ongoing viability of such governance.

8.2 Countering the Degeneration Threat

Sustainability and degeneration are opposites. So, while my research foregrounds questions of sustainability in player-governance, the threat of degeneration also needs considering. Do the rationales of player-governance contain tendencies that may lead to the formation of oligarchies in these firms? Is there a risk that a small clique of members will gradually, perhaps even unwittingly or with good intent, accumulate authority and reduce democratic decision-making? Does this risk grow as the firms become older and founding members move on? If so, how are the PGOs

B. Long, *Democratising Orchestras*, Music Business Research,
https://doi.org/10.1007/978-3-032-17399-7_8

studied countering such risks and sustaining genuinely participatory player-governance? Such questions sit at the heart of this chapter, and the current section's overview of the "degeneration thesis" (Cornforth, 1995, p. 488). In what follows I explore how PGOs sustain their governance in the face of these degenerative tendencies.

Theoretical and empirical studies over more than a century have failed to reach general agreement on whether labour-management, and in this case player-governance, is inherently degenerative (Dow, 2018; Pencavel, 2013). In this study, I did not seek to prove or disprove the degeneration thesis; instead, I regard degeneration as a risk or threat. Risks and threats do not inevitably materialise, and when they do, they can be reduced or countered. The threat of degeneration in PGOs needs to be contextualised. There are factors involved beyond the economic considerations that feature prominently in the theoretical writing on degeneration in LMFs (Ben-Ner, 1988a; Cornforth, 1995; Dow, 2003, 2018; Rothschild & Russell, 1986; Stryjan, 1989). In the case of PGOs, degeneration in participatory decision-making may result from an unwillingness of members to take on governance work. Creating and sustaining an environment in which PGO members are willing to take on such activity means more than offering economic incentives (Charmettant, 2024). The opportunity to be involved in artistic decision-making is critical. Equally, a virtuous cycle of engagement, commitment, and sense of responsibility that is fostered by player-governance can, in turn, boost the readiness of members to contribute to the sustainability of player-governance by taking on governance roles.

Player-governed orchestras face further degenerative threats to their governance. Among these threats is declining member commitment to player-governance if, for example, other motivations for joining become dominant. The six firms studied in this research all offer potential members attractive artistic and professional opportunities that may relegate any part played by player-governance to insignificance. In a sector characterised by widespread precarious employment (Williamson & Cloonan, 2016), the PGOs studied offer modest employment security, even if they do not offer the high levels of protection that musicians in tenured orchestras enjoy. There is, then, a risk that new members are primarily attracted by the artistic opportunities and work offered, and have little interest in player-governance as an idea or in practically supporting it by taking on governance roles.

Lack of preparedness to take on governance roles among new members may spawn a leadership group whose connection to the broader membership becomes tenuous. This can occur if other members free-ride on the governance and management work of the core group. A PGO drifting towards oligarchic control by a small coterie of quasi-permanent artistic leaders, or a traditional artistic director, jeopardises the engagement and commitment that are fostered by player-governance. The shared artistic decision-making that is fostered by participation, and the possibility of renegotiating the traditional hierarchies of orchestral work may also be jeopardised. Such a danger is exacerbated if there is a widespread tendency for principal players to avoid the potential for peer animosity that may result from governance work. That situation may further reduce the pool of potential governance officers. This potential disinterest in, or apathy towards, the principles and practice of player-governance is an additional degenerative threat to the sustainability of PGOs.

In Chaps. 4, 5 and this chapter I analysed and explored the essential governance features of the PGOs featured in this book. The attention now shifts to their responses to the risk of degeneration, and thus how they sustain their governance structures. The essential findings in the following three sections are grouped under rubrics that label how these PGOs sustain player-governance: adaptability, social interaction, and the fostering of musical quality. The next section looks at how these PGOs implement adaptive and flexible approaches to participation as responses to degeneration and as tools to foster governance sustainability. Maximising member involvement in decision-making within these PGOs is central to the sustainability of their governance structures. However, the logics of adaptation and responsiveness come up against counteracting factors. In particular, the acknowledgement and balancing of the hierarchies of work in orchestras are critical. These PGOs illustrate the essential role of adaptability and how they foster, institutionalise, and carefully balance it with other drivers.

8.3 Adaptability Builds Sustainability

That the flexibility of player-governance is essential to its longevity was clearly enunciated at various points in the three interview-based chapters. Adaptability and sustainability go hand in hand. The PGOs studied are not orthodox LMFs, even if their control models overlap with many of the conditions for labour-management that were explored in Chap. 2. PGOs and their workers use practices that necessitate adaptive approaches to the principles of labour-management theories. By pursuing such adaptive processes, these PGOs demonstrate how control by workers operates in contexts beyond the firms typically scrutinised in the LMF literature. What follows outlines how these PGOs adapt labour-management to the dynamics, drivers, and pressures of orchestras and their musicians and, in so doing, how they create specialised and customised governance systems.

The concept of adaptability in firms has been the subject of wide-ranging research, including articles on the connection between adaptability and innovativeness (Tuominen et al., 2004), competitive advantage (Reeves & Deimler, 2011), profitability (Takii, 2007), and adaptability in approaches to the market (Oktemgil & Greenley, 1997). However, flexibility and adaptability have received scant attention in the LMF literature. Theorists often treat LMFs as desiccated, standardised, and static, thereby ignoring firms' dynamic contexts and the diverse labour conditions of their workers. A branch of the literature does posit that LMFs and producer cooperatives display evolutionary tendencies approximating to a life cycle (Batstone, 1983; Ben-Ner, 1988a; Stryjan, 1989). Generally, though, theorists in the field have not considered labour-management's flexibility, malleability, and transformative potential. Such omissions are perhaps unavoidable in high-level theories. In response, empirical and focused studies like this book contribute to the field by foregrounding labour-management's adaptability and evolutionary possibilities.

Chapter 2 described how, based on relevant theories, orchestras were suitable sites for labour-management. But they are also hybrid, multidimensional organisations, and sustaining player-governance in these firms requires that it is adaptable and flexible to suit their changing needs. The ability of PGOs to embrace and negotiate their fundamental multidimensionality spans their attempts to sustain their firms' governance. This adaptability reappeared at various points during the interviews presented in Chaps. 4, 5 and this chapter. A diverse range of factors, practices, and logics combine to sustain player-governance in the organisations studied. However, none of these factors alone can counteract the potential for degeneration or obviate the need for ongoing vigilance and awareness. Player-governance, like labour-management more broadly, is a continuous process of multilateral balancing and renegotiation rather than a steady state of being or a point of arrival. Charting the ability of complex and hybrid organisations such as orchestras to adapt labour-management to their needs is one of the essential contributions this book makes.

Like orchestras themselves, orchestral workers are considerably more complex and diverse than the hypothetical workers described in most of the labour-management literature. The musicians interviewed for this research bring unique human capital and work practices to player-governance. They also have specific demands and expectations of labour-management. Deep and long-term commitments to their profession mark these workers. Musicians own their tools of trade (instruments). Their training not only begins at a very early age but emphasises the development of individual and soloistic skills (Bennett, 2005, 2008). The work routines of orchestral players combine ensemble teamwork with solitary preparation and practice away from the organisation. PGO members embody high levels of individual entrepreneurship and identification with their specific work. Yet orchestral work is team-focused and the musicians interviewed are not entrepreneurs in the individualistic sense often associated with that term. Orchestral players are individualistic team workers. The tensions inherent in such a formulation necessitate a broad and adaptive conceptualisation of workers in LMFs.

8.3.1 Orchestras' Competing Logics and Hybrid Governance Structures Call for Adaptability in Labour-Management

The need of PGOs and their members to continuously balance conflicting and competing logics, interests, and drivers was the most prominent recurring element in the governance structures and operations of the firms studied for this book. Competing economic rationales were observed at the setup stage. Conflicting artistic and economic logics are involved when deciding that some musicians are enfranchised while others are engaged as supernumeraries and management staff are employed as hired labour. Balancing the competing ideas involved when musicians take artistic control, but still share it with authority figures such as conductors, is also essential to sustaining player-governance. In addition, competing interests must be managed when peers undertake mutual monitoring with the aim of optimising performance. All of these elements are best understood as an adaptive embrace and management of a multidimensionality and hybridity that is essential to player-governance. At each of these inflection points, these PGOs are ready to adapt the fundamentals of labour-management to create a sustainable balancing of the conflicting logics they embody.

As a result of the factors described above, no single labour-management paradigm suffices to describe the governance structures observed in the PGOs considered in this book. These firms do not fit neatly into a single governance model. They display features of the classical labour-management studied in the literature, but differ through their widespread and systematic use of hired labour. In this respect, their structures display elements of professional partnerships and knowledge-intensive firms. However, these PGOs do not require their members to contribute to firm capital, nor do they create the tradable shares in their firms that are typical of law firms, medical practices, or business consultancies (Hansmann, 1990). The profit sharing that is central to most LMFs is not relevant to these firms. Instead of clearly aligning with any single organisational model, the PGOs studied seek to balance and align multiple logics, competing organisational identities, and dispersed, multilateral power structures.

Some of the factors observed in these PGOs are, nevertheless, common to all orchestras and ensembles. They serve artistic logics that also direct management decisions while adhering to the principles of (not-for-profit) commercial operations. PGOs incorporate further logics that add other dimensions to the already complex management and governance structures of orchestras. Preeminent among these additional dimensions is, of course, their participatory and democratic decision-making practices. These infuse the operations of PGOs. In some instances, they build strengths (through high levels of engagement, commitment, and responsibility). In others, they add complexity, for example, when it comes to mutual monitoring, managing generational change, and recruitment. The ability and extent to which these PGOs are able to understand, embrace, and harness the complex multidimensionality that is the essence of player-governance determines in large part their governance and organisational sustainability.

8.3.2 *Fields of Tension: Artistic*

The PGOs considered in this study attempt to combine and resolve two main areas of tension. The first exists between the perspectives of highly trained professionals seeking to exercise greater control over their artistic work than is available in comparable organisations, while still availing themselves of efficiencies that evolved in the traditional hierarchical model of orchestral operation. In the second field of conflicting pressures, PGO members form a group of workers seeking to maximise their employment security in a sector characterised by high levels of precarious work and while working within the varying labour-demand structures of music performance. Here too tensions can arise when these desires come up against the commercial realities of orchestra management. The responses of the PGOs studied to these fields of tension demonstrate the crucial role adaptability and flexibility assume in player-governance.

Members' control of artistic decision-making is the most fundamental feature of the PGOs researched. Every aspect of these firms' operations is impacted by artistic decisions. Such deliberations determine who—if anyone—conducts, who is invited to perform as a soloist, indeed, who plays in the orchestra or ensemble in any given project or performance. Such decisions also establish and maintain the musical profiles and brands of these PGOs. This need among musicians to exercise control of the musical aspects of their work was described in the interviews as "crucial" and the "defining element" in player-governance. It stems from players' deep-seated desires to contribute their knowledge of programming, artistic trends and opportunities, and to increase buy-in, engagement with, and commitment to the core of their work as orchestral musicians. In turn, exercising artistic control builds engagement, satisfaction, commitment, and a strong sense of ownership. Taking artistic control is a central element in player-governance.

Another of the most pervasive examples of multidimensionality in the PGOs considered manifests itself in the basic operating models and identities of these firms. As an organisational form, the orchestra evolved and achieved its initial organisational and artistic apotheosis in late eighteenth-century Europe. Orchestras' adherence to hierarchical control mirrored wider social, political, and economic thinking of that time. By the second half of the twentieth century, those social, political, and economic parameters had been substantially revised and realigned. By then, the role and powers of conductors and music directors in the orchestral hierarchy were beginning to seem anachronistic (Koivunen, 2003). Orchestral musicians increasingly had the skills of highly trained professionals. Treating them as cogs in a machine was outdated. Yet, as the PGOs in this study demonstrated, some elements of the traditional orchestral hierarchy boost artistic efficiency and therefore may merit retention. Closely coordinated action by a large group of performers is the central aim of orchestras and ensembles. Achieving this in the studied PGOs involves judicious use of the leadership and organisational skills of hierarchical authority figures, primary amongst whom are conductors, but on terms and within boundaries set by members. The result is an adaptive amalgam of competing demands: the desire to harness the efficiency of hierarchical organisation, and the demand for musicians to retain control over their work and the high-level artistic decisions it involves. Adapting the flat-hierarchy thinking of labour-management so as to judiciously retain efficient elements of orchestral hierarchy is central to the governance and performance models these PGOs have implemented. Player-governance is sustainable when members are able to understand, embrace, and harness the competing logics that characterise multiple aspects of artistic operations and governance.

8.3.3 *Fields of Tension: Job Security and Hired Labour*

Economic factors also result in tensions that call for flexibility and adaptability. For PGOs, the primary economic driver is the reduction of precarious employment among musicians. The firms in the study were in part established to reduce the exposure of members to precarious work. These PGOs' success in this endeavour is, though, tempered by the reality that they all continue to offer work on a semi-freelance basis. Membership offers more employment security than that available to musicians who rely on short-term engagements, but these PGOs do not offer the tenured positions that many musicians in symphony and theatre orchestras enjoy. Members have a clear incentive to create tenured positions for themselves, but the unpredictable demand structures for musician labour in orchestras mean that doing so would threaten the economic viability and sustainability of their PGOs. The members of the PGOs studied resist the temptation to contract each other on terms that would threaten organisational sustainability, for example, by offering tenure and fixed-hours contracts in the face of the variability in demand for the services of individual players. In exercising such prudence, they prioritise organisational sustainability over short-term employment interests and provide a clear demonstration that organisational sustainability and player-governance can be successfully combined when adaptability is added to the mix.

At the same time an important subset of the workers in these PGOs—the management staff—are engaged as hired labour, typically using fixed-hours, full-entitlement contracts. This results in a paradoxical situation in which the members (musicians) engage management staff on more secure terms than they are able to offer themselves. The divergent treatments of musicians and management staff are based on the different dynamics of the respective labour markets. When considering precarious work in the sector, the PGOs studied clearly "look two ways at once" (Jackall & Levin, 1984, p. 11) in their arrangements for different workers. In Sect. 7.1, I explored the challenges of establishing the most sustainable franchise in a PGO. My analysis of the PGOs I studied indicates that the LMF literature overstates the risk of degeneration created by the engagement of hired labour. The firms studied have managed to counteract the forces observed by Dow (2003, 2018), Pencavel (2013), and others, while being able to successfully embrace the multidimensionality this balancing creates. They make regular use of hired musician labour and their management teams do not become members. But strengths that emerge from player-governance, such as enhanced engagement and commitment to the firm, along with the democratic norms that infused these PGOs from the outset, combine to counteract any temptation to reduce the number of members or to increase the amount of hired labour used.

As their founding members retire, generational change is a challenge for some of the PGOs studied. However, it is not resulting in a cross-generational weakening of player-governance, and new members are being recruited to replace founders. In such cases, being engaged as a supernumerary is often a prelude to membership. The use of such hired labour among musicians further illustrates how the embracing of multiple dimensions constitutes a pillar of the governance and operational models employed by PGOs. They balance the risks of degeneration that the literature highlights with a strongly anchored commitment to player-governance that is buttressed by the positives garnered from the greater engagement and commitment engendered by musicians' artistic control.

The PGOs studied can, then, be seen as an embodiment of the desire to give orchestras an operational model that is more closely aligned with wider political, economic, and social trends towards the greater worker "voice" (Wilkinson et al., 2014) inherent in labour-management, while retaining the useful elements of their traditional hierarchical practices. The PGOs in the study use adaptive governance structures that are comfortable with hybridity. They do not revolutionise the operating and governance structures of orchestras they inherited from several centuries of development. Instead, they adapt, expand, and update those models while embracing flexible understandings of labour-management. The orchestras and ensemble I considered add new elements such as participatory and democratic decision-making to the world of orchestras, while taking on new objectives and concerns, including the desire to offer musicians greater employment security than they have as freelancers.

This section analysed and described how the PGOs studied step outside the boundaries of the theoretical literature's thinking on LMFs. The degeneration hypothesis highlighted by many thinkers on labour-management makes little allowance for the responsive and adaptive evolutionary potential displayed by PGOs. The governance sustainability these firms have achieved is, nonetheless, to a large extent rooted in the adaptability of player-governance. Their form of labour-management has proven able to meld elements of control by workers with key features and practices specific to orchestras and their workers.

This section focused on firms and their adaptability. The next directs the spotlight onto the workers in PGOs.

8.4 How Social Energy Counters Degeneration

The findings presented in this section highlight the social dynamics of PGOs. The LMF literature typically takes firms as the unit of analysis rather than the interactions of members and other stakeholders. The dominance of economists in the field has meant that the key debates have pitted LMFs against capital-controlled firms (Ben-Ner, 1988b; Pencavel & Craig, 1994), sought to explain the rarity of labour-management (Dow, 2003), or pondered the threat of degeneration (Cornforth, 1995; Diefenbach, 2018; Pencavel, 2013). This section treats identity-making and democratisation as critical components of these firms. What follows deepens the literature by presenting findings on the role of member and employee interactions and social energy in PGOs. The findings show that negotiating fluid organisational identities plays a key role in sustaining player-governance, and that a flexible, context-specific and pragmatic approach to participation underpins these PGOs.

I have borrowed and adapted the idea of social energy from the cultural and literary scholar Stephen Greenblatt (1988) (see also Robson, 2008). He proposed social energy as an analytic lens in his study of Shakespearean theatre and its historical context. The concept of social capital now enjoys wider currency, but Greenblatt's idea has attractive and complementary aspects. Attaching the term "capital" to a social construct gives the phenomenon an economic gloss. It hints at individualistic, transactional and acquisitive qualities that are antithetical to social interaction. Social energy, on the other hand, comes closer to the flowing, reactive, generative nature of much social exchange. Social capital fuels social energy, but the contemporary focus on the capital element of the process overshadows subsequent forms of energy and activity. The musicians and orchestral employees who gave interviews for this study call on their social capital as part of their work, but it is the social energy, dynamics, and interactions that most strongly emerged and play the most significant part in countering degeneration in these PGOs.

This preferencing of social energy as an explanatory construct also aligns well with the essence of orchestral work. Orchestras embody and build on social and creative energies. Teamwork is core to their onstage operations. These dynamics run through most aspects of player-governance canvassed in this book, be it the realignment of the orchestra–conductor/leader relationship, the redirection of authority between musicians and management, or the challenges of mutual monitoring required by player-governance.

What follows has a two-part structure based around aspects of member and employee social energies. My initial focus is the formation and continuous negotiation of shared intra-organisational identities and the self-reinforcing roles they play in sustaining player-governance. In the second substantive section, I consider how multiple elements of participation counter degenerative tendencies in control by members.

8.4.1 The Orchestra as Collective Idea: Intra-Organisational Identity and Sustainability

Creating, negotiating, and balancing multiple and fluid intra-organisational identities are critical ingredients of the social energy observed among PGO members and staff. A range of ideas on company identity have been explored in the management, organisational, and psychology literatures (Bartel et al., 2007; Watkiss & Glynn, 2016; Whetten, 2006). Here the emphasis falls on those conceptualisations that members and other internal stakeholders develop for their orchestras. Under consideration is how PGO members and employees regard and identify with their firms and how these relationships contribute to the structure's sustainability. PGO brands and marketplace identities play roles in their commercial success. First, though, the study of PGOs calls for an appreciation of how members and employees regard and identify with their firms. Understanding PGOs means considering the identities their stakeholders give them.

From this internal perspective, a firm's identity is not a "property of the organization" (Watkiss & Glynn, 2016, p. 319). Instead, members and other stakeholders individually and collectively fashion an idea of what the firm represents, what its mission and purpose are, and how they, as members, identify with this construct (Watts, 2010). In the words of Watkiss and Glynn (2016), "the locus of identity resides in the interpretive schemas of the various organizational members" (p. 319). Such identities are vital in the PGOs studied. Player-governance involves members' negotiating, shaping, and managing a "collective sense of 'what we do' as an organisation" (ibid.). Control by musicians includes their power and responsibility to shape and direct the vision, mission, and identity they give to their firms.

Pratt (2016) built further on such concepts, locating a "normative-utilitarian dimension" (p. 107) in organisational identities. On this spectrum, "utilitarian identities represent a 'for-profit,' 'monetary,' or 'economic' focused self-definition" while "normative identities, by contrast, are non-economic and can represent a variety of religious, cultural, aesthetic, and similarly non-monetary focused identities" (ibid). Pratt's bifurcation mirrors the commercial/artistic hybridity at the core of orchestras. How do PGOs reconcile these bifurcated organisational identities? Do the high levels of engagement and commitment the interviewees articulated shape how they think about their PGOs? Do these PGOs maintain a collective internal identity as their founding members leave? If so, does it evolve? What is the link between sustaining such an identity and sustaining player-governance? These and similar questions underlie what follows.

The identities, visions, and missions of the PGOs studied are not (or are no longer) those of individual founders who exercise almost unfettered control. Instead, these firms embody the shared ideas and creativity of their founding members or of those who introduced player-governance. To these founding visions are added the interest and thinking of musicians who joined after the setup phase. This diversity of experiences means that creating shared, open, and fluid identities is central to player-governance. These identities and the continuing negotiation that shapes them emerged from comments made by several interviewees. Mario described understanding his orchestra as either an embodiment of its current members' thinking or as an "open container" that future members could continue to develop. He outlined several scenarios, ranging from the orchestra as an inclusive "life-form" to one in which the firm only works for a subgroup. Others highlighted a sense of ownership and collective "spirit" in their PGOs. The intra-organisational identities collectively forged by these PGO members reflect the participatory essence of labour-management.

The differing identities described by Mario and other interviewees echo the deep-seated challenges that shape control by musicians. The sustainability of such governance requires members to move beyond individual interests and thinking. It calls for a collective "idea" of the orchestra, as Mario put it. This understanding, in turn, must become an "open container" with the flexibility to adapt and evolve in response to membership changes. The last founding member of several of the studied PGOs will retire in the next few years; then, the idea of each orchestra will be institutionalised as an ongoing firm and more than a personal project of visionary founders. This evolution from a newly established "stage-of-life project" (Mario) and experiment in participatory governance to a responsive firm that can accommodate members' coming and going is crucial to long-term governance viability. Such a development tests the ability of new PGOs to institutionalise control by musicians. Sustained player-governance demands a fluid, multifaceted, and regenerative shared identity of the type I observed in the PGOs studied for this book.

The organisational identities of these PGOs embody their plurality as artistic and commercial firms. A normative identity, in Pratt's (2016) sense, is fostered when members take artistic control. Making essential musical decisions such as repertoire planning, the engagement of conductors and soloists, and building orchestra brands allows musicians to create normative identities for their firms. Doing so mirrors the utilitarian identity associated with addressing employment security concerns. Musicians' desire to exert control over their work is key to creating a shared "idea" of their PGOs, defining their firms, and fostering the engagement and commitment that are central to the sustainability of player-governance.

Intra-organisational identity is, then, a construct in a two-way relationship with members who play active roles in shaping the collective ideas of their PGOs. The resulting identities—while remaining fluid and the subject of constant negotiation—in turn act as objects of engagement, commitment, and perceived responsibility. Player-governance amplifies these identity negotiations when the high levels of engagement, commitment, and sense of responsibility that it offers, demands, and fosters increase members' identification with their firms. Members shape collective, bottom-up identities. These constructs then shape the interactions between members by providing "performative repertoires" (Watkiss & Glynn, 2016, p. 324) to which members relate. Player-governance creates opportunities and fora for musicians to shape the internal ideas of their PGOs, while also allowing players to develop strong identificatory bonds with their PGOs and the identities they embody. Identity and identification exist in a virtuous and sustainable cycle of social energy.

Sustaining control by musicians depends on protecting and fostering this circle. Devoid of such a circle's reinforcing energy, PGOs face declining engagement and members' pursuit of outside interests, as Richard mentioned. This loss of engagement may then endanger musicians' willingness to take on the committee and board work at the core of player-governance. Keeping members engaged is a vital role for intra-organisational identities. The recurrent generating of these shared visions and "interpretive schemas" (Watkiss & Glynn, 2016, p. 319) is crucial for the survival of control by musicians. Player-governance creates both openings and challenges for the fostering and negotiating of these identities. Its participatory ethos means that members' ideas concerning their PGOs are bottom-up constructs built on democratic decision-making, sensemaking (Weick, 1995), and social energy (Greenblatt, 1988). Such identities, in turn, clear the way for high levels of engagement, sense of responsibility, and commitment to the firm. The result is a self-fortifying cycle that sustains these PGOs' governance. Constructing a shared organisational identity goes hand in hand with sustaining player-governance. From this discussion of the orchestra as shared idea and identity, I move to consider member participation in player-governance, the next key ingredient.

8.4.2 *Pragmatic Democratisation, Participation, and Governance Sustainability*

Two contrasting approaches were observed in the ways these PGOs deal with participatory decision-making. Member decision-making is shaped by these PGOs' adapting of democracy to the specifics of work and authority in orchestras. Remoulding artistic hierarchies—in particular, the orchestra–conductor relationship—contrasts with the democratising of decision-making observed in the governance realm. In most cases, my interviewees see benefits in retaining some hierarchy in music performance. PGO members are prepared to delegate considerable control to conductors or performance directors, thus exploiting any benefits from having "a little bit of autocracy" (Martin). In some situations, there may be musical imperatives to the use of a conductor, for example, when works with many performers needing central coordination are on the programme. Nevertheless, five of the six firms studied operate without an artistic or musical director, though some conductors also serve as artistic partners, a role that involves them providing advice on artistic planning. Only one of the firms in the study has a music director. These PGOs thus embrace performance hierarchies at members' discretion and when using conductors boosts efficiency and artistic quality.

Authority structures are much flatter in the governance and management contexts than on stage. In those contexts, a drive to flatten decision-making power is clearly apparent. The interviewees repeatedly emphasised the primacy of their retaining governance control. Some spoke of "empowering ourselves", others of the orchestra belonging to the members and of wanting to "find our own way" (Sophie). Two approaches thus emerge: the delegation of authority and the retaining of control hierarchies in musical production alongside flattened control structures and participatory decision-making in the governance context. Such hybridity illustrates what might be thought of as pragmatic democratisation. This approach responds to and sustains control by musicians. It girds these firms' hybridity and their balancing of competing logics and energies as they seek to sustain their governance structures. The labour-management literature makes little allowance for such flexibility and pragmatism. These findings on the pragmatic application of democratic thinking enrich the understanding of LMFs and player-governance in the orchestra world.

The pragmatic democratisation adopted by PGOs can, however, cause friction when governance hierarchies do not align with musical proficiency or seniority. Angela, a section leader who does not have a governance role, alluded to the problems that can arise when the two realms collide. Richard described how the pressures of solo performance required of section leaders might make them less likely to take on what he called "highly exposed positions" in governance. A further polarity emerges from the pragmatic democratisation model. It materialises between direct and representative democracy and the disparate types and levels of participation these two poles represent. Balancing these polarities of hierarchy and participation is a central challenge for player-governance and its sustainability.

What is at stake if the PGOs studied are unable to sustainably balance the structural polarities of orchestra management and governance? What indicates that the dynamics are unbalanced? Efficiency is the first factor to consider. Direct democracy may create efficiency costs if all members are involved in routine decision-making (Dow, 2018). Failing to retain a balance between direct and representative democracy imposes potentially unsustainable costs on PGOs (ibid.). The weakening of a PGO's participatory decision-making becomes the most acute degenerative danger if it goes too far towards preferencing representative over direct democracy. Perceptions of disenfranchisement can emerge if members feel that their voices are given insufficient weight in a governance system that moves too far toward representative democracy. Any efficiency benefits of such a move must be balanced against the needs for members to sense that their membership and enfranchisement have meaning.

To sustain player-governance, the PGOs in this research ensure that the proportion of players who are engaged as supernumeraries does not grow to the point at which members function as an oligarchy. The risk here of a tendency towards oligarchy and subsequent degeneration in participation is not of a financial nature, but rather is based on musical or organisational seniority or competence. Degeneration into a structure characterised by an enfranchised membership that declines as a share of the total workforce and that is devoid of genuinely participatory decision-making is the greatest risk for a PGO that is unable to balance the competing hierarchies, polarities, and tensions at the heart of player-governance.

The role of participation in these PGOs, nevertheless, concerns more than balancing the various drivers that shared decision-making involves. Participation also melds engagement, loyalty, and human capital. The literature suggests that engagement is key to retaining workers and can "significantly affect employee retention, productivity and loyalty" (Lockwood, 2007, p. 2). The interviewees' ideas also showed how participation fosters elements such as engagement and commitment, which in turn are frequently linked to governance sustainability and organisational success. Engagement plays a further crucial role in sectors—such as music performance—that rely on high levels of human capital and retaining essential workers (Callan & Lawrence, 2009). Despite orchestras' dependence on their players' skills, most offer musicians very limited opportunities for career progression (Piperek, 1981). In the absence of vertical career advancement, these PGOs create alternative opportunities for professional development in the form of participation and engagement in governance and management. Such openings help generate sustained member engagement and commitment. Members' participation in the control of their PGOs builds engagement and loyalty while harnessing their human capital to the success of these firms.

Kahn's (1990) emphasis on engagement's alignment between "preferred self" tasks, and organisations is instructive. He observed that "people who are personally engaged keep their selves within a role, without sacrificing one for the other" (ibid., p. 700). My interviewees preferred terms such as "personality" to "preferred self", but when Richard spoke of "someone's personality [being] active and present" and player-governance ensuring "you are allowed to be present as a personality", it became clear that engagement and sustained high-level performance were intimately linked in these PGOs. Such observations suggest a reconceptualisation of Macey et al.'s (2009) model of engagement away from their linear, unidirectional understanding to one that is circular, as depicted in Fig. 8.1. This revised model also features an element that can be conceived of as akin to a feedback loop, through which organisational citizenship behaviours (OCBs) (Podsakoff et al., 2016) contribute to the sustainability of the engagement-facilitating environment that Macey et al. (2009) position at the beginning of their model.

In this understanding, player-governance functions as an environment that fosters feelings of engagement among musicians. This engagement then supports OCBs such as serving on governance committees, developing concert programmes,

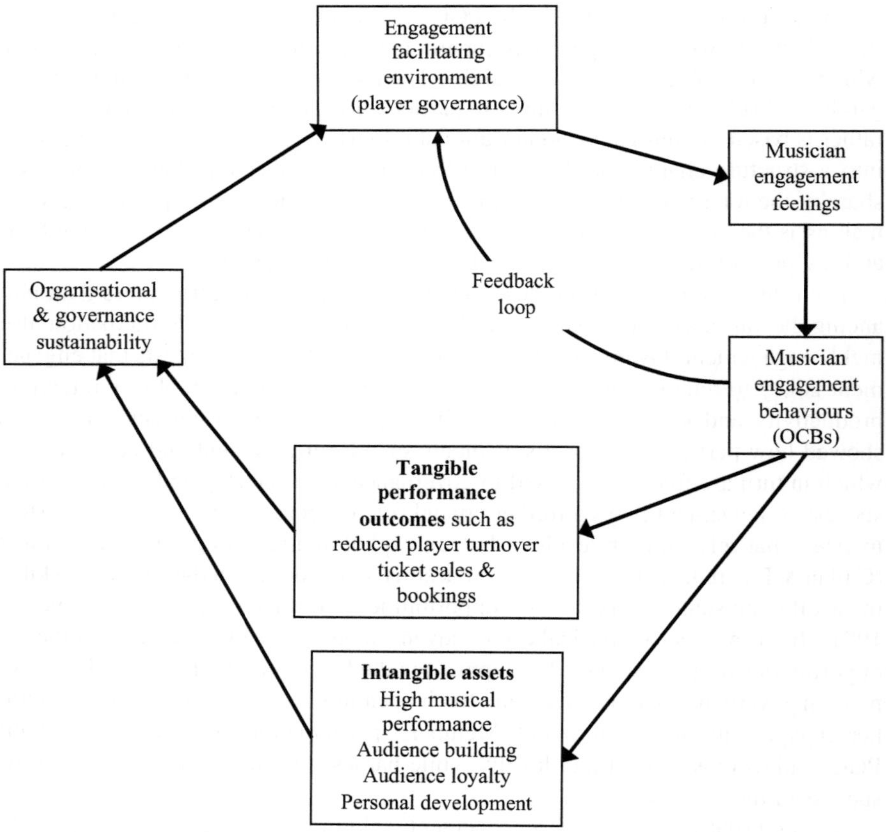

Fig. 8.1 Cyclical conception of the engagement model proposed by Macey et al. (2009)

or educational projects. A further virtuous circle becomes apparent. Player-governance makes engagement and commitment possible, while the behaviours that result from that engagement and commitment help make player-governance sustainable. Other tangible performance outcomes and intangible assets are also founded on and supported by engagement behaviours among musicians. Continuing around the circle, these provide the foundations of governance sustainability.

This section covered some of the core challenges of player-governance. Participation, in its myriad forms, is the defining element of the PGOs I researched for this book. The central element of the sustainability of player-governance consists of member participation in decision-making, of the engagement, commitment, and sense of responsibility that members develop and that can create a mutually supportive, virtuous circle, and the collective, participatory negotiation of intra-organisational identities. Participation in these PGOs is a complex field. Frictions can arise between the parallel sites of decision-making—governance and performance. The former aspires to flat and high-participation hierarchies, while in performance, members retain more of the traditional hierarchies embodied by conductors and section leaders, even if these control structures are fundamentally renegotiated and rebalanced by player-governance. The various participation strategies, responses, and processes developed by the PGOs in the research cohort demonstrate that player-governance is sustainable and that successful management of participation is a potent antidote to the risk of degeneration.

The third cluster of findings congeals around the theme of performance optimisation and its connection to governance sustainability. A sustainable governance structure must also be one that fosters and facilitates high performance. The central challenge here is achieving and maintaining peak performance in a context of mutual monitoring by musicians. It is to this theme that the discussion now turns.

8.5 Musical Quality, Player-Governance, Sustainability

The third group of findings concerns the relationship between player-governance and musical quality. The ability to perform regularly at the highest possible level is essential for an orchestra or ensemble (Lagrosen & Lagrosen, 2017). Governance and management systems must facilitate and support great music-making. If player-governance cannot enable sustained high-quality performance, the model itself will prove unsustainable, the victim not so much of degeneration as of marketplace rejection. The findings of this section highlight the difficulties associated with mutual monitoring, recruitment, and generational change in PGOs. It also shows that these PGOs, nevertheless, implement player-governance such that it contributes to and supports high musical quality.

The details of mutual monitoring vary between LMFs. The basic principle, though, is that the members monitor the work of their peers and decide on any actions necessary to address performance deficiencies. A lack of objective measures for musicians' artistic proficiency is, though, a challenge for peer monitoring in orchestras. Performance optimisation in these PGOs becomes complicated because the mutual monitoring systems they use become contested in the absence of clear and generally accepted quality measures. Without such gauges, musicians' monitoring of each other creates a range of interpersonal and psychological dynamics that raises the stakes involved in performance monitoring.

In some cases, these raised stakes include disillusionment with player-governance to the point at which some members long for a "bad guy" monitor in the form of a music director/conductor. This tension is the focus of the first subsection below. The second aspect considered—generational change—may follow from performance problems, but the discussion also deals with the importance of maintaining player-governance as post-foundation members join and founders move on. The final subsection highlights the unusual, multi-step nature of the recruitment processes required by these PGOs as they take on hired labour before, in some cases, enfranchising such players as members.

8.5.1 Mutual Monitoring and Governance Sustainability

The labour-management literature mostly holds that mutual monitoring among workers is more effective and efficient than hierarchical supervision (Ben-Ner, 1988a; Hansmann, 1990, 1996). Dow (2001) noted that "mutual monitoring is cheap and accurate compared with monitoring by supervisors" (p. 214). In a similar vein, Bowles and Gintis (1993) argued that one of the reasons for the "superior efficiency of the democratic firm" is that it has "monitoring mechanisms unavailable or prohibitively expensive for the capitalist firm" (p. 93). Hansmann (1990) added the idea of self-monitoring and argued that "by encouraging both self-monitoring and mutual monitoring, worker ownership may offer an important efficiency advantage over investor ownership where monitoring workers is difficult" (p. 1762). Alchian and Demsetz (1972) extrapolated such thinking to different industries and concluded that the possibility of mutual monitoring favours partnerships of the type observed in PGOs. They found that

> Team production in artistic or professional intellectual skills will more likely be by partnerships than other types of team production. This amounts to market-organized team activity and to a non-employer status. Self-monitoring partnerships, therefore, will be used rather than employer-employee contracts, and these organizations will be small to prevent an excessive dilution of efforts through shirking. (Alchian & Demsetz, 1972, p. 790)

Among the PGOs studied, the use of mutual monitoring proved more complex and multifaceted than suggested by these authors. My research indicates that mutual monitoring in PGOs is not as cheap and accurate as the literature assumes. Theoretical approaches risk oversimplifying the role of workers in organisational monitoring. The psychological burden on workers involved in monitoring colleagues—and in being monitored—can be considerable, but is not generally acknowledged in the literature, with its focus on financial costs. Bowles and Gintis

(1993) were a rare exception when they acknowledged that "it may be argued that mutual monitoring introduces sufficient discord within a work team to undermine the positive effect of participation on worker productivity" (p. 93). They, nevertheless, concluded that "mutual monitoring in a democratic setting should strengthen the participation effect, in part by enhancing the perception of equal contribution among members, and hence of reducing the incentive to free-ride" (ibid.). Mutual monitoring is essential to player-governance, but my research finds that it imposes considerable burdens on members.

The principal monitors in externally governed orchestras are conductors (or instrumental performance directors) and section leaders. The days when conductors could expose, embarrass, and even dismiss individual players during rehearsals are now generally past. Music directors (who are practically all conductors), nonetheless, retain a central role in performance monitoring, assessing the abilities of applicants in auditions, and resolving difficulties when individual musicians are not playing at the required level (Glynn, 2008). Section leaders also play a role in performance monitoring, usually in tandem with music directors. Peer-to-peer monitoring may occur within hierarchically organised orchestras, but it is generally informal and ad hoc. In effect, performance monitoring in externally governed orchestras is, then, similar to that in other hierarchically organised firms.

Whatever the governance model, the mechanics of monitoring the performance of orchestral musicians are fraught with peril. The central challenge for monitors is the lack of objective and widely accepted measures. None of the conventional yardsticks from other sectors, such as piece rates, revenue generated, or client feedback, are applicable in monitoring individual orchestral musicians. Players' performance may even vary from day to day or as a function of the works on a programme. Modern orchestras perform works from many historical periods and styles. Players are expected to master the various performance practices, sound ideals, and styles required by such breadth, but not all do. Players' performance quality—if definable at all—may vary between works, further complicating any evaluation of their overall proficiency.

PGOs' use of mutual monitoring may help them achieve and sustain high performance in such a challenging context. Mutual monitoring among orchestral players can be more effective than in its hierarchical, conductor-led counterpart when monitoring is difficult or when it strengthens the "participation effect" (Bowles & Gintis, 1993, p. 93). Such benefits can, in turn, boost the sustainability of player-governance, but the extent to which these positives manifest reflects how successfully PGOs manage mutual monitoring. Mutual monitoring also brings burdens, as the interviewees made clear. The central tension that emerges from the research occurs between the hierarchical nature of performance monitoring and the low-hierarchy logic of player-governance. Players' taking control of artistic decision-making in a PGO creates opportunities, but also brings with it responsibilities for the optimisation of performance quality.

Musicians who were trained in hierarchically organised structures may find it difficult to overtly question colleagues' playing. Susanna highlighted the dilemma when such players take on mutual monitoring in PGOs. Players may doubt their right to monitor a peer's performance, yet, as she noted, they have not transferred that right to any other monitor. The interviewees spoke of the difficulties inherent in monitoring their peers' playing, describing the process with words, including "extremely contentious", "super painful", "totally difficult", "brutal", "really awful", and "absolutely the hardest thing we have to do". Indeed, some interviewees mentioned the attractions of an authority figure who would take responsibility for the difficult decisions that are sometimes involved. In few other aspects of the PGO model was the tension between shared responsibility and hierarchy so clear and so present in members' thinking.

The interviewees confirmed that mutual monitoring had the effect of distributing or socialising the tensions inherent in quality management, particularly in the absence of objective and agreed measures. In systems of hierarchically organised monitoring in which a music director assumes the role of the primary monitor, musicians may experience a sense of solidarity with each other as problems of individual performance are identified and resolved. Such a monitor focuses on any resentments of players, allowing them to "all hate the dictator together" (Susanna). Such negativity is between the monitor and the monitored. Mutual monitoring makes any destructive energy multilateral, while potentially reducing solidarity. The collegiality at the heart of player-governance is threatened. The sustainability of player-governance in the face of mutual monitoring is, then, a question of balancing the positive—higher participation and reduced hierarchy—and the burdensome elements it entails, while containing the tensions it creates as much as possible.

8.5.2 Generational Change

The LMF literature highlights concerns about the risk of degeneration in worker participation when members leave their firms. Ben-Ner (1988a) wrote that

> In the long run a worker-owned firm with collective ownership of its assets can expect a gradual reduction in the size of its membership due to retirements and quits accompanied by a continuous increase in the share of hired wage laborers in its workforce. (p. 300)

My research shows that PGOs place considerable importance on counteracting this degenerative tendency. Indeed, despite the burdens of lengthy, multi-stage recruitment procedures, PGOs continue to take on members, even if only to replace departures rather than to increase membership. Engagement as hired labour often serves as the first step to membership. In small, human capital-dependent firms such as the PGOs in this book's research cohort, supernumerary musicians constitute a pool of potential members. An essential difference between the LMFs of the theoretical literature and these PGOs is the lack of entitlement to residual earnings among members of the latter due to their non-profit status. In its absence, members may even have an incentive to increase the number of members. Doing so increases the number of people available to take on governance roles, spreads any financial liabilities and legal responsibilities, and helps sustain player-governance. This temptation is, nonetheless, balanced by the complex music-specific mechanisms that determine demand for musicians' labour in orchestras and ensembles.

Nevertheless, a further dilemma emerges for PGOs. On the one hand, player-governance fosters a strong engagement with and commitment to the organisation among members. On the other, the strength of this bond makes it hard for retirees to deal with separation from the organisation. The members of the PGOs studied have a strong sense of ownership. Such firms might find it easier to delegate control over questions of artistic quality—including those about age-related declines in proficiency—to a music director or chief conductor, yet this would remove one of the central pillars of player-governance: player control over artistic decision-making. Agreeing on a retirement age, perhaps that used in relevant national social welfare systems, is unlikely to help. Considerable deterioration in proficiency may set in among some professional musicians before they reach their sixties (Gembris & Heye, 2014), though others demonstrate very high proficiency until the age of sixty-five or beyond (Brodsky, 2025).

Age-related drops in player proficiency, along with retirements and other member departures, threaten the sustainability of player-governance if the remaining members take on replacement players as hired labour rather than as members. Ben-Ner's prediction quoted at the start of this subsection would, in that case, represent a genuine threat to the sustainability of player-governance. The PGOs considered show no sign of such a tendency, however. Taking on new members in a not-for-profit context does not come with the same disincentives that accompany the expansion of membership in profit-sharing LMFs.

8.5.3 Recruitment's Role in Governance Sustainability

The recruitment of members who are prepared to actively support player-governance is essential to its sustainability. One of the threats it faces comes from the potential for a reduction in membership density if supernumerary players are blocked from becoming members. Yet, while auditions provide a familiar and relatively reliable means of establishing a musician's instrumental proficiency, determining whether a potential member will flourish in and contribute to the sustaining of player-governance—in Sophie's words, discovering "how they tick, what they are like in such a community"—is much less straightforward. Walter commented on the length of time required to become a member in his PGO, noting the use of "several stages" and emphasising that "it's not just a straight audition and probation period, as in most orchestras". He felt that this made "a big difference" and, stressing continuity, added that "partly the reason the orchestra has remained the way it is, is the very strong method of recruitment".

This multi-step nature of recruitment observed in the PGOs studied shines light on related questions in the LMF literature. Theoretical approaches to membership in LMFs are critical of the employment of non-members (hired labour). They see it as a threat to the sustainability of labour-management if the number of enfranchised members shrinks to the point at which decisions are made by a small number of members (Dow, 2018; Pencavel, 2013). Most of the PGOs studied offer initial engagements on a hired-labour basis. Full membership remains open to these players if, after a familiarisation and socialisation phase, both parties are amenable. The use of hired labour thus plays an important role in these PGOs and serves as a form of selection, socialisation, and familiarisation that contributes to the strength and sustainability of player-governance. It ensures that recruits to membership are well aligned with the governance ethos of their PGO.

In my analysis of the interviews, three themes emerged about recruitment, and in particular recruitment to full, enfranchised membership: its centrality to the operation and sustainability of PGOs, the importance of factors beyond musical proficiency, and the amount of time involved. For the PGOs I researched, getting recruitment right means assessing potential members' suitability as business partners, not just their proficiency as performers. Assessment of the former needs more time than recruitment in externally governed orchestras (Lehman, 1995). Multistage processes result, with many members starting as supernumerary, hired labour before transitioning to membership. Player-governance thus imposes recruitment costs, though the result is a process that reflects the centrality of hiring the best possible players, something Sophie and other interviewees felt was critical to the success of PGOs. Some interviewees viewed the thoroughness of recruitment as an important element of their PGO's success and sustainability, while others felt that the time involved was burdensome. In fact, it is both.

The insecurity of freelance orchestral work may mean that potential new members in these PGOs are attracted to audition primarily by the modest improvement in job security that they offer, rather than any particular commitment to the principles, aspirations, and ideals of player-governance. If this prioritisation were widespread, these orchestras would run the risk of degeneration in their player-governance as founders who were committed to player-governance were replaced by recruits who, in their search for the opportunity to work with a good orchestra, might even be ambivalent about such governance. In the face of such risks, the firms I researched have introduced recruitment processes that are especially thorough and that address the need to establish what Sophie called "what they are like in such a community". Extended pre-membership probation periods are also central to successful recruitment to these PGOs. For Sebastian, an audition was only the beginning of the recruitment process, a prerequisite, and the subsequent interactions with a player were "much more important than what they demonstrate in an audition".

Socialisation is at work in PGOs alongside a system of filtering of potential members. Herbert observed that "someone who plays with us regularly already knows, they know everyone, they know how everyone ticks, how it works". Maria described the years of familiarity with potential members that is common in PGOs. For potential members, this period of socialisation plays a more important role than in an externally governed orchestra because successful candidature is typically dependent on the support of two-thirds or more of members. For the organisation, socialisation serves to screen new members for alignment with the values of the membership and the governance model, to discover, in Sophie's words, "what they are like in such a community". For the sustainability of PGOs, this is a core element of recruitment. New members must be fine musicians and must, in most cases, also be able and willing to help make governance decisions. It is, moreover, important that fresh ideas can be voiced in decision-making committees, and it is essential for the model's sustainability that new members feel that their suggestions, perspectives, and concerns are as valued as those of more established members. Achieving this is a further element of successful recruitment, and the responsibility falls on existing members.

The three aspects of performance optimisation in the PGOs studied place significant responsibility on members. Monitoring performance, managing retirements, and recruitment of suitable members are three pillars of high-level performance. Optimisation lays bare some of the tensions that underlie player-governance and that call for astute balancing and management. Many of the interviewees found the monitoring of their peers' performance or dealing with age-related drops in proficiency burdensome, and at times even longed for an external monitor to take on such tasks. However, they recognised that doing so would be inimical to player-governance. The ability to recruit members who are willing and able to sustain player-governance as well as being excellent instrumentalists is, perhaps, the most fundamental task in sustaining player-governance. Engaging potential members as supernumeraries may run the risk of degeneration towards an oligarchic structure, but if judiciously managed, it can allow PGOs to assess the suitability of potential new members while also allowing such musicians to decide whether they want to commit to sustaining player-governance.

8.6 The Three Pillars of Sustainable Player-Governance

In this book, I set out to understand and then explain how democratic governance by musicians works in a group of five orchestras and one ensemble. The preceding chapters presented a deep dive into the advantages of such governance tempered with a recognition of the challenges it presents. The central question concerns the sustainability of player-governance. Ultimately one of the key tests of any governance model is its potential longevity. Without being sustainable over years and decades, a governance system would only be suitable for the start-up phase of any enterprise.

Many drivers appear to militate against player-governance in the long term. Democratic decision-making may slip down the list of priorities when founding members are gradually replaced as part of generational change. Founders may have incentives to withhold membership from later recruits and an oligarchy may gradually replace the original democratic structures. Yet the case study organisations I looked at have achieved governance sustainability. They have built adaptive and evolutionary models that harness the benefits while taming or at least navigating the perils and burdens.

The sustainability in governance that these firms have achieved stands on three pillars. The first of these combines various parameters that have music-making and artistic choices in common. The case study PGOs give wide-ranging programming and artistic personnel decisions to members but generally retain a leadership role for authority figures such as conductors. Achieving and keeping the highest possible performance standards involves mutual monitoring by playing members. This monitoring can create difficulties but is also central to player-governance.

The second pillar undergoing player-governance consists of several parts related to organisational work. Choices about membership categories, eligibility criteria, recruitment, and voting franchises constitute the core of this pillar. The ability of these organisations to adapt the ideas of labour-management to the realities of orchestras is key to the sustainability of their governance models. The optimising of participatory and democratic decision-making sits atop this pillar.

The final of the three pillars brings together elements that have individual musicians at their heart. A governance system that offers members little is unlikely to prove enduring. Player-governance goes some way towards improving the job security for players in an industry characterised by insecure work. Feelings of engagement, commitment, and responsibility are important, if less tangible, benefits that accrue to musicians in PGOs. Such forms of affective engagement in turn contribute to organisational identities that build solidarity and in so doing help sustain player-governance. Such virtuous circles appear at various places in the PGO case studies this book investigated. They represent a key feature of player-governance.

It is not an aim of this book to advocate for or "sell" player-governance in orchestras or democratic decision-making in performing arts companies more generally. Nor have I tried to show that this way of running an orchestra is in any sense superior to other forms of governance. As orchestras and ensembles continued to be founded anew, player-governance may be a viable organisational system but "off-the-shelf" governance templates are unlikely to succeed. Each of my case studies has found its own way, responding to its context and evolving as it navigates a highly competitive, demanding marketplace and labour market. Indeed, adaptability is a key ingredient of these PGOs. Others who seek to follow in their footsteps will need to chart their own journeys. I hope this study may encourage those who are tempted to give musicians greater control over their orchestras and ensembles while also alerting them to the stumbling blocks on the road. May fortune favour the brave.

References

Alchian, A. A., & Demsetz, H. (1972). Production, information costs, and economic organization. *The American Economic Review, 62*(5), 777–795. https://www.jstor.org/stable/1815199

Bartel, C., Blader, S. L., & Wrzesniewski, A. (Eds.). (2007). *Identity and the modern organization*. Lawrence Erlbaum Associates.

Batstone, E. (1983). Organization and orientation: A life cycle model of French co-operatives. *Economic & Industrial Democracy, 4*(2), 139–161. https://doi.org/10.1177/0143831X8342002

Ben-Ner, A. (1988a). The life cycle of worker-owned firms in market economies. *Journal of Economic Behavior & Organization, 10*(3), 287–313. https://doi.org/10.1016/0167-2681(88)90052-2
Ben-Ner, A. (1988b). Comparative empirical observations on worker-owned and capitalist firms. *International Journal of Industrial Organization, 6*(1), 7–31. https://doi.org/10.1016/0167-7187(88)90003-3
Bennett, D. E.. (2005). *Classical instrumental musicians: Educating for sustainable professional practice* (Doctoral dissertation). University of Western Australia. https://api.research--repository.uwa.edu.au/portalfiles/portal/33544367/Bennett_Dawn_Elizabeth_2005.pdf
Bennett, D. (2008). *Understanding the classical music profession: The past, the present and strategies for the future*. Ashgate.
Bowles, S., & Gintis, H. (1993). A political and economic case for the democratic enterprise. *Economics and Philosophy, 9*(1), 75–100. https://doi.org/10.1017/S0266267100005125
Brodsky, W. (2025). *Seasoned musicians playing beyond the 5th decade: A case study on symphony orchestra lifestyle and ageing*. Oxford University Press. https://doi.org/10.1093/9780198956501.001.0001
Callan, V. J., & S. A. Lawrence. (2009). Building employee engagement, job satisfaction, health, and retention. In *The Oxford handbook of organizational well being*. Oxford University Press. https://doi.org/10.1093/oxfordhb/9780199211913.003.0017
Charmettant, H. (2024). Where is democracy nestled? Reflections on organizational degeneration based on an artists' cooperative. *Journal of Participation and Employee Ownership, 7*(3), 213–228. https://doi.org/10.1108/JPEO-12-2022-0031
Cornforth, C. (1995). Patterns of cooperative management: Beyond the degeneration thesis. *Economic and Industrial Democracy, 16*(4), 487–523. https://doi.org/10.1177/0143831X95164002
Diefenbach, T. (2018). Why Michels' 'Iron law of oligarchy' is not an Iron law – and how democratic organisations can stay 'Oligarchy-Free'. *Organization Studies, 40*(4), 545–562. https://doi.org/10.1177/0170840617751007
Dow, G. (2001). Allocating control over firms: Stock markets versus membership markets. *Review of Industrial Organization, 1*(2), 201–218. https://www.jstor.org/stable/41798995
Dow, G. (2003). *Governing the firm: Workers' control in theory and practice*. Cambridge University Press.
Dow, G. (2018). *The labor-managed firm: Theoretical foundations*. Cambridge University Press.
Gembris, H., & Heye, A. (2014). Growing older in a symphony orchestra: The development of the age-related self-concept and the self-estimated performance of professional musicians in a lifespan perspective. *Musicae Scientiae, 18*(4), 371–391. https://doi.org/10.1177/1029864914548912
Glynn, M. (2008). Maestro or manager? Examining the role of the music director in a symphony orchestra. In J. Lampel, J. Shamsie, & T. Lant (Eds.), *The business of culture: Strategic perspectives on entertainment and media*. Taylor & Francis.
Greenblatt, S. (1988). *Shakespearean negotiations: The circulation of social energy in Renaissance England*. University of California Press.
Hansmann, H. (1990). When does worker ownership work? ESOPs, law firms, codetermination, and economic democracy. *Yale Law Journal, 99*(8), 1749–1816. https://doi.org/10.2307/796676
Hansmann, H. (1996). *The ownership of enterprise*. The Belknap Press of Harvard University Press.
Jackall, R., & Levin, H. M. (1984). Work in America and the cooperative movement. In R. Jackall & H. M. Levin (Eds.), *Worker cooperatives in America*. University of California Press.
Kahn, W. A. (1990). Psychological conditions of personal engagement and disengagement at work. *Academy of Management Journal, 33*(4), 692–724. https://doi.org/10.2307/256287
Koivunen, N. (2003). *Leadership in symphony orchestras, discursive and aesthetic practices* (Doctoral dissertation). University of Tampere. https://trepo.tuni.fi/handle/10024/67230

Lagrosen, Y., & Lagrosen, S. (2017). Aesthetic service quality – A study of a symphony orchestra. *Total Quality Management, 28*(3-4), 318–330. https://doi.org/10.1080/14783363.2015.1082419
Lehman, E. V. (1995). Recruitment practices in American and British symphony orchestras: Contrasts and consequences. *The Journal of Arts Management, Law, and Society, 24*(4), 325–343. https://doi.org/10.1080/10632921.1995.9941778
Lockwood, N. R. (2007). Leveraging employee engagement for competitive advantage: HR's strategic role. *HR Magazine, 52*(3), 1–11.
Macey, W. H., Schneider, W., Barbera, K. M., & Young, S. A. (Eds.). (2009). *Employee engagement: Tools for analysis, practice, and competitive advantage*. Wiley.
Michels, R. 2000 (1915). *Political parties: A sociological study of the oligarchical tendencies of modern democracy* (E. Paul, & C. Paul, Trans.). Batoche Books.
Oktemgil, M., & Greenley, G. (1997). Consequences of high and low adaptive capability in UK companies. *European Journal of Marketing, 31*(7–8), 445–466. https://doi.org/10.1108/03090569710176619
Pencavel, J. (2013). The economics of worker cooperatives. In *Elgar research reviews in economics*. Edward Elgar. https://doi.org/10.4337/9781784710545.
Pencavel, J., & Craig, B. (1994). The empirical performance of orthodox models of the firm: Conventional firms and worker cooperatives. *Journal of Political Economy, 102*(4), 718–744. http://www.jstor.org/stable/2138762
Piperek, M. (1981). *Stress and music: Medical, psychological, sociological, and legal strain factors in a symphony orchestra musician's profession: A study commissioned by the Vienna Symphony* (L. Katschinka, I. Kurz, & M. Verber. Trans.) Braumüller.
Podsakoff, P., Mackenzie, S., & Podsakoff, N. (Eds.). (2016). *The Oxford handbook of organizational citizenship behaviour*. Oxford University Press.
Pratt, M. G. (2016). Hybrid and multiple organizational identities. Chap. 6. In M. G. Pratt, M. Schultz, B. E. Ashforth, & D. Ravasi (Eds.), *The Oxford handbook of organizational identity*. Oxford University Press. https://doi.org/10.1093/oxfordhb/9780199689576.013.28
Reeves, M., & Deimler, M. (2011). Adaptability: The new competitive advantage. *Harvard Business Review, 7–8*, 134–141.
Robson, M. (2008). *Stephen Greenblatt*. Routledge. https://doi.org/10.4324/9780203408018
Rothschild, J., & Russell, R. (1986). Alternatives to bureaucracy: Democratic participation in the economy. *Annual Review of Sociology, 12*, 307. https://doi.org/10.1146/annurev.so.12.080186.001515
Stryjan, Y. (1989). *Impossible organizations: Self-Management and organizational reproduction*. Greenwood Press.
Takii, K. (2007). The value of adaptability—Through the analysis of a Firm's prediction ability. *Journal of Economics and Business, 59*, 144–162. https://doi.org/10.1016/j.jeconbus.2006.02.001
Tuominen, M., Rajala, A., & Möller, K. (2004). How does adaptability drive firm innovativeness? *Journal of Business Research, 57*(5), 495–506. https://doi.org/10.1016/S0148-2963(02)00316-8
Watkiss, L., & Glynn, M. A. (2016). *Materiality and identity, How organizational products, artifacts and practices instantiate organizational identity*. Oxford University Press. https://doi.org/10.1093/oxfordhb/9780199689576.013.10
Watts, S. (2010). Identification and the cultural organization: How the concept of identification can impact the constituencies who work within cultural organizations. *Journal of Arts Management, Law & Society, 40*(3), 200–216. https://doi.org/10.1080/10632921.2010.506173.
Weick, K. E. (1995). *Sensemaking in organizations*. Sage Publications.
Whetten, D. A. (2006). Albert and Whetten revisited: Strengthening the concept of organizational identity. *Journal of Management Inquiry, 15*(3), 219–234. https://doi.org/10.1177/1056492606291200
Wilkinson, A., Donaghey, J., Dundon, T., & Freeman, R. (Eds.). (2014). *Handbook of research on employee voice*. Edward Elgar.
Williamson, J., & Cloonan, M. (2016). *Players' work time: A history of the British Musicians' Union, 1893-2013*. Manchester University Press.

Appendix 1

Database of Major Player-Governed Orchestras and Ensembles Organised by Year of Foundation

Orchestra or ensemble name	Established	Operational base	Indicative no. of members	Player-governed since[a]
Vienna Philharmonic	1842	Vienna	135	
Berlin Philharmonic	1882	Berlin	123	
London Symphony Orchestra	1904	London	100	
London Philharmonic	1932	London	67	1939
Philharmonia Orchestra	1945	London	80	1964
Royal Philharmonic Orchestra	1946	London	82	1963
London Mozart Players	1949	London	40	2014
Orpheus Chamber Orchestra	1972	New York	26	
Tafelmusik	1979	Toronto, Canada	17	
Basel Sinfonietta	1980	Basel, Switzerland	138	
Deutsche Kammerphilharmonie Bremen	1980	Bremen, Germany	41	
Ensemble Modern	1980	Frankfurt, Germany	22	
Chamber Orchestra of Europe	1981	London	60	
Orchestra of the Age of Enlightenment	1986	London	54	
Freiburg Baroque Orchestra	1987	Freiburg, Germany	22	
L'Orquestra Simfònica del Vallès	1987	Spain (Catalonia)	40	

(continued)

B. Long, *Democratising Orchestras*, Music Business Research,
https://doi.org/10.1007/978-3-032-17399-7

Orchestra or ensemble name	Established	Operational base	Indicative no. of members	Player-governed since[a]
Ensemble Musikfabrik	1990	Cologne, Germany	15	1995
Louisiana Philharmonic	1991	New Orleans, USA	77	
Ensemble Resonanz	1994	Hamburg, Germany	18	
Mahler Chamber Orchestra	1997	Berlin	47	
Kammerakademie Potsdam	2001	Potsdam, Germany	34	
The Knights	2004	New York	35	
A Far Cry	2007	Boston, USA	17	

[a]In cases of player-governance being introduced after the foundation

MIX
Papier aus verantwortungsvollen Quellen
Paper from responsible sources
FSC® C105338

If you have any concerns about our products,
you can contact us on
ProductSafety@springernature.com

In case Publisher is established outside the EU,
the EU authorized representative is:
Springer Nature Customer Service Center GmbH
Europaplatz 3, 69115 Heidelberg, Germany

Printed by Libri Plureos GmbH
in Hamburg, Germany